POST MORTEM

Private Eye Productions Limited
6 Carlisle Street, London, W1D 3BN

www.private-eye.co.uk

First published in Great Britain by Private Eye Productions Limited 2025
1 3 5 7 9 10 8 6 4 2
Copyright © Private Eye Productions Limited / Richard Brooks 2025

Richard Brooks has asserted his right to be identified as the author of this work
in accordance with the Copyright, Designs and Patents Act 1988
Edited by Stephen Patience
Design by Glenn Orton
Cover photographs: Getty Images

A catalogue record for this book is available from the British Library
PB ISBN 978-1-901784-76-3
All rights reserved. No part of this publication may be
reproduced, stored in a retrieval system, or transmitted,
in any form or by any means, electronic, mechanical,
photocopying, recording or otherwise, without the
prior permission of the publishers

Printed and bound in Great Britain by Clays Limited, Suffolk NR35 1ED

"It's only because of their stupidity that they're able to be so sure of themselves."

Franz Kafka, *The Trial*, 1925

PRIVATE EYE

How the Post Office, the British government and a global IT company ruined the lives of thousands of innocent people

by Richard Brooks

Contents

	Foreword	XI
	Introduction	1
1	**A NEW DAWN** Dreams of IT utopia turn into computer nightmares	11
2	**FRAMED** The Post Office deploys Horizon against its sub-postmasters and ignores an expert's exposé of the system	23
3	**WALES OF PROTEST** The Post Office stifles early dissent and crushes any opposition	33
4	**COMMERCIAL BREAK** Financial freedom for the Post Office tightens the shackles on the sub-postmasters…	41
5	**NO CRIME AND PUNISHMENT** The Post Office coerces sub-postmasters into false confessions	49
6	**ARTICLES OF FAITH** Resistance takes shape; the Post Office takes cover	65
7	**ROUGH INJUSTICE** The defence of Horizon justifies misleading the courts and inflicting grievous harm	74
8	**SECOND COMMERCIAL BREAK** A new regime promises a bright future for the Post Office, but makes protecting the brand more essential than ever	81

9	**EYE-OPENER**	86
	Private Eye picks up the story, MPs get organised and the Post Office tries to look concerned	
10	**BRAVE REVIEW**	98
	The independent experts prove a little too independent	
11	**SEE NO EVIL**	114
	Hopes for the independent review turn to ashes, and keeping a lid on the scandal becomes a conspiracy to cover up	
12	**INSIDE JOB**	130
	A Fujitsu whistleblower breaks cover; new brooms keep sweeping under the carpet; and Alan Bates finds backers to put their money where his mouth is…	
13	**ALL OUT LAW**	141
	Alan Bates gets his day in court, while the Post Office and Fujitsu plumb new depths to deny justice	
14	**DRAMATIC DEVELOPMENTS**	158
	Campaigning sub-postmasters secure a public inquiry; a TV drama forces government to act; but for too many the ordeal goes on	
15	**SEARCHING INQUIRY**	174
	A public reckoning and heroic attempts to evade it – 2,214,858 pages of evidence, 780 witness statements and 298 witness appearances. A few highlights, and plenty of lowlights…	
16	**CONCLUSION**	192
	Ending the litany of scandal…	

Acknowledgements	199
Appendix I	201
Key officials	
Appendix II	204
Timeline of events	
Index	207

Foreword

by Sir Alan Bates

WHEN you are up against a foe that is so arrogant, prepared to lie about facts, totally ignorant of the technology it stands by, and under the control of incompetent management with oversight that is blind and utterly ineffective, then you have a battle on your hands – especially when your adversary has government-backed pockets to keep the truth at bay.

Some might say that sums up the Post Office Horizon scandal; others may say it covers all government scandals. So when you know you are right, and everyone else is wrong, it is hard to get a handhold to start to climb out of the gutter into which the Post Office threw so many innocent people. Yet a handhold is something that *Private Eye* has continued to offer us, ever since its first article on the subject, "Computer says no", in late September 2011.

A key factor in our battle, especially in the early days, was that Post Office's main strategy was the control of the narrative. It relied upon weasel wording, outright lies and misdirecting the growing number of MPs at Westminster who were coming forward to support our campaign. In this it was ably supported by Whitehall's civil-service masters, who were meant to be keeping an eye on things; if they were, it was a blind one. Year after year Post Office waved its flags – "Horizon is robust" and "Sub-postmasters are thieves" – up and down the corridors of Whitehall and Westminster. But the continual cutting and satirical voice of *Private Eye*, raising home truths about the events and the senior personnel involved, was helping expose some of the less palatable facts about Post Office.

When other media had moved on from our story, having been spun away by Post Office's "deny the truth" department – its press office – *Private Eye* continued to publish hard-hitting articles and gave comfort and encouragement to many of the victims who felt they were being ignored. In the early years these articles might only appear in a short column at the back of an issue, yet as time went on these slowly crept forward in the magazine until they arrived on the front cover and you could hardly turn a page without finding yet another article about the scandalous antics of Post Office and its compatriots. By this time, it should have become compulsory reading in Whitehall.

I think it is fair to say that Westminster has noticeably failed to act on this a number of times over the years. Parliamentarians were probably diverted from looking too closely at the growing outcry by their Whitehall servants; it has become clear to me during all my years of campaigning that the might of Whitehall has been allowed to lead Westminster along. This is often in a subtle, rarely overt way; the bureaucracy steers a course to suit its own agenda. I for one do not need the outcome of the Williams inquiry to know just how much Whitehall's failures helped keep a lid on the Horizon debacle for so many years.

Yet it is *Private Eye* which, issue after issue, has kept dragging the dirt into the sunlight – albeit at times dicing with a court visit. Such sterling work has to be done, and long may it continue to shine a light on those who'd rather stay on the shady side of the street. Apart from the ongoing fallout from Horizon, the scandal does seem to have given an impetus to other campaigns. Rarely a week goes by when at least one or two other campaigners are in contact, looking for the magic formula to raise their issue to the level we achieved. But if there was a formula, I never found it – it was just a long hard grind, day after day, year after year.

Yet issue after issue, *Private Eye* lifts the lid on so many of the scurrilous events and those whose actions often impact the lives of everyone, which would otherwise be missed. It is renowned for highlighting the nonsense that goes on behind closed doors, often with great cartoons or by lambasting those in power, continuing the centuries-old tradition of British political satire.

Richard Brooks, the author of this book, has from day one been *Private Eye*'s regular contributor on the Post Office Horizon scandal. I have had many conversations with him over the years about this major corporation abusing its powers and being out of control while its owner, the government, chose to remain ignorant of the damage it was inflicting. His many pieces have reflected the utter stupidity and nonsense surrounding a scandal that has inflicted so much suffering on so many hard-working people.

So thank you Richard, and thank you Ian, and all at *Private Eye*. Long may the *Eye* keep focused on exposing the truly unscrupulous and nonsensical side of life.

Introduction

BY 2011, *Private Eye* had been covering wasteful mega-IT projects – in everything from tax collection to healthcare – for more than a decade. So, when I filed our first report on mounting complaints about the Post Office's Horizon system, it was as "the next phase in the lifecycle of botched computer projects – malfunction".

The story this time was about more than "just" hundreds of millions or billions of pounds being poured down the drain (though that kind of money had been squandered in the development of Horizon). I had spoken to sub-postmasters who were living with the devastating consequences of having been accused of stealing money on the evidence of what they were sure was a fatally flawed IT system.

The Post Office nevertheless told the *Eye* that there were "no issues" with Horizon. Visible errors, as simple as the system registering the wrong class of stamp sold, as well as regular freezes and crashes, blatantly contradicted this. But to accept any fault, concluded our report, "would be to admit that the computer [system] on which it depends is a pig in a poke that has not only wasted billions but might now be dispensing miscarriages of justice as well".[1]

The pushback was immediate. The Post Office's chief operating officer wrote to the editor, insisting that the organisation "takes meticulous care to ensure that the Horizon computer system in branches nationwide is fully accurate at all times", adding piously that this was because "public money is entrusted to the Post Office". The letter was published beneath one from a sub-postmaster who remained anonymous for fear of the repercussions. "You are treated like rubbish by them," he said. "They answer to no one."[2] Other sub-postmasters, he said, "are too scared to say anything as they are worried that they will be shut down by [the] Post Office". In the space of two issues of the magazine,

---
1 *Eye* 1298, September 2011
2 *Eye* 1299, October 2011

a picture of injustice, denial and vindictiveness became painfully clear. Some of those sub-postmasters – a number convicted in court, others sacked, all financially ruined and most personally shattered – had quietly come together as the Justice for Subpostmasters Alliance. (*Sub-postmaster* encompassed many women, who would previously have been *sub-postmistresses*, and the alliance's members would also include post office staff who were similarly affected.) This group, reported the *Eye*, "reckons the total affected could run into thousands". Another zero would eventually have to be added to that. But the man behind the burgeoning movement was an understated sort of chap.

∼

In June 2019, a court looking at claims brought against the Post Office by Alan Bates and 554 others heard something remarkable about the cash shortfall that a newly installed IT system had thrown up at his branch in Craig-y-Don, in north Wales, 18 years earlier.

"A correct assessment of cash holdings could not be made because the Horizon system intermittently adds the previous day's cash holdings to the daily declaration," a Post Office auditor had reported back in 2001.[3] Bates hadn't been told about this fault or the fact that the Post Office was aware of a significant malfunction in its new IT system, either then or in the years since. Instead, after losing his Post Office branch because he wouldn't accept false figures generated by Horizon, he was left to wage a two-decade battle to expose the truth.

In what became one of the most consequential campaigns for justice in British history, Alan Bates uncovered far more than IT glitches. He showed how an institution of the British state used its flawed technology to prosecute, punish and impoverish thousands of sub-postmasters in the widest miscarriage of justice and campaign of persecution of its own citizens on record.

Around 1,000 sub-postmasters and their staff were convicted using data from the flawed IT system, usually over branch shortfalls but also for allegations of pension and other payment frauds. Around 700 were prosecuted by the Post Office itself, most of the rest by Scottish and Northern Irish independent prosecutors;[4] 236 people were imprisoned.[5] Claims under various schemes for

---

[3] *Alan Bates & Others v Post Office Ltd*, Judgment No. 6, "Horizon Issues", 16 December 2019
[4] corporate.postoffice.co.uk/horizon-scandal-pages/faqs.
Post Office remediation unit director Simon Recaldin, witness statement to inquiry, 4 November 2024, public inquiry ref WITN09890500, shows 697 convictions from 764 Horizon-era prosecutions conducted by the Post Office in England and Wales
[5] bbc.co.uk/news/business-67956962. In Scotland there were 141 convictions: gov.scot/publications/foi-202400431750. In Northern Ireland the figure is put at 29: ppsni.gov.uk/news/public-prosecution-service-northern-ireland-statement-re-post-office-horizon-convictions

financial redress reveal more than 10,000 other victims, including those falsely suspended or sacked and forced to "repay" sums they never owed, and many who plugged shortfalls from their own pockets. Anecdotal evidence indicates others whose lives were routinely made a misery by struggling night after night to make their branch accounts balance but who have not sought compensation.

The Post Office puts the amount that sub-postmasters wrongly "repaid" at £36m, although some believe it to be much higher. But even this figure translates into thousands of pounds taken from businesses with modest profits. The numbers of sub-postmasters across the UK was around 17,000 at the start of the century and 11,000 by 2013, when Horizon-based prosecutions (though not unjustified civil action) effectively ended. One Post Office estimate put the number to have used the Horizon system during this period at around 25,000.[6] It seems probable that most sub-postmasters were victims to some extent of the Post Office scandal.

Behind these bare numbers lies a litany of suffering, from lost liberty to unjustly ruined reputations, stolen livelihoods, family breakdowns and depression. Thirteen suicides have been linked to the scandal.[7] Scores of victims have died before receiving exoneration, never mind compensation. One of the leading law firms for sub-postmasters surveyed a group of its clients and, in the 102 responses, found: 51 who said they had been ostracised by their communities; 18 bankruptcies; and 23 marriage breakdowns.[8] Extrapolate those numbers across the thousands of victims and the picture is of a tidal wave of human misery. Even then the bald statistics mask the different reality for each affected sub-postmaster and the impact on those around them, from employees they sometimes suspected and sacked, to children scarred by bullying and lost educational opportunities, and elderly parents watching a son or daughter jailed.

It would be hard to argue that this doesn't represent mass abuse by the British state. Even after prosecutions of sub-postmasters based on Horizon (mis)information ceased, it persisted through six more years of lies and cover-ups until a judge in the Alan Bates case ruled that the Post Office's treatment of sub-postmasters was "oppressive" and the Horizon system that became its instrument of torture was "not remotely robust".[9] When the first convictions were overturned in 2021, a Court of Appeal judge ruled that prosecutions had not only been wrong but were an "affront to justice".[10]

Such findings did not mark the end of the sub-postmasters' ordeal,

---

6 corporate.postoffice.co.uk/horizon-scandal-pages/faqs
7 *Post Office Horizon IT Inquiry Report Volume 1*, 8 July 2025
8 Howe & Co survey, cited in closing submissions by Sam Stein KC at inquiry, 16 December 2024
9 *Bates v Post Office* Judgment No. 6, 16 December 2019
10 *Jo Hamilton & Others v Post Office* appeal judgment, 23 April 2021

however, as both government and Post Office dragged their feet on overturning false convictions and paying for the suffering they had inflicted. It would take a drama on ITV in January 2024 to force both to face up to their responsibilities and accelerate the wheels of justice and – still inadequately – of redress. All the while, those implicated in the scandal spun their way through the public inquiry set up after Bates's victory, recalling in detail what mitigated their culpability and forgetting what proved or aggravated it.

∼

For the Post Office, its masters in Whitehall and its IT supplier Fujitsu, one word defined the stance to be taken against allegations of IT malfunction: Horizon was "robust". Many, perhaps most, of those with any involvement with the system knew for sure that it was not. Others convinced themselves it *was* robust. Those at the top of the chain demanded to be told it was robust, in the face of evidence that it wasn't. When he was later asked if his experience had been Orwellian, Alan Bates replied "It's the same old mantra… 'War is peace, slavery is freedom, ignorance is strength.' I think I would add a fourth one to that… 'Horizon is robust.'"[11] At one point, Post Office chief executive (from 2012) Paula Vennells sought to change the language so that "bugs" mentioned by colleagues, which belied the claimed robustness of Horizon, became benign "exceptions" and "anomalies".

The roll call of those who toed the line – whether they believed it or not or were themselves misled – is an august one. It includes: government ministers accountable to MPs in parliament; senior civil servants sworn to behave in the public interest; highly paid Post Office executives professing their regard for sub-postmasters; non-executive directors whose job it was to hold them to account; lawyers bound by professional standards to act truthfully in the interests of justice; and accountants whose job it was not to turn a blind eye.

These groups collectively failed to use the common sense that would have told them something was seriously wrong. Why would so many sub-postmasters, all having gone through checks before appointment, steal on such a vast scale, especially when they would know that missing funds would quickly become apparent? And why, in all reports of convictions – both internally and in press coverage of convictions – was there never any sign of the ill-gotten gains (sometimes even after intrusive searches)? Significant thefts invariably come with at least some indication of where the money went,

---

11 Ian Hislop and Helen Lewis, *Orwell vs Kafka* episode 1, Radio 4, 8 June 2024

usually on gambling or other addictions, lavish spending or debt repayments. But somehow the same sub-postmasters who were stupid enough to crudely steal large sums of cash – essentially the allegation in most cases – were also criminal masterminds who could hide all trace of any benefit.

What official "thinking" there was about the apparent sub-postmaster crime wave amounted to prejudiced notions of, in the words of the Post Office's managing director in the late 2000s, "subbies with their hands in the till".[12] Sub-postmasters were often struggling financially and large amounts of cash, it was thought, were simply too tempting. One senior Post Office investigator had written a dissertation for an MSc course on crime risk, shortly before the roll-out of Horizon, with the title *There Must Be Some Mistake*. He would tell the public inquiry this was chosen "with complete irony".[13] The sub-postmasters were at it, in other words.

The precise effects on the levels of sub-postmaster prosecutions caused by the introduction of Horizon are obscured by poor data. But figures supplied by the Post Office show that comparable prosecutions were ramping up in the couple of years before the introduction of Horizon, from single-digit levels in the early and mid-1990s to 70 in 1998 and 101 in 1999. Over the next decade they average around 70. Horizon appeared to be riding a wave of heightened prosecutorial interest dating from the days that it was being developed. A precursor IT system called Capture, used in hundreds of branches from around 1992, has since also emerged as highly flawed and the source of wrongful prosecutions. It may well be that this scandal really began before Horizon. But once the system was in, there is no question that it became the tool with which to make the false allegations. Perhaps the most telling trend in the statistics is that the proportion of prosecutions relating to relatively simple "shortfalls", as opposed to more complex pensions or Giro frauds, increased dramatically – from around 30 percent of total prosecutions in 2000 to around 70 percent in 2005 and 90 percent by 2008. With the numbers of investigators being gradually cut over this period, it seems they were learning that Horizon shortfalls produced easy prosecutorial wins.[14]

When it came to denying the scandal, the Post Office defied logic. There were more than 2bn transactions successfully going through the system every year, went the argument, so it must be robust. Nobody appeared sufficiently numerate to realise that this gave no reassurance. A very large number had to be multiplied by the error rate to give an idea of how often a system might go wrong

---

12 Email from Alan Cook to Mary Fagan, October 2009, public inquiry ref POL00158368
13 David Pardoe, witness statement to inquiry, 24 October 2023, public inquiry ref WITN08170100
14 Simon Recaldin, witness statement to inquiry, 4 November 2024, WITN09890500

and, in this case, potentially generate spurious figures. Of course, technicians, managers and executives did understand this; they just didn't want to.

Anybody developing or running IT, or even using it, knew that all software has bugs and errors. The Fujitsu engineers and managers certainly knew, right from the chaotic development of Horizon, that there were flaws. As did many of the Post Office's investigators, lawyers and bosses. Yet, in a culture of complicity and fear, none wanted to say so. Such was the refusal to confront reality that when *Private Eye* wrote its first story on the scandal in 2011, the Post Office issued the technologically illiterate rebuttal that "the Horizon computer system in branches nationwide is fully accurate at all times".[15]

So when sub-postmasters began joining Bates's Justice for Subpostmasters Alliance in droves – with detailed, cogent accounts of their experiences, often supported by their MPs – why did the mass denial persist? Largely because it was essential that it did so. The Post Office's focus was commercial success, with subsidy-free independence from government the holy grail. This was pursued through cost-cutting and "transformation" initiatives, treating the organisation as an entirely economic operator rather than also a social one, which executives were heavily incentivised to deliver. Financial imperatives shaped how the Post Office's leadership and its government shareholder viewed the Horizon IT system from launch right through to handling the tragic consequences of its inadequacy.

This was always a short-sighted strategy, demonstrated by the prosecution of sub-postmaster Jo Hamilton – seen distraught as phantom shortfalls flash on her screen in the 2024 ITV drama *Mr Bates vs the Post Office*. Before being hounded into court and coerced into a guilty plea, she had been not just a sub-postmaster but a pillar of her community, assisting elderly residents with getting their pension payments and much else. Yet, as her counsel at the public inquiry, Tim Moloney KC, later put it, "Post Office didn't and/or wouldn't see the wealth in that".[16] (More wonkishly, a think tank puts the annual "social value" of the Post Office at £3.8bn).[17]

Too much hung on Horizon's failings not being exposed. The costs would sink the government's financial ambitions for the Post Office and possibly the organisation itself. To avert this existential crisis, lies and wilful blindness pervaded the organisation. Questioning Paula Vennells on behalf of other sub-postmasters at the public inquiry, Sam Stein KC put to her that "the risk was too great; looking under that rock, you're going to find a

---

15 *Eye* 1298, September 2011
16 Tim Moloney KC, closing statement to Phase 4 of inquiry, 2 February 2024
17 London Economics analysis for the Post Office, 2023

problem, it's going to devastate the Post Office, ruin it, and you couldn't let that happen, could you, Ms Vennells?" The best she could respond was that "I loved the Post Office."[18]

For accused sub-postmasters, this blindness turned into the most mendacious treatment. Each was told by investigators that he or she was the only one reporting problems with Horizon. Then, coerced into admitting liability to minimise punishment but maximise the Post Office's financial recoveries (of amounts not due), they were often forced to agree never to mention flaws in the IT system. The dishonesty of these tactics mattered not to the Post Office's investigators, lawyers and managers. As Kafka wrote in *The Trial*, it was "not necessary to accept everything is true; one must only accept it as necessary".

∼

The role of sub-postmaster has a more important place in British social history than the modest job title suggests. The first regional postmasters began work with the creation of the General Post Office under Charles II in 1660, supervising the major "posts" between which mail was passed in a relay delivery system. Over the following decades, as the postal system became more widely used, local shopkeepers and traders who acted as "sub-postmasters" away from these centres began to play an increasingly prominent role.

The numbers of letters to be handled grew exponentially with the arrival and expansion of the railway network in the 19th century. By the outbreak of the First World War, 23,000 sub-post offices, alongside 1,100 main – or Crown – offices in larger towns, were dealing with a large chunk of the 6bn letters posted annually, and had become hubs of local communities. Their importance grew throughout the war, as they began to make payments to wives of men on active service as well as paying the recently introduced state pension.[19] By the time of the Second World War, helping to administer the rationing system, local sub-post offices had become critical community services and an object of public affection.

Unlike postmasters, sub-postmasters were always agents rather than employees of the Post Office. They were nevertheless bound by strict rules and responsible for losses of public money in a rigid and disciplinarian culture dating from the days of highwaymen holding up the King's Mail. As early as

---

18 Paula Vennells, inquiry evidence, 24 May 2024
19 For an authoritative history of the Post Office, see Duncan Campbell-Smith's *Masters of the Post: The Authorised History of the Royal Mail* (Allen Lane, 2011)

1683, the General Post Office's assistant solicitor's job included "the detection and carrying on of all prosecutions against persons for robbing the mails and other fraudulent practices".[20] A "missing letter branch" established in the early 19th century became a more general investigation branch in 1908 and, following major reforms in the late 1960s under Labour postmaster general Tony Benn, the investigations division that would deploy Horizon against sub-postmasters. Mistrust of, and even prejudice towards, sub-postmasters had deep roots.

The essence of the sub-postmaster role had changed little by the turn of the 21st century. It was governed by a contract making the relationship with the Post Office explicit. "The sub-postmaster is responsible for all losses caused through his own negligence, carelessness or error," this read. "Deficiencies due to such losses must be made good without delay."[21] With a new computer system tracking every movement infallibly (according to the Post Office), the belief that apparent losses must be the sub-postmaster's fault became Holy Writ – to the point that any need to show "negligence, carelessness or error" was forgotten.

The contract amounted to an extreme imbalance of power, in which sub-postmasters were forced to work as the Post Office demanded, with the shoddy tools it mandated. They had no choice but to surrender to the IT system imposed on them, while also being liable for its errors. At the same time, they didn't have the employment rights that normally come with a master-servant relationship, and usually worked for less than the minimum wage.

When things inevitably went wrong in a branch and the Post Office's apparatchiks descended, the sub-postmaster's ordeal began in earnest. The conduct of the investigators – blindly loyal and set apart from the sub-postmasters, over whom they had the whip hand – would echo behaviour associated with infamous psychological studies such as the Stanford experiment of the 1970s, where those given authority in a simulated prison environment became aggressive and abusive; or Stanley Milgram's experiment of the 1960s, in which participants inflicted electric shocks on others when ordered to do so. For Ed Henry KC, counsel representing many of the affected sub-postmasters at the public inquiry, the Post Office power structures, dogmas and consequent actions brought to mind Voltaire: "Those who can make you believe absurdities would have you commit atrocities."[22]

When it comes to the lies and cover-up – which were always essential

---

20 Duncan Atkinson KC, expert report to inquiry, EXPG0000002
21 *Bates v Post Office* Judgment No. 3, "Common Issues", 15 March 2019
22 Ed Henry KC, closing statement to inquiry, 16 December 2024

parts of the persecution – psychologists will doubtless find huge cognitive dissonance among the legions of professionals, executives, civil servants and ministers who believed what it comforted them to believe, not what the evidence told them.

∽

If Alan Bates, armed with some prior experience of "electronic point of sale" IT systems as well as remarkable fortitude, had not pursued his and other even harsher cases for so long, the Post Office scandal would not have been exposed. Thousands of innocent men and women would have gone without redress and with their names permanently besmirched.

Bates – assisted by a handful of MPs, notably James Arbuthnot, as well as other campaigning sub-postmasters and a belatedly growing band of journalists – had to overcome the orchestrated resistance of both a mighty corporation and government. At every level, the truth was concealed from him and the other sub-postmasters. Investigators lied to them. Lawyers manipulated evidence that would go before the courts. Managers buried Horizon's manifold faults, ensuring that senior executives officially saw only the partial picture they wanted to see: the one that would keep the financial results show on the road. Board directors, who should have been probing as the list of credible complaints from sub-postmasters lengthened, acquiesced in the cover-up. On the rare occasions that they did "lift the rock", they swiftly replaced it before the nasty secrets beneath could escape.

At the apex of this corrupted pyramid were indifferent politicians with higher priorities and short attention spans, dismissing the escalating human catastrophe as a matter for the "arm's length" Post Office – although this came at the cost of thousands of blighted lives and mounting costs to the taxpayer.

Three of those lives belong to: Seema Misra, who was pregnant when jailed in 2010 over a missing £70,000, of which there was no other sign; father-of-two Lee Castleton, bankrupted with a £350,000 bill in order to deter others from taking a stand; and Tracy Felstead, despatched to Holloway prison aged 19 for a theft that didn't happen. Small wonder that their counsel invoked Voltaire, or that he also called the Post Office Horizon IT scandal "as dark a chapter in our governmental, corporate and legal history as can be imagined".[23]

This is *Private Eye's* account of those political, institutional, professional and personal failures – offered in the hope that the lessons of the Post Office scandal will guard against such abuses in future.

---

23 Henry, closing statement to inquiry, 17 May 2023

1

A NEW DAWN

Dreams of IT utopia turn into computer nightmares

THE Horizon system was born in a time of technological hope. Nowhere was the optimism greater than in Britain's corridors of power. As the internet age dawned, information technology would transform the country's outdated public services and institutions.

Although the cutting edge of IT was to be found across the Atlantic, when the John Major government decided to modernise the system of paying pensions and benefits to people who took their books to the post office every week, it handed the task to a British company called International Computers Ltd (ICL).

ICL had begun life in a previous spasm of official techno-enthusiasm, a creation of Harold Wilson's 1968 Industrial Expansion Act and reportedly the brainchild of his minister of technology, Tony Benn. Bringing together smaller British computer companies and given a large grant, ICL was to be Britain's answer to IBM, the US giant of the postwar mainframe computer age.

The company wasn't, alas, to achieve anything like that prominence. It lagged behind its rivals, becoming increasingly reliant on Asian postwar success story Fujitsu, not least for the microchips that were truly transforming the power of IT. By 1990 it was 80 percent owned by the Japanese company.

ICL nevertheless retained its place at the heart of the drive to automate UK public services. It was the natural choice when, in 1996, Tory social security secretary Peter Lilley unveiled a plan to install a new IT system for post offices that would link up with an electronic card system for benefits payments, replacing the old order books. This would eliminate around £150m of fraud every year and provide seamless accounting for Britain's post offices' largest source of business. Project Horizon, said Lilley, brought the post office network "into line with the best retail practice",[1] enabling it to sell a

---

[1] Announcement by social security secretary Peter Lilley, 15 May 1996, POL00089859

wider range of services and, in doing so, become less dependent on benefits payments.

The contract for all this would be between his government and the Post Office on the one hand and ICL subsidiary company ICL Pathway on the other. Its offering had scored worst on official bidding criteria, apart from cost and (with grim irony, given the following years' events) reduction of risk for the Post Office. But following the recession of the early 1990s, government funds were short and the British IT industry needed all the help it could get. So the cheapest option it was.

Financial engineering

Information technology wasn't the only area in which mid-1990s government ministers were intent on innovation. Investment in hardware and software, just like that in more concrete infrastructure, required funding. That would mean more borrowing, which a fiscally conservative government wanted to avoid. A more imaginative alternative was needed.

The early thinking behind the private finance initiative (PFI) was captured in a 1993 pamphlet, *The Opportunities for Private Funding in the NHS*, written by new Tory MP David Willetts. It set out how public service assets could be financed, built and owned by private companies and supplied to the public sector over the following years for an annual fee. These would repay the private company's funding and interest costs, plus a profit on top. Crucially, the taxpayer's future obligations would not be counted as government debt. This novel funding method, most commonly used for hospitals, prisons and roads, could also work for investment-hungry information technology projects such as Horizon.

The chancellor of the time, Ken Clarke, had insisted on an important condition for the use of PFI: that the risks of failure or extra costs in any project were transferred to the private sector. When it came to complex IT projects with detailed specifications full of unknown consequences, this was a recipe for confusion and wrangling. With Horizon, it didn't help that adaptation to legacy systems and products was also a big part of the job. Questions about who among the Department of Social Security, Post Office and ICL bore what responsibilities, plus a host of technical difficulties, bedevilled the project from the start. After nearly two years and several millions of pounds spent on consultants, by late 1997 ICL Pathway had failed to deliver the agreed progress and had been served with a notice for a breach of contract by the new Labour government. The project was already going pear-shaped.

Political choices

Having informed ICL that it was failing and been met with complaints from Fujitsu in Tokyo about excessive interference, Tony Blair's New Labour government had to decide what to do with the expensive IT fiasco on its hands. First, it turned to the head of chancellor Gordon Brown's PFI taskforce, veteran banker Adrian Montague. The expert panel he convened saw the dysfunction in the development of the Horizon IT system at the heart of the project, with all parties incapable of delivering on their side of the bargain. On the technical level, his team doubted whether the vintage Riposte messaging system, used by the Horizon software to send information from one point in a closed system to another, was capable of operating with an online networked system (dealing, for example, with the still fairly new National Lottery sales). There was, said Montague, "some risk around scaleability [sic] and robustness because the system has had to be tested at the level of component parts", i.e. not as a whole.[2] For what was set to be the largest non-military IT system in Europe, with tens of thousands of terminals and billions of transactions annually, this was not reassuring.

Montague set out the government's options, which boiled down to: ploughing on regardless; dropping the benefit payment card element; or scrapping the whole thing. The subsequent inter-departmental squabbling featured a who's who of New Labour luminaries. In one Whitehall showdown that summer, according to one of his civil servants, social security secretary Alistair Darling "put the case strongly for an urgent decision to cancel the project" (which was straining his budget considerably). The minister responsible for the Post Office, Ian McCartney, disagreed and "presented the case for option 1 [carrying on with the whole project]".[3]

McCartney would soon be off to Japan, reporting back from Fujitsu that "if the government cancelled the project, it would put at risk the [proposed] flotation of ICL, [which] would in turn put jobs and investment at risk". He was backed by our man in Tokyo telling Blair of "profound implications" for bilateral relations. Over at the Treasury, chief secretary Stephen Byers also favoured continuation, fearing a huge compensation bill that could follow cancellation.

Such was Horizon's importance across many ministerial briefs that the final call would be made right at the top. That December, Blair was briefed by the head of his policy unit, Geoff Mulgan, on what the spad judged an "increasingly flawed" project. It was "centred around a technology, the benefit

---
2 PFI Taskforce Horizon panel report, July 1998, POL00028094
3 Sarah Graham, briefing note for Benefits Agency chief executive Peter Mathison, 4 August 1998

payment card, that is both overengineered – and very expensive – and likely soon to be obsolete".[4]

But the deal was critical for Fujitsu's and ICL's plans. Scrapping Horizon would "lead to a heavy loss (£200m) this year" for ICL, said Mulgan. It would probably force the resignation of the chief executive and "put them in a protracted legal battle with government". Cancellation would also be "destabilising" for the country's post office network since "sub-postmasters fear that without Horizon they will lose their customer base" (for handling benefit payments). On the other hand, carrying on with the Tories' benefit payment card would hold up the move to paying benefits directly into bank accounts, which was how New Labour saw the future. Darling's social security department thus estimated it "would save £800m if the project was cancelled".

Mulgan noted in passing that the business secretary ultimately responsible for the Post Office, Peter Mandelson, had "largely kept out of the discussions".[5] That was to change dramatically as soon as Mulgan fired off his missive summarising the rival views. Mandelson immediately made an impassioned plea for the full Horizon package. Not only would terminating the programme damage the post office network, but: "Our relations with Fujitsu, a major inward investor into the UK over the past decade, would be severely damaged, as would the credibility of PFI."[6] For a New Labour government that had set itself stringent debt rules, while also promising transformational investment, the latter was not to be underestimated.

But even Mandelson could see that this alone didn't justify foisting a hopeless system on the Post Office, so he added that "the basic development work has been thoroughly evaluated by experts who have pronounced it viable, robust…" Here was one of the first defences of the system to use the reassuring but helpfully vague word that would cause so much harm down the years. And it was already inaccurate. Neither the Montague report to which Mandelson appears to have been referring, nor any other group of experts, had pronounced Horizon "robust".

The New Labour guru nevertheless prevailed. Blair – who had met ICL chairman Michio Naruto not long beforehand to discuss the contract – had a "clear preference", wrote his principal private secretary Jeremy Heywood four days later, "to avoid cancelling the project". The government "should retain the [benefit payment card] but seek to ensure that over time it… provides

---

4 Letter from Geoff Mulgan to Tony Blair, 9 December 1998, CBO00100001_072
5 Ibid
6 Letter from Peter Mandelson to Treasury minister Stephen Byers, 10 December 1998, BEIS0000418

an effective transition path to a satisfactory long-term position".[7] Pleasing a critical supplier, given the government's wider IT ambitions, and sparing the blushes of the PFI programme together trumped getting the technology right. And, of course, the legendary New Labour spin machine was not in the market for bad-news announcements about botched IT and cancelled contracts.[8]

Unhappy customer

The idea of going full steam ahead was, however, once again to prove wishful thinking. Commercial negotiations dragged on, while ICL's software engineers and their hapless Post Office counterparts continued to botch. With ICL complaining about the fortunes it had already sunk into the programme and the cost-conscious Treasury resisting further financial commitments, talks soon collapsed.

Both sides were left trying to save face and limit the damage: in ICL's case, to its reputation and Fujitsu's plan to float the company on the stock market; and in the government's, to priorities such as the cherished private finance initiative. So, in May 1999, they salvaged a pared-down version of the Horizon system from the wreckage. It would be used for post office branch transactions and accounting, but without the benefit card payment system that had been central to the Horizon project in the first place. When the National Audit Office looked at the fiasco a year later, it would put the wasted costs at £127m for the Department of Social Security, £571m for the Post Office and £180m for ICL.

The Post Office became a reluctant party to a half-baked deal hatched over its head. Just a few days before the agreement was struck, chairman Neville Bain, a New Zealander who had spent his career in industry before joining the Post Office in May 1998 with a modernising mandate, had griped about a "conspiracy" between the Treasury and consultants from KPMG over numbers that justified going ahead with Horizon.[9] A Treasury official noted that the Post Office "believe the Horizon hardware and software is probably sub-optimal as the platform for providing network banking and modern government services".[10] Its leaders couldn't even say "whether the Horizon hardware and software is preferable to the system they might procure following termination". The new system didn't exactly have management buy-in.

But sign up they had to. As the group chief executive from the time, 32-

---
7 Memo from Jeremy Heywood to Mulgan, 14 December 1998, CBO00000009
8 The internal government debates were considered in the inquiry. Many of the original documents were unearthed by campaigner Eleanor Shaikh and are expertly dissected in her paper *Origins of a Disaster* (Bath Publishing, 2022)
9 DTI memo from Christopher Woolard (PPS to Byers) to David Sibbick, 12 May 1999, BEIS0000440
10 Treasury briefing to ministers, 14 May 1999, POL00039931

year Post Office veteran John Roberts, would tell the public inquiry more than 23 years later, "basically, we were put at the end of a gun and it was a yes/no choice and, in the end, we said yes – but I don't think we said yes with a great deal of enthusiasm". [11] Another senior figure in the Post Office Horizon delivery team, David Smith, recalled that "the leaders at [the Post Office] felt that they had been shafted by a government/[ICL] Pathway stitch up",[12] with the message "sign this or all the other things you want you can forget". He added that Post Office MD Dave Miller "said at the time 'I have the same feelings about Pathway as I would have for the man who had just shoved 15 inches of bayonet up my posterior'." Miller would later deny having made the remark.

It didn't help that the Post Office itself was in some turmoil. Upon arriving as chairman in 1998, Bain had opened the door to faddish management consultants and created a blizzard of initiatives and reviews. The Shaping for Competitive Success programme, for example, turned the Post Office into an "internal marketplace" with 10 business units and 11 support units all functioning as profit centres contracting with each other. The result, wrote Post Office historian Duncan Campbell-Smith in 2011, was that "no one really knew what was happening to the business at all". [13]

All this left an unhappy and distracted customer using a substandard product, under the supervision of an image-conscious government that wanted to put an early headache behind it. In a prompt "lessons from the Horizon project" memo on the shambles in May 1999, Blair's spad Geoff Mulgan said it was "misconceived from the start – has faced continual delays and problems [and]… has delivered in the end a far from optimal solution".[14] Horizon was a "timebomb" that should have been dealt with sooner after the 1997 election. The episode had shown "the absence of any strategic grip on plans for government IT" and "the relative lack of competence of the Post Office and their failure to develop a proper business strategy". Meanwhile, "nearly all the facts presented to ministers turned out to be unreliable". They were refrains that would echo down the next two decades.

Horizon's flaw show

Under the new deal, the more limited Horizon system still had to be formally "accepted" as up to the job. The experience in branches where it was trialled, however, showed just how far off the mark it remained.

---

11 Anthony John Roberts, inquiry evidence, 20 October 2022
12 David Smith, PowerPoint presentation *The Story of Horizon and Horizon Online*, September 2010, FUJ00098040
13 Duncan Campbell-Smith, *Masters of the Post*
14 Memo from Mulgan to Blair, 20 May 1999

Over the summer of 1999, internal Post Office reports recorded that "evidence from the live trial shows that the counter system is unstable and lacking the 'industrial strength' necessary".[15] So-called "acceptance incidents", including system freezes and unrecorded or duplicated transactions, were proliferating into the hundreds. Ominously, reported officials, "error levels are currently running at twice the normal pre-Horizon baseline". In one week alone, comparing "the underlying transaction stream to summary totals on the cash account", there were "2,451 differences experienced in 67 outlets", out of around 300 in the trial.[16] A note on "receipts and payments mismatch" recorded a "large number of incidents" in which cash balances didn't correspond with revenue and expenditure.[17]

The central principle of the double-entry book-keeping system, on which sound accounting has been based for centuries, is that every transaction leads to two entries of identical value – for example, an increase in sales and a corresponding rise in cash. So, as the official wrote, the mismatch "exposes a lack of integrity in the double-entry accounting functions of the Horizon system".[18] It was something that, at this point at least, the Post Office's auditors appreciated. The faulty IT, wrote beancounter Ernst & Young the same month, "gives us concern as to the ability of [the Post Office] to produce statutory accounts to a suitable degree of integrity".[19] In other words, Horizon was messing up the Post Office's own accounts too.

Post Office officials fully understood the gravity of this. A report on "system stability" in August 1999 recorded: "The ICL Pathway system is an integral part of [the Post Office's] client accounting system – indeed the service is an accounting service" and it "accounts for turnover of £140bn per annum involving some 3bn transactions".[20] The memo's author also understood something that Post Office directors would fail to, or affect not to, for the next two decades: "Given the scale of this system even relatively small defects are capable of generating errors within the accounts of very significant amounts." So serious was the risk that "the potential is for these write-offs to be significantly threatening the business performance against shareholder targets and potentially as a going concern". Horizon's defects were, in other words, already known to be an existential matter for the 400-year-old institution.

In the Post Office's stifling culture, however, this was the kind of danger

---

15 Internal Post Office memo, 15 August 1999, POL00028337
16 Post Office memo, 10 August 1999, POL00030393
17 Post Office document, 15 August 1999, POL00028338
18 Ibid
19 Letter from Ernst & Young to David Miller, 23 August 1999, POL00090839
20 Post Office memo, POL00028337

for even senior executives to gloss over in discussions with directors. Minutes from a July 1999 board meeting recorded that, subject to concerns over training for sub-postmasters on the new system, "David Miller [the network managing director] considered the system robust and fit for service" (although the minutes also recorded that "members were concerned that a number of technical issues remained unresolved").[21] Never mind that Miller and his boss, Post Office managing director Stuart Sweetman, who was on the main Post Office board, were fully aware of the software issues and problems that sub-postmasters trialling the system were experiencing.[22]

So was the government. The previous month, a Horizon working party meeting chaired by trade minister Ian McCartney had discussed, according to an attendee from the National Federation of Sub-Postmasters (NFSP), "very serious issues still to confront, including training and systems difficulties". Federation officials were discovering, even in this trial phase, "difficulties and trauma being experienced by some sub-postmasters". They felt that "a tragedy was not far away if something was not altered soon".[23]

Such warnings did not, however, weigh in the decision-making of McCartney and his boss back at the Department for Trade and Industry, now Stephen Byers (following Mandelson's resignation over an undeclared loan). Their focus was on limiting the costs that were ramping up daily and avoiding scaling back Horizon again. That could entail another nine-figure compensation payout to ICL and set back wider ambitions for the post office network, such as greater financial services business to compensate for the intended full automation of benefits payments by 2003. McCartney, said the NFSP men, was "emphatic that he would not accept slippage" and was dismissive of complaints.[24] "If there were problems with software, training etc then these should have been flagged up earlier".[25] The junior minister, who one of the sub-postmasters' counsel would tell the inquiry 23 years later was "woefully reckless",[26] had a simple if wildly optimistic message: "You will make it work."[27]

With nobody prepared to countermand the Post Office's sole shareholder, a system that was never going to "work" properly was never going to be rejected either. In late September 1999, Horizon duly achieved "acceptance", heralding

---

21 Post Office board meeting minutes, 20 July 1999, POL00000352
22 Miller and Sweetman, inquiry evidence, 28 October-1 November 2022
23 Report of National Federation of Sub-Postmasters NEC meeting, NFSP00000471
24 Ibid
25 Notes on NFSP Horizon working group meeting, 22 June 1999, NFSP00000203
26 Ed Henry KC, closing statement on Phase 2 of inquiry, 7 December 2022, SUBS0000018
27 NFSP00000471

its rollout to around 20,000 post offices over the next couple of years. The full "acceptance criteria" were far from being met, but the timetable demanded the go-ahead.

Further conditions had been imposed in return for this concession. But these were also immediately missed. By late November, "the overall level of errors [had] greatly exceeded the 0.6 percent target level – by an order of magnitude or more", said Post Office contract manager Keith Baines.[28] The future looked bleak too. ICL was developing new software to track bugs and there was bad news here, too: "Also, there have been new incidents that it seems would not have been trapped by the integrity control you are developing," Baines told Miller in November.

ICL's code of dishonour

Just like New Labour, ICL and its Japanese parent Fujitsu had more pressing concerns than the quality of a new IT system. ICL chief executive Keith Todd had repeatedly promised that the loss-making company would float on the stock market by the end of 2000 – generating a handsome payout on his own share options – and the last thing he needed was failure on its most important contract.

He knew, however, that ICL's work on Horizon had been catastrophic from the outset. As early as October 1997, consultants from PA Consulting Group were telling the company that it had "seriously misjudged" the work required.[29] As errors and effects in the software mounted in the autumn of 1998, ICL asked one of its development managers and an auditor to form a taskforce to get to the heart of the issues.

Particularly problematic was the EPOSS (electronic point of sale system) used by Post Office counters. This translated entries on the Horizon screen by the sub-postmaster or staff member into the IT events that would ultimately determine the branch's results, and thus how much cash there should be at the end of the day. The taskforce reported "significant deficiencies". Its authors, Horizon deputy development manager David McDonnell and internal auditor Jan Holmes, concluded bluntly: "Whoever wrote this code clearly has no understanding of elementary mathematics or the most basic rules of programming."[30] In technical terms, the code was, one insider from the time would later tell journalist Nick Wallis, "a bag of shit". The system was "a prototype that had been bloated and hacked together afterwards for several

---

28 Email from Keith Baines to Miller, 18 November 1999, POL00028550
29 PA Consulting Group review, 1 October 1997, POL00028092
30 Report on the EPOSS PinICL Task Force, 18 September 1998, FUJ00080690

years, and then pushed screaming and kicking out of the door. It should never have seen the light of day. Never."[31]

But still the ICL executives persisted with it. Todd sought to limit testing to a "model office" before reluctantly accepting the need for extensive live trials. The thinking seemed to be that a Whac-A-Mole approach of fixing bugs when they arose would suffice. It didn't, and errors continued to sprout. In October 1999, an audit found the same pattern of frequent bugs and errors. "The figures indicate that the problems facing EPOSS during the task force period have not diminished."[32] ICL, concluded Jan Holmes, should think about rewriting the code.

For the heavily incentivised ICL executives, however, the race was on to get the system into post office branches. They didn't alert the Post Office to the technical fiasco at their end, even though the effect was mayhem in the trial branches.[33] The company rejected the idea of what would be an expensive and delaying rewrite. "Effectively," wrote ICL Pathway's Horizon programme director Mike Coombs, "as a management team we have accepted the ongoing cost of maintenance rather than the cost of a rewrite."[34] In other words, we'll wing it.

For the higher-ups at ICL, the small matter of an IT company botching its IT programmes was eclipsed by commercial priorities. Todd's commercial and legal director Richard Christou, a lawyer turned hard-nosed commercial negotiator, succeeded him as chief executive in August 2000. He inherited a company losing tens of millions of pounds annually and would turn it around by riding the wave of outsourcing by the government that was ICL's largest client – on everything from healthcare IT to defence. Christou had led the bidding and negotiations on the Post Office deal and saw it as his baby. In later life he would reflect on it as his proudest achievement. "I did that, nobody else did," he would tell an interviewer in 2019. "They still have the contract, 25 years later, and it's been their most profitable."[35]

With Christou at the helm over the following years, his baby became a very difficult child. It continued to be plagued by bugs and defects but, in the dash for cash, these didn't enter his calculations. The taskforce updates listing the latest IT fiascos were not something that he or the ICL board would bother with, despite the timebombs they were planting in the company and in the Post Office. It was all, Christou would tell the public

---

31 *Computer Weekly*, 19 February 2021
32 ICL Pathway development audit, 28 October 1999, FUJ00079782
33 Henry closing Phase 2
34 ICL Pathway schedule of corrective actions, 10 May 2000, WITN04600104
35 archivesit.org.uk/interviews/richard-christou/

inquiry in 2024, "a technical issue and it's not something that would have been raised at board level".[36]

Preoccupied with near-term commercial costs, those around the boardroom tables both in ICL and at the Post Office's HQ in London's Old Street lacked any curiosity about the IT system on which their businesses depended. Guarding immediate financial interests above all else, they limited the bad technical news they received and ignored what they did.

Instruments of torture

Unfortunately for the sub-postmasters, just as their need for protection from rogue IT was about to become critical, techno-mania was getting everywhere. It even infected Britain's dusty legal establishment. In 1997, this culminated in a transformative recommendation from the Law Commission – a statutory body of judges, academics and senior lawyers – for the repeal of an important piece of criminal evidential law.[37]

Since 1984 computer evidence had been admissible in prosecutions only if it could be shown that the technology was operating properly. As one judge warned in the late 1980s: "[Computers] do occasionally malfunction. Software systems often have 'bugs'… Realistically, therefore, computers must be regarded as imperfect devices."[38]

By the late 1990s, however, the big brains of the legal profession believed that this law "serves no useful purpose". Technological progress meant it was "increasingly impractical to examine (and therefore certify) all the intricacies of computer operation". Its repeal would throw the burden of proof back on to defendants, lumbering them with an old common-law principle that "in the absence of evidence to the contrary, the courts will presume that mechanical instruments were in order at the material time". (This was a standard adopted to allow coppers in court to rely on their watches for the correct time they'd nabbed somebody.)

In its enthusiasm to embrace the new information age, the commission thought that reversion to the old ways would not "result in a conviction merely because the defence had failed to adduce evidence of malfunction it was in no position to advance". Although access to (and usually control of) the machines tended to be in the hands of prosecutors rather than defendants, the "regime would work fairly". They were reassured by support from prosecutors including the Crown Prosecution Service, the Inland Revenue (now HM

---

36 Richard Christou, inquiry evidence, 19 June 2024
37 Law Commission, *Evidence in Criminal Proceedings: Hearsay and Related Topics*, 1997
38 Mr Justice Steyn, *R v Minors*, 14 December 1988

Revenue & Customs) and, tellingly, the Post Office itself. In mid-1999, just as the mother of all malfunctioning computer programs was being unleashed, the change was duly enacted.

What the commission thought implausible – convictions because defendants couldn't show IT malfunction – in fact almost perfectly described what would happen over the following years. The contract for the Horizon system explicitly required ICL Pathway to provide data to the Post Office for use in prosecutions, but not to any accused sub-postmaster.

As the Horizon system rolled out across the country, planting its corrupted technology in post office branches from the Lizard to Shetland at the rate of hundreds every month, the legal dice had been decisively loaded against sub-postmasters.

2

FRAMED

The Post Office deploys Horizon against its sub-postmasters and ignores an expert's exposé of the system

THE Post Office's attitude towards sub-postmasters, as independent small businesspeople who stood apart from the corporate body, was already one of suspicion and high-handedness. It was born of centuries of protectiveness towards the King's Mail (which, until 1837, it remained a capital offence to interfere with) and then of the money passing through the country's post offices and sub-post offices. In the modern era, it was drilled into staff that they were, above all, stewards of public money. Of itself, this was reasonable; the treatment of sub-postmasters that it was used to justify was anything but.

The Post Office began prosecuting nearly 150 years before the country's first police force, making it the oldest criminal investigations body in the world. It continued to do so for 330 years, even after the Crown Prosecution Service was established in the 1980s following a Royal Commission. It had found that sometimes biased and often substandard police prosecutions needed a dose of objectivity applied to them before getting near a court.

Although other organisations, such as transport authorities and charities like the RSPCA, also conduct private prosecutions, right up until 2013 the Post Office was the only body to maintain its own large, dedicated team of investigators and prosecution lawyers to take on serious crimes committed by what might be considered its own people. This came with certain limitations, such as not having powers of arrest or search and seizure. But, without these powers and, more importantly, the rules and discipline constraining them, Post Office investigators routinely cut corners – in everything from the way they collected evidence to explaining sub-postmasters' rights to them. They were, in short, amateurish.

With even the Post Office's senior executives often unaware that their own organisation rather than the CPS was prosecuting sub-postmasters, by the time Horizon was rolled out, the investigation division's 100 or so investigators[1] – part of the Post Office's wider security division – were already a law unto themselves. Most had risen through the organisation, had little formal training and were subject to no independent oversight in the way that police officers were, however imperfectly, by the Independent Police Complaints Commission (as it was until 2018).

False accounts

At the turn of the 21st century, Pamela Lock had been the sub-postmaster in Cwmdu in Swansea for 25 years, working alongside her husband Geoffrey's successful bakery business and providing the kind of community service for which the post office existed. In a quarter of a century, she'd had no problems with her branch accounts beyond the odd minor discrepancy that she could always track back through the paperwork. That changed the moment Horizon was installed in her branch in January 2000.

As with so many sub-postmasters at the time, Mrs Lock had no real computer experience. But, having received just two and a half days' training, she started performing all the transactions she had previously recorded on paper through the new system. Shortfalls began to appear almost immediately. Her repeated calls to the Post Office's Network Business Support Centre helpline in Chesterfield proved useless. She was falsely reassured that the discrepancies would somehow resolve themselves. They didn't. They accumulated weekly and after six months ran to £31,000. But, in order to keep trading, she had been forced to declare weekly that the books balanced. One morning that July, Post Office auditors arrived, discovered the shortfall, asked where the missing money was, and – as it never actually existed and was therefore nowhere to be seen – shut Mrs Lock's branch down.

Within weeks, Post Office investigators were badgering her with the same question. They suggested she employ a forensic accountant. She did. The beancounter reported that the Locks' finances showed no suggestion of them having benefited from the £31,000 or any money improperly. But this cut no ice with the investigators; they had the unimpeachable Horizon shortfall number and that was enough for them. (In another case around the same time, investigators inadvertently gave away the Kafkaesque position that suspects were in by asking London counter clerk Tracy Felstead "Can you demonstrate how you did not steal the money?")[2]

In November 2001, Pamela Lock stood in the dock of Swansea Crown Court and pleaded guilty to three counts of false accounting. She had been

---
1 Anthony Marsh, inquiry evidence, 5 July 2023
2 Court of Appeal judgment, *Hamilton & Others v Post Office*, 2021

advised to do so by her lawyer in return for a theft charge being dropped. She was ordered to repay the balance of the shortfall she hadn't already funded. The story of the conviction and her photograph hit the front page of that day's widely read *South Wales Evening Post*. She received a community service sentence but, more importantly, lost her post office branch and standing in the community she'd served. Her staff lost their jobs. Locals were angry that they now had to travel further afield for the services she had offered. Before long, the Locks were forced to sell the bakery business, too, and retire. Three years later Geoffrey died, his ill health brought on, Mrs Lock believes, by stress.

As Pamela Lock would later put it: "How could a woman work as a postmaster for 25 years without problems of any kind and then suddenly change and become dishonest and inept?"[3] That was an obvious question that the Post Office investigators did not bother to ask. Or, more likely, did not want to ask. Their evidence was, in effect, a defective stock-take from "auditors" who had not even looked into the IT records. But, with the law on computer evidence stacked in their favour, it sufficed to get the Post Office the desired result. The destruction of the Locks' lives was incidental.

Successful challenge

Convictions such as Pamela Lock's showed what easy prey sub-postmasters now were. They were being held liable for any branch losses, real or imaginary, under their one-sided and wilfully misinterpreted contract. They were also under extreme weekly pressure to sign off trading statements every Wednesday. If they didn't, they wouldn't be able to open their post office the following day. But if they acknowledged a shortfall, even when convinced it was caused by the faulty Horizon system, they could expect ruinous financial demands very soon.

A further possibility involved moving the shortfall to a "suspense account", a form of bookkeeping limbo that stalled recovery by the Post Office, but this was allowed only with the approval of a regional manager. Many, like Mrs Lock, would feel compelled to submit incorrect statements claiming that their accounts balanced in order to survive. This then presented the opportunity for easy convictions. Hundreds would plead guilty to the lesser offence of false accounting in an effective deal that (usually) kept them out of prison. Then the Post Office would be able to deploy stronger criminal financial powers to "recover" the money that had never been taken in the first place.

It was clear from very early on that evidence-free prosecutions such as Pamela Lock's were unmerited. If challenged with some of the real evidence

---

3 Pamela Lock, quoted in closing submissions by Sam Stein KC at inquiry, 16 December 2024

that investigators were denying sub-postmasters, they often didn't stand up. In Northern Ireland, Maureen McKelvey had been running her post office branch in the village of Clanabogan, near Omagh, for a decade when Horizon was foisted on her. Money immediately began to "disappear". She was spun the standard lines: that she was the only one with difficulties (half of sub-postmasters would report being told this) and that discrepancies would right themselves. They didn't, forcing her to put £25,000 in from the shop she ran alongside the post office. When an audit in 2001 found another shortfall, she was immediately suspended and charged with theft.

It took five years for the case to come to court. Despite the toll this took on her physical and mental health, Mrs McKelvey maintained her innocence and pleaded not guilty at Dungannon Crown Court. Fortuitously, a selection of shortfalls randomly selected to put before the jury showed that one had cropped up when a stand-in official from the main Omagh post office had covered for her. (The Post Office's investigator in the case, Suzanne Winter, had omitted any mention of this in her report to the Police Service of Northern Ireland, which ran prosecutions in the province; had she done so, the prosecution might have been avoided.)

Maureen McKelvey was duly acquitted, the judge calling the Post Office's case a "sham".[4] But even then the Post Office denied her the vindication she'd earned. Post Office security officials whisked her away from the courtroom, telling her she was not allowed to talk to the assembled press. She would later describe the organisation's behaviour as "'Mafia' like".[5]

Broken records

These early cases typified the co-ordinated callousness, and ineptness, of the Post Office. Its auditors, the first ones on the scene when it came to branch shortfalls, did not in fact audit. They weren't qualified in either accounting or IT systems, and received little training for their role. They were glorified stock-takers who compared what was left in a branch at any point with what the Horizon system said there should be.

The "investigators" to whom the auditors' findings were passed – who'd generally had three weeks' training before being unleashed on work that could put people behind bars – didn't actually investigate the IT evidence on which they based prosecutions and other sanctions. As Maureen McKelvey's investigator, Suzanne Winter, would eventually admit, "I did not know of any problem with the

---
4 Quoted by Christopher Jacobs at inquiry, 26 January 2024
5 Maureen McKelvey, witness statement to inquiry, WITN03700100

Horizon system."⁶ She didn't know because she didn't try to find out if there were any. This was despite the obligation implicit in her job title and the possibilities of IT errors having been raised with her by both Mrs McKelvey and a previously suspected sub-postmaster. In the earlier case, Winter had even received a report from a firm of forensic accountants employed by the sub-postmaster, suggesting that false accounting entries could have been down to IT errors. She would later claim that she had been repeatedly told by her superiors that Horizon was 100 percent reliable and that "if you started to challenge too much, it didn't go well".⁷

The occasional IT-related enquiries the Post Office sleuths did make were limited to "audit record queries" (ARQs), made to a team in ICL, or Fujitsu Services as it was renamed in April 2002. But, under a service agreement, even these were limited. Any requests above this limit would incur costs the Post Office could do without. Defence requests for Horizon data were often therefore resisted, and Post Office investigators were told by ICL that they had hit the monthly allocation.⁸ The upshot was the absurd Catch-22 situation in which, as one Post Office head of investigations would later admit, the Post Office would "only investigate if there is a Horizon System fault, if there is already evidence of a Horizon System fault".⁹

In any event, it was always known by Fujitsu and the Post Office that the information produced through an ARQ – essentially a record of keys supposedly pressed in a Post Office branch, but treating duplications or omissions of entries as genuine – wasn't capable of establishing the absence of glitches. A "network banking prosecution support policy" drawn up in 2002 had envisaged far greater information being provided by the IT company, such as more detailed "event logs" that showed everything affecting a branch's IT record. But auditors and investigators were conveniently not trained in examining such records – and didn't ask for them.¹⁰

Bug life

Had investigators been motivated and equipped to delve deeper into the underlying computer records, they would have understood the hopelessness of the Horizon code and the chaos at the Fujitsu HQ in Bracknell that was wrestling with it.

One of the vanishingly few whistleblowers to come forward at any point in the scandal, former Fujitsu software engineer Richard Roll, would much

---

6 Suzanne Winter, inquiry evidence, 26 January 2024
7 Ibid
8 Judgment in *Hamilton* appeal, 23 April 2021, and Gary Thomas, inquiry evidence, 7 December 2023
9 Anthony Marsh, inquiry evidence, 5 March 2023
10 Ed Henry KC, closing statement on Phase 4 of inquiry, 2 February 2024

later tell the *Eye* that, in the early 2000s, a dedicated team was running "a constant rolling programme of patches to fix the bugs". Fearing financial penalties on the company's key contract, it "would basically tell the Post Office what they wanted to hear".[11] He would also reveal how software engineers regularly altered branch accounts from Bracknell in order to correct mistakes, entering transactions as if they were the sub-postmaster. (Oddly enough, the value of such "transaction corrections" was vastly higher when fixing mistaken surpluses that favoured sub-postmasters than it was for putting right erroneous sub-postmaster deficits – where the preferred option was for them to cough up.) This "remote access" was about as obvious a sign as possible that the IT was misfiring but, like the bugs themselves, would be covered up for a couple of decades.

Those "bugs, errors and defects" – already well known within Fujitsu and bearing names such as the "Callendar Square/Falkirk bug" (after the branch where it was identified), "reversals", "data tree build failure discrepancies", "Girobank discrepancies", "phantom transactions", "reconciliation issues" – had been proliferating across the Horizon-benighted post office network since roll-out. The spurious branch figures they threw up could be absurd; as early as July 1999 one branch showed an impossible cash discrepancy of £1.08m. Fujitsu's logs noted this as "due [to] a known software error that has no [*sic*] been resolved" (in the usual botching, patch-and-mend fashion).[12]

Any independent technical examination of Horizon in action would paint a very unflattering picture. The Post Office was about to be presented with just that.

Critical friend

Another woman who dared to question her treatment was Julie Wolstenholme, sub-postmaster at the Cleveleys branch in Lancashire. She had recently taken it over from her parents, who'd run it successfully from 1990. After Horizon's installation in February 2000 she began to experience relentless malfunctions. "The system was crashing up to six times per day," she would later testify. "Ghost transactions and, more importantly, excessive misbalances [were appearing]... the system would alter, swap or delete of its own accord."[13]

Mrs Wolstenholme made 90 calls to the helpdesk, usually being told to reboot the system, which didn't work. By November, with shortfalls mounting, she called the helpdesk one more time. On this occasion an official admitted

---

11 Richard Brooks and Nick Wallis, *Justice Lost in the Post* special report, *Eye* 1519, April 2020
12 *Bates v Post Office*, Judgment No. 6, "Horizon Issues", 16 December 2019
13 Julie Kay (formerly Wolstenholme), witness statement to inquiry, WITN09020100

there were IT problems. She rang her retail network manager, Elaine Tagg – who had previously visited the Cleveleys branch and encountered problems of her own with Horizon – and told her she wouldn't use Horizon until matters were resolved. The manager arrived at the office the same day with a letter suspending Mrs Wolstenholme and demanding what was now a £15,000 shortfall.

Even though she wasn't prosecuted, the increasingly familiar toll of consequences – lost home, broken relationship, suspicion in the community and impoverishment – followed for Julie Wolstenholme. But she also turned the tables on the Post Office. While it sued her for the shortfall, she counter-claimed for wrongful termination of her contract on the grounds that she had been forced to use an IT system that wasn't up to the job.

The ensuing battle should have presented a golden opportunity for the Post Office and ICL/Fujitsu to face the truth of their shambolic IT system. Instead, they saw the case as a mortal threat. The Post Office's IT risk register was updated to read: "Damage to reputation of Post Office and potential future financial losses if PO loses court case relating to reliability of Horizon accounting data at Cleveleys Branch Office".[14] Exposing the IT system's fallibility would compromise all that mattered most to the Post Office.

This defensive reaction followed an order from the court that an expert be appointed to look at Horizon's operation in the Cleveleys branch. In January 2004, Law Society-accredited IT specialist Jason Coyne was jointly instructed by both sides to examine 90 "fault logs", ie Mrs Wolstenholme's complaints to the helpdesk. He concluded that 63 of them were "without doubt system-related failures" and that "the technology installed at the Cleveleys sub-post office was clearly defective in elements of its hardware, software or interfaces".[15] Most of the errors "could not be attributed to being of Mrs Wolstenholme's making or operation of the system".

Rather than taking seriously this reality check on an IT system operating in almost every Post Office branch in the UK, the Post Office's executives, lawyers and investigators, along with Fujitsu's IT engineers, instinctively covered up. The software support centre manager who was presented with Coyne's report, career Fujitsu man Steve Parker, was particularly dismissive. "Any technology that runs 24 hours a day will have hardware defects that require fixing," he wrote to Fujitsu audit manager Jan Holmes. "This is normal business."[16] As for Coyne's view that the level of discrepancies was "worrying",

---

14 Post Office risk-opps and forecast analysis, period 1 2004/05, POL00120833
15 Jason Coyne, witness statement to inquiry, WITN00210101
16 Email from Steve Parker to Jan Holmes at Fujitsu, 17 February 2004, WITN04600304

Parker said: "No way... Almost all accounting errors in computer systems are caused by user error. GIGO principle [garbage-in-garbage-out]." Coyne would later describe this view as "delusional".[17] The same could have been said of Parker's comment – remarkable for somebody with such experience of Horizon – that "17,000 PMs [sub-postmasters] are not complaining of misbalancing and transactions."[18]

Over at Post Office HQ, the people who had fretted over the development of the system before roll-out were also trying to bury the problem. Keith Baines, the contracts manager who four years earlier had reported that errors in branches trialling Horizon were exceeding targets by "an order of magnitude", now contacted his counterpart at Fujitsu in mild panic. "As I'm sure you will understand, Post Office is concerned by these findings, not only in relation to this particular case," he wrote to commercial and finance director Colin Lenton-Smith, "but also because of any precedent that this may set and that may be used by Post Office's agents [sub-postmasters] to support claims that the Horizon System is causing errors in their branch accounts."[19]

Drafting a response to Coyne's findings, Fujitsu audit manager Jan Holmes grew irritated. "I've done a bit more to this but if I continue I fear I might call him a git, or something worse," he wrote.[20] Holmes's intolerance of criticism of Horizon was bizarre given that he had been one of the co-authors of the 1998 report into the EPOSS part of Horizon that had listed a host of faults and concluded that the code-writers must have had "no understanding of elementary mathematics or the most basic rules of programming".[21] He'd authored a later report saying it "continues to be unstable".[22] But Holmes was never the most consistent. He had also given evidence in the 2002 prosecution of 19-year-old Tracy Felstead that the Horizon system was operating properly at the Camberwell Green Post Office, where she worked, despite all he knew of Horizon's failings. At his relatively senior level in Fujitsu, threats to expose Horizon were clearly a severe annoyance.

Fujitsu's and the Post Office's interests in Julie Wolstenholme's case were closely aligned. As she stood her ground and a trial date loomed, the shared priority to limit the wider damage morphed into a plan to silence the troublesome sub-postmaster. By April 2004, Holmes told Lenton-Smith that

---

17 Coyne, inquiry evidence, 26 July 2023
18 WITN04600304
19 Letter from Keith Baines to Colin Lenton-Smith, 5 February 2004, POL00095375
20 Email from Holmes to Lenton-Smith, 11 March 2004, FUJ00121557
21 FUJ00080690
22 ICL Pathway schedule of corrective actions, 22 November 1999, FUJ00079783

the Post Office lawyer in charge of civil cases, Mandy Talbot, thought that "the safest way to manage this is to throw money at it and get a confidentiality agreement signed".[23] Talbot, he said, "wants, if possible, to keep it out of the public domain", which was "unlikely to happen if it goes to court".

Without the backing required to face the financial jeopardy of a trial, Julie Wolstenholme had to settle her case, for an amount that would never reflect her true losses. A note from the Post Office's barrister advising on the settlement terms gave away what its game was. "I am asked to take into particular account that the Post Office is anxious for the negative computer expert's [Coyne's] report to be given as little publicity as possible," he wrote.[24] Mrs Wolstenholme was duly silenced with a non-disclosure agreement. All was signed off by none other than network managing director David Miller, who had been programme director for Horizon in the late 1990s and knew intimately the errors that the system was capable of producing.[25]

State of denial

The Post Office had bought the silence that it and Fujitsu needed. But deep residual concerns were revealed in a reflective email from Fujitsu's Jan Holmes to Colin Lenton-Smith at the Post Office that August, on the subject of "risk position on litigation support". It was laced with the disdain for sub-postmasters felt across the two organisations.

"Although Cleveleys may appear to be closed it could be construed that [the Post Office] bought off Mrs Wolstenholme rather than defend their system," wrote Holmes. "Even if a gagging order is placed on the woman she apparently had a gaggle of postmasters lined up to support her case and they will be well aware of what the final outcome was. I'm sure that they will not be keeping quiet."[26]

A similar dispute had blown up in the meantime at the Shobnall Road branch in Burton-on-Trent. For that, Fujitsu had been asked to provide "a witness statement to the effect that nothing contained in the [Fujitsu service centre calls] could have caused, or be described as, a system malfunction". Alas, reported Holmes: "Comments made by engineers that 'keyboards can cause phantom transactions' do not help the Post Office's position." The exasperated Fujitsu man summed up the dire situation: "How many more Cleveleys and Shobnall Road howlers exist in the [helpline] archive? Two

---

23 Email from Holmes to Lenton-Smith, 7 June 2004, FUJ00121637
24 Advice from SA Brochwicz-Lewinski, 26 July 2004, POL00118229
25 David Miller, inquiry evidence, 16 April 2024
26 Email from Holmes to Lenton-Smith and William Mitchell, 20 August 2004, FUJ00121724

out of two is a bit of a worry." His company's support of the Post Office's legal cases "warrants a bit more thought".[27]

If it ever happened, that thought did not include any consideration of whether the Post Office should be using an obviously woeful IT system in an increasing number of prosecutions, which hit 94 in 2004. Nor was there any suggestion that the investigators and prosecutors ought to be informed of Jason Coyne's findings about technological defects. Fujitsu and Post Office executives took the easier, and more profitable, option of doubling down. The party line, it was agreed, was to remain as Keith Baines had put it in a thoroughly misleading witness statement for the Wolstenholme case: "Any faults that occurred in the Horizon computer system were eliminated once they were identified… All sub-postmasters were fully trained in the use of the Horizon equipment. The system was fully tested before it was used by the Post Office and it is fit for its purpose. The system itself does not create losses."[28] Never mind that this was wrong on every point; it was the necessary position.

"It's got your fingerprints all over it"

---
27 Ibid
28 Baines, witness statement in *POCL v Wolstenholme*, 14 October 2003, POL00118250

3

WALES OF PROTEST

The Post Office stifles early dissent and crushes any opposition

LEADING the "gaggle of sub-postmasters", honking increasingly loudly about their mistreatment over branch "shortfalls", was a certain Mr Alan Bates of Craig-y-Don in Llandudno. His contract had been terminated a few months before Julie Wolstenholme was forced to settle her case, following his sustained refusal to "make good" an unidentifiable shortfall of just over £1,000 that he had transferred to a Post Office "suspense account". He'd successfully managed to pinpoint a £5,000 Horizon error, bringing the shortfall down from £6,000 and, fortunately for thousands of sub-postmasters, stubbornly refused to pay up for the rest.

Bates, 49 at the time, had been particularly irked by the Post Office's refusal to let him see the record of Horizon entries for his branch, which disappeared from a sub-postmaster's view at the end of the weekly accounting period. It seemed an obvious unfairness when at the same time he was presumed by Post Office managers to be liable for the "shortfall" that this data was generating. Bates had offered to repay the amount if it could be shown, in line with his contract, that it was down to his "negligence, carelessness or error". But, with the burden of proof inverted and without the information to show it was not due to these things, he was, like Kafka's protagonist in *The Trial*, "condemned not only when he's innocent, but also in ignorance".

Alan and his partner Suzanne lost their livelihoods and the £100,000 that they had invested in the branch and its linked haberdashery shop, together known as the Wool Post. He was advised that legal action against the Post Office would merely heap more financial misery on them. So, conscious that others were almost certainly experiencing similar problems, he decided on a different tack.

What became a historic campaign for justice started with a letter to the *North Wales Weekly News* in October 2003 explaining a story that "all began in October 2000 when the Post Office installed the Horizon computer system". Alongside Bates's letter, two locals complained of how elderly customers would have to travel into Llandudno because of the loss of the "well run" Wool Post with its "friendly atmosphere". A steely-eyed Bates was pictured outside the business he'd just lost. "I can assure everyone I will not give up on the issue until the Craig-y-Don post office returns to the Wool Post," he wrote, adding – in words that might now raise a wry smile – "whether it takes three months or three years."[1]

Bates was planting the seeds of the initiative that would eventually defeat his tormentor. He created the Postofficevictims.org website and emblazoned the name on a banner above the shop. This was the movement that would bring victims together and ultimately prove that their experiences were not their fault but that of the Post Office and its misuse of the Horizon IT system.

An insecure institution already up to its neck in malpractice would do whatever it took to hide this truth for many more years. It would even conspire to commit crimes of its own to maintain its fictions.

Uncivil proceedings

The sub-postmaster at South Marine Drive in Bridlington, on the Yorkshire coast, could not have been more open with the Post Office about the trouble he began to encounter in January 2004.

Thirty-five-year-old former RAF technician Lee Castleton and his wife Lisa-Marie had taken on the branch and newsagent attached to it six months earlier, seeking a new life with their two young children. For a while they encountered few problems. When discrepancies began to appear, Lee was straight on to the Post Office's helpline, only to be reassured vaguely that all would work itself out. It didn't. Discrepancies cropped up increasingly regularly over the following weeks. With 91 calls to the helpline proving fruitless, an exasperated Lee called for the auditors to come in.

On 23 March 2004, Post Office auditor Helen Rose arrived and confirmed a £25,756 shortfall. Lee's regional manager immediately suspended him. With locals soon suspecting and even taunting his family, he set about trying to get the bottom of the problem. His efforts were met with the same refusal to supply the needed information that Alan Bates had faced. Demands for payment followed as his family's lives spiralled into despair.

Yet when the Post Office's demands for money went to Scarborough County Court almost two years after his suspension, the Post Office failed to turn up. It was Lee's counter-claim for damages for his wrongful suspension that succeeded – although not, alas, for long. He was to get the full Post Office

---

[1] *North Wales Weekly News*, 23 October 2003

double whammy of amateurishness followed by vindictiveness. Realising the significance of its defeat, the Post Office reinstated its claims, this time for hearing before the High Court.

So important did the Post Office consider the Castleton case that its senior civil lawyer, Mandy Talbot, was prepared to further the organisation's corporate interests, seemingly without stopping to question whether they were at odds with the interests of justice. At one point early in 2006, Stephen Dilley, a solicitor from the Post Office's external civil lawyers, Bond Pearce (now Womble Bond Dickinson), reported that Talbot's "view is that the PO must not show any weakness and even if this case will cost a lot, there are broader issues at stake other than just Castleton's claim: if the PO are seen to compromise on Castleton, then 'the whole system will come crashing down' i.e. it will egg on other sub-postmasters to issue speculative claims."[2] Soon before the trial, Talbot wrote that a judgment against Castleton "will be of tremendous use in convincing other postmasters to think twice about their allegations".[3]

It was obvious from the numbers alone that this was not a genuine claim for recompense of losses. Spending more than £300,000 of public money that would never be recovered was, remarked Post Office counsel Richard Morgan, "madness". The case against Castleton was a commercial initiative – protecting the Horizon system and the Post Office brand – for which the law was not intended.

No tactics were too underhand. When Morgan asked Talbot ahead of the court case whether the Post Office knew of any issues with Horizon, she failed to mention the damning Coyne report produced for the Wolstenholme case, in which she had been so closely involved not that long before. She did at one point tell her Post Office colleagues that "Fujitsu should be able to check the system with particular reference to Marine Drive [at the relevant time] to confirm whether or not they have found any evidence of the problems complained of by Castleton", and state that "I need to know whether there's any justification for this allegation."[4] But, conveniently, she heard nothing more, and didn't follow it up.

The Fujitsu team were equally determined to do whatever it took to win. Ahead of the trial, the company's litigation support manager, Peter Sewell, wrote to Andy Dunks, a Fujitsu security analyst who was due to appear as a witness. "That Castleton is a nasty chap and will be all out to rubbish the FJ

---

[2] Email from Stephen Dilley to Julian Summerhayes, 24 February 2006, WITN09510100
[3] Email by Mandy Talbot, 9 November 2006, POL00113909. For these aspects of the *Castleton* case, see in particular inquiry appearances of Talbot, 28 September 2023, and Richard Morgan and Stephen Dilly, 22 September 2023
[4] Email from Talbot to colleagues, 1 December 2005, POL00071202

name," he said. It was "up to you to maintain absolute strength and integrity no matter what the prosecution throw at you".[5] While this betrayed a certain misunderstanding of the legal process (neither the Post Office nor Fujitsu was being prosecuted), and perhaps of the word "integrity", it was certainly on-message. Sewell concluded: "We will all be behind you hoping you come through unscathed. Bless you." Dunks responded: "I had to pause halfway through reading it to wipe away a small tear."[6] None of which sounded like preparation for giving objective evidence in a court of law.

At least one member of the Post Office team didn't want the case to go ahead. Two days before the hearing, solicitor Stephen Dilley rang Castleton, who couldn't afford legal representation, trying to persuade him to concede. When Lee explained that he was pushing on, if only to get some answers, he recalled Dilley telling him: "But Lee, we are the Post Office, we will ruin you."[7] He would later deny having said this, but he would not have been wrong and may even have felt justified in giving the warning.

Immoral bankruptcy

Post Office Ltd v Castleton, heard in the High Court in London over six days in December 2006 and January 2007, encapsulated the sub-postmasters' legal bind. By signing off weekly balances showing shortfalls, Castleton had given what the law calls an "account stated". The courts would presume this to be an acceptance of the financial position. "The statement of the account, though not its validity, is admitted," said His Honour Judge Richard Havery QC at the trial. "Accordingly, the burden of proof lies on Mr Castleton to show that the account is wrong."[8] But that, of course, was an impossible hurdle to get over, given the further legal presumption of computing accuracy and the inability of sub-postmasters to access underlying IT records.

The Post Office rubbed Castleton's nose in this impossible predicament. Not only was he liable but, said its counsel Richard Morgan gratuitously, he was "a thief". In another assault on his character, in keeping with the campaign to demonise Castleton, the auditor Helen Rose made the false allegation that he had smelled of alcohol when she visited his branch.

Castleton did have some evidence. His temporary successors had also experienced discrepancies. The sub-postmaster at the South Marine Drive branch by the time of the trial was having repeated problems with debit cards

---

5 Email from Peter Sewell to Andy Dunks, 7 December 2006, FUJ00154750
6 FUJ00154750
7 Lee Castleton, witness statement, WITN03730100
8 *Post Office Ltd v Lee Castleton* judgment, 22 January 2007, POL00004325

and was, in the judge's own words, "convinced that the problem was with the Horizon system".⁹ Lee also knew of complaints of errors at another branch. The key witness in the case, a softly spoken senior Fujitsu IT engineer working in its software support centre called Anne Chambers, admitted these were caused by a bug – the Callendar Square one – but reassured the judge there was no evidence of it at South Marine Drive.

Chambers had prepared for the case with a more senior IT engineer, Gareth Jenkins, whose false evidence in other cases would become infamous. He'd told Dilley that "it is certain that the most likely explanation [for the shortfalls] is misoperation or fraud" and had "firmed up" Chambers's written evidence.¹⁰ She had also been instructed by colleagues in Fujitsu's security and customer services divisions not to mention so-called "Horizon Known Error Logs", the very name of which was a bit of a giveaway, and complied with the request. She knew, too, that Fujitsu support services staff could remotely insert transactions into branch accounts, posing as the sub-postmaster, but chose not to mention this. Nor did she raise a "known fault" that was causing the system to register stamps as missing at Marine Drive.

The most important man in the courtroom, Judge Havery, was nevertheless convinced by Chambers. The Fujitsu engineer had, he said, "concluded that there was no evidence whatsoever of any problem with the system".¹¹ She was "a clear, knowledgeable and reliable witness, and I accept her evidence". And that was more or less that for Lee Castleton. The shortfalls, said Havery, were "real deficiencies and as such are irrefutable evidence that Marine Drive was not properly managed at the material time". The Post Office had been entitled to terminate his contract. "Moreover," added the judge, "the losses must have been caused by his own error or that of his assistants." With his bill for the shortfall and the Post Office's legal costs approaching £350,000, bankruptcy and years of hardship followed for the Castleton family.

At the Post Office, joy abounded. Talbot emailed colleagues that "the judgment has entirely vindicated the Horizon system".¹² Head of branch accounting Rod Ismay, who understood the system-wide importance of Horizon integrity, replied "great news". Then, straying slightly beyond a beancounter's brief, he added "What can we do on a proactive comms front here?" *Post Office v Castleton* had always been a show trial.

One woman, though, was troubled. Through what she had and hadn't

---

9 Ibid
10 Gareth Jenkins, inquiry evidence, 25 June 2024
11 POL00004325
12 Email from Talbot to colleagues, 22 January 2007, POL00090437

said at her employer's bidding, Anne Chambers had misled the High Court about Horizon. As she put it in a regretful "afterthought" document a week later, "Fujitsu made a major legal blunder by not disclosing all the relevant evidence that was in existence."[13]

Pride and prejudice

The Post Office and Fujitsu groupthink, dictating that shortfalls must be down to sub-postmasters' mistakes or more probably frauds, was clearly so strong that it could make senior and, it seemed, otherwise normal people behave deceitfully and vindictively towards sub-postmasters. It also appeared to be near universal, capturing the auditors, investigators, regional managers, IT engineers and even lawyers. Any enlightened idea of questioning the IT system was squashed or, at best, ignored. Speaking out against the Post Office dogma or the obvious malpractice that it fostered was unthinkable. One former executive responsible for the Post Office's contracts with sub-postmasters, John Breeden, would later tell the public inquiry that protecting the "very, very strong brand" was "just part of the DNA of the business".[14] But this, he agreed, came at the expense of doing the right thing by sub-postmasters.

There were good historic reasons for the strength of the Post Office brand. But the fierce protectiveness towards it, which would ultimately suffocate the organisation, reflected the staleness and insularity of the institution. Many of those holding the sub-postmasters' fates in their hands knew little beyond the Post Office. Investigators had often worked their way up from the counter in Crown offices – those branches run directly by the company – with little broader perspective than a belief that the Post Office was always right. Suzanne Winter, for example, the investigator in the Maureen McKelvey case, had joined the Post Office in 1976 as a counter clerk. Promotion came by not rocking boats – which raising concerns over fairness, justice or the reliability of Horizon certainly would. Much the same went for the principal ICL/Fujitsu engineers relied upon by the Post Office in its mistreatment of sub-postmasters in criminal and civil cases. Gareth Jenkins and Anne Chambers were both graduate mathematicians who had joined the company in 1973 and 1978 respectively. At every turn, sub-postmasters were up against company men and women.

Longstanding, unquestioning loyalty to the brand and the institution distanced staff from sub-postmasters. The latter were outside the command-and-control bureaucracy of the 12,000-strong central organisation. They were

---
13 Anne Chambers, *Afterthoughts on the Castleton Case*, 29 January 2007, FUJ00152299
14 John Breeden, inquiry evidence, 17 October 2023

more entrepreneurial and more ethnically diverse. A 2024 survey suggested 43 percent were from minority ethnic groups. Post Office investigators, as far as could be seen, were white. This separation eroded empathy and produced a prejudice that could turn into outright discrimination and racism. For a time, for example, the Post Office labelled fraud suspects as: "Indian/Pakistani types", "Negroid types" and "Chinese/Japanese types".[15] (At Fujitsu, support centre staff responsible for a Horizon helpline talked of "another Patel scamming again",[16] one staffer later saying "you'd just hear it constantly on the floor").[17] No evidence of racial bias can be seen in matters such as prosecution decisions, but the presence of such attitudes betrayed the belittling of sub-postmasters.

Further up the chain, among bosses equally steeped in Post Office culture, the prevailing attitude was of indifference to the sub-postmasters' plights and how they were landed in them. For the top brass, investigations, prosecutions and dismissals, with the financial recoveries that followed, served the historically important purpose of tackling losses to the Post Office through fraud and error. In the modern corporate world, they allowed them to tick the box for addressing this "risk". The details of how it was done were not something for them to dwell on.

Even the Post Office's head of security from 1999 to 2006, encompassing investigations, would later claim not to have had any awareness of problems with Horizon, which his investigators were being told about almost daily. Tony Marsh, who had started as a postman in 1981 and been promoted through the Crown office setup and the security branch, would tell the inquiry that, with capable people beneath him, "I never really needed to get hands-on in the investigations space." One level below him, his national investigations manager merely rubber-stamped prosecution recommendations from investigators without questioning them.[18] Meanwhile, sitting above the security operation, David Miller, Post Office chief operating officer from 2000 to 2006, chose not to tell Marsh or his investigators what he knew about problems with Horizon from his time as programme manager during its bug-infested implementation.[19]

This was a conspiracy of silence at senior levels. Its essential dishonesty was typified by what happened when, in 2004, Marsh had received a copy of the Coyne report produced for Julie Wolstenholme's case, in which Horizon

---

15 List of identity codes, inquiry evidence, undated, POL00115674
16 Amandeep Singh, witness statement, 13 January 2023, WITN06660100
17 Singh, inquiry evidence, 7 March 2023
18 Anthony Utting, inquiry evidence, 17 November 2023
19 Tony Marsh's inquiry evidence, 5 July 2023, was that nobody told him about Horizon's flaws; David Miller could not recall doing so, 16 April 2024

was called "clearly defective". He took it to Miller. Marsh rubbished it in front of him and Miller didn't read it. Everybody wanted to wish it away.[20]

At the top of the Post Office tree, setting these men's priorities, there was little interest in the lives of sub-postmasters. The chief executive between 1995 and 2002, John Roberts (who had joined in 1967), was aware from the painful birthing of Horizon that the system was far from error-free. But he knew nothing about its use in prosecutions, he would testify. His successor from 2002 until 2005, ex-banker David Mills, was not even aware until the end of his tenure that the Post Office conducted its own prosecutions. This was despite more than 200 Horizon shortfall convictions being secured in the period. Mills's board, preoccupied with addressing £1m-a-day losses at what he would call a "burning ship" of a business, didn't discuss such matters either.

Horizon's arrival had been accompanied by a shift in the Post Office's difficult social-commercial balance. Corporate changes around the same time turbo-charged incentives to put financial performance above all else, and eroded accountability. Even with Horizon's fatal flaws established, internally at least, this shift guaranteed that thousands more sub-postmasters would be victimised and that the only response to challenges would be cover-ups.

---

20 Miller, inquiry evidence, 16 April 2024, says that Marsh "was dismissive of that report"

4

COMMERCIAL BREAK

Financial freedom for the Post Office tightens the shackles on the sub-postmasters…

THE Post Office had been on a commercialising trajectory since Harold Wilson's minister of technology, Tony Benn, made it a public corporation as opposed to a department of state in 1969. He had wanted a "great leap forward" and freedom from the strictures of civil service rules and financial controls.[1]

From the time Margaret Thatcher's government got into its privatisation stride in the 1980s, the prospect of the Post Office going the same way as British Telecom (split from the Post Office in 1981; sold off in 1984) hovered persistently in the background, even though the prime minister publicly rejected the idea ahead of the 1987 general election. She was "not prepared to have the Queen's head privatised" (translation: lose votes in marginal constituencies that liked their local post offices as they were).

The organisation was, however, refashioned to resemble other large businesses. In 1986, reforming chairman Ron Dearing separated the Post Office into four units under an over-arching Post Office Corporation. These were: Post Office Counters Ltd, responsible for all post office branches; Royal Mail letters; a parcels division that became Parcelforce in 1990; and Girobank (which would be sold off in 1990). For sub-postmasters, out went distinctly non-entrepreneurial "cost-plus" payments that ensured they at least kept their heads above water but gave no incentive to increase sales. They were replaced by more market-rate-based payments for the services and products they provided on behalf of the Post Office, such as selling stamps, and for the government, such as driving licence applications.

When recession bit in the early 1990s, the new settlement put increasing strain on branches and made those in some locations uneconomical, causing more than 600 to disappear between 1990 and 1995. The Post Office itself began shedding the town centre Crown offices that were expensive to run and

---

1 Campbell-Smith, *Masters of the Post*

occupied valuable land, handing their roles to franchises in supermarkets and other large retailers. The 1,340 Crown offices in 1990 were almost halved to 700 by 1995 (the latest number is around 115).[2]

This scaling-back was, however, soon accompanied by a turnaround in the Post Office group's overall financial fortunes. Mail volumes ballooned, from less than 14bn in 1988/89 to almost 20bn in 1999/2000, inflated by the rise of direct-mail marketing and economic recovery.[3] Between 1993/94 and 1997/98 the Post Office's profits rose from just below £200m to nearer £450m. While Post Office Counters Ltd made only a modest contribution to this – around the £35m mark – it remained critical to the overall effort, as the public face of the organisation.

But new threats were looming. The rise of electronic communication had begun, and by the mid-1990s was obviously going to be transformational, as was the opening up of mail markets at home and abroad. With financial storm clouds gathering, it might have been hoped that the cash being generated would have been invested to prepare the business. But the mid-1990s Treasury was grappling with post-recession fiscal challenges, which attracted it to the private finance initiative and snaffled around three-quarters of the Post Office's profits in tax and dividends. For chancellor Ken Clarke, this bounty was some consolation for the fizzling out, in 1995, of the John Major government's half-hearted attempts to resurrect privatisation under trade secretary Michael Heseltine's "Project Lion".

What the late 1990s Post Office lacked in financial resource, it tried to make up for in modernising zeal. While the New Labour government also rejected privatisation (despite Tony Blair's initial enthusiasm), its 1997 manifesto had promised greater "commercial freedom" for the organisation. The Post Office was soon in the grip of new chairman Neville Bain's management consultancy-led initiatives, with faddish names such as the Competitive Overhead Strategic Structure Programme and the Shaping for Competitive Success project that fractured the group into an "internal marketplace". This approach had been deployed disastrously at the BBC and elsewhere, and produced equally unimpressive results at the Post Office.

Along with the self-inflicted problems, chief executive John Roberts and his management were struggling with weighty matters such as the need to modernise distribution centres and letter delivery systems to compete in a new postal services market, plus overseas acquisitions such as the 1999 deal for German Parcels (now, as GLS, the Royal Mail group's most profitable part).

---

2 commonslibrary.parliament.uk/research-briefings/SN02585/
3 postalmuseum.org/wp-content/uploads/2016/10/11_Letters_delivered_by_Royal_Mail_1920_2010.pdf

So when it came to the nightmare that was the development and deployment of the Horizon IT system, it suited a preoccupied Post Office board to turn a blind eye to fundamental flaws and go along with the escalating hype about the technology's commercial possibilities.

Arms of the state

Between the signing of the Horizon deal with ICL in May 1999 and "acceptance" of the calamitous IT system in September that year, Labour's Blairite business secretary Stephen Byers launched a white paper on Post Office reform with the subtitle *A World Class Service for the 21st Century.*

For all the aspiration, to a network of post office branches that grew and relied on 19th- and 20th-century developments such as mass letter-sending and the welfare state, the 21st looked challenging. Emails were eating into the volume of mail and stamp sales. Government departments were moving services away from post offices and on to the emergent internet. But the new Horizon IT system, predicted Byers, would come to the rescue. It would enable more financial services to be offered across Post Office counters and "deliver the government's ambitions to interface with citizens in a modern, convenient, efficient and coherent manner through the increasing use of IT".[4] *Counter Revolution*, a report from Tony Blair's performance and innovation unit, was even more hopeful. With Horizon in place, Post Office branches could become "one-stop shops for government information and transactions", provide the outlet for a "Universal Bank to combat financial exclusion" and act as e-commerce distribution centres.[5]

For sub-postmasters a change to the Post Office's corporate status was to prove more momentous than any of these innovations. Under the 2000 Postal Services Act that followed Byers's white paper, the Post Office corporation became a "public limited company" of the sort more commonly found on the stock market. Although still government-owned, it would be subject to the more business-orientated aspects of company law. As the white paper explained, it would be "absolutely clear that the directors owe their duties to the company (not directly to the government as owner) and will require the government as owner to exercise its interests effectively".[6] In other words, directors will serve corporate interests and ministers won't interfere. A new independent regulator, the Postal Services Commission (Postcomm), would replace government oversight. Its remit was to cover

---

4 *Hansard*, 15 July 1999
5 Commons public administration committee, 17 January 2001
6 Post Office Reform white paper, 8 July 1999

service levels and market operations but not the post office network or Britain's sub-postmasters.

In Whitehall jargon, the Post Office became an "arm's-length" business. Whitehall would henceforth have no involvement in operational matters, and ministers would be able disclaim liability when things went wrong. Just as the PFI scheme at the root of many of Horizon's failings took financial liabilities off the government's books, the new deal would absolve it of responsibility for their consequences. And in 2003, the Post Office was put further beyond ministerial accountability by the creation of an additional buffer, a new Shareholder Executive. This was to act as steward of public shareholdings – bringing, the theory went, more acumen to the government's role as shareholder in around 20 companies including the Post Office, Channel 4 and the Royal Mint. Unfortunately, the bankers and consultants enlisted to staff the new body and sit on the Post Office board would prove even less interested in sub-postmasters than the civil servants and ministers that preceded them.

The arm's-length arrangement was a typically New Labour "third way" solution, very different from full state ownership and management, but stopping well short of what would have been a politically vexed privatisation (especially with Alan Johnson, who had led the Communication Workers Union's 1990s opposition to privatisation, installed as postal services minister from the middle of 1999). Like many such solutions, it left a large gap in accountability for what remained an important public business and service.

Fashion victim

As part of the New Labour changes, Byers also instigated a rebrand, deciding the Post Office name that had served well for 340 years should become "Consignia". The head of the consultancy outfit behind the name explained: "It's got consign in it. It's got a link with insignia, so there is this kind of royalty-ish thing."[7] (The Queen was said to have been miffed that she wasn't consulted.) Like the private finance initiative, this was another move entirely in keeping with the mood of the times. As with other risible corporate rebrands (such as accountancy firm PwC's consultancy arm becoming "Monday"), it did not last. Consignia was consigned to history the year after it was adopted.

The Post Office group didn't, however, revert to being the Post Office Corporation, but became Royal Mail Holdings plc. The Post Office name had been relegated in the corporate pecking order below the Royal Mail name that had first appeared on stagecoaches a mere couple of hundred

---

7 news.bbc.co.uk/1/hi/business/2002480.stm

years or so before. Post Office Counters Ltd, dealing with the branch network, became simply Post Office Ltd.

The rethink could be ascribed to a hard-nosed retailer who replaced Neville Bain as chairman in 2002. Allan Leighton, a bullet-headed former Asda chief executive credited with having turned the supermarket around in the late 1990s, had been brought in a year earlier. The intention was that he could do something similar for the Consignia group and the post office branch network, which had plunged into losses at the turn of the 21st century (not helped by the £571m Horizon accounting write-down of 1999/2000).

Not only did Leighton dump the Consignia brand; he also scrapped the "internal market" setup and returned to the kind of structure that Ron Dearing had created in the 1980s. So far, so sensible. The captain of industry would be credited with steadying the ship for a while. But he couldn't hold back a tide of adverse challenges for the Royal Mail group in the first few years of the 21st century.

The Royal Mail business was simultaneously suffering not just from the rise of electronic communications but soon the opening up of letter delivery to competition. Royal Mail still had to provide the expensive "last mile" delivery services while, gradually from 2003 and then fully by 2006, competitors could muscle in on more lucrative parts of the business. Then there were growing demands to plug deficits in the £15bn Post Office pension scheme, as a stock-market downturn and the consequences of having taken a long contributions holiday in the 1990s hit home. On top of all this, modernisation entailed thousands of job losses and was met with extensive industrial action. By 2006/07 the financial stability secured by Leighton and the man he brought in from the Football Association as chief executive, Adam Crozier, was crumbling.

The Post Office's branch network business had 21st-century problems of its own, including Horizon. By 2002, Post Office Ltd's directors were recording that "the incremental costs of running the Horizon system has turned counter services into a fundamentally unprofitable operation". This was about to be exacerbated by losing the job of handing out benefit payments, estimated to provide around £400m of income, the following year.[8] Leighton's choice to run the Post Office part of the Royal Mail group, David Mills, would call it a "burning ship". The former HSBC banker tried to keep it afloat by slashing the number of sub-post offices (from 17,743 in 2000 to 13,884 in 2005), relying on Horizon coming good and facilitating financial service sales in those that survived.[9]

---

8 Post Office Ltd 2001/02 accounts, note 3
9 commonslibrary.parliament.uk/research-briefings/SN02585/

Corporate men

In the upper reaches of Royal Mail Group plc, executives were handsomely incentivised to deliver on financial performance (80 percent of their bonus calculation) and less so on other matters (20 percent was based on customer service targets). Even Leighton, a non-executive chairman of the sort who would normally be paid a flat fee to focus on high corporate standards while executives chased the money, picked up bonuses of more than £160,000 a year. Crozier was in a different league still, with incentive schemes that would take his pay from Royal Mail over a seven-year tenure to £9.6m. Even at the fusty old Post Office Ltd, chief executive David Mills received bonuses 96 percent weighted towards financial targets and a not-worth-getting-out-of-bed-for 4 percent related to customer service.[10] Senior managers, one or two levels down from his board, enjoyed similarly financially directed bonuses if the group fulfilled its "renewal plan" of turning around losses.

This was a different world from the one that the sub-postmasters were inhabiting, although one man did try to make contact with the aliens in the Royal Mail boardroom. It was, unsurprisingly, Alan Bates. In 2003, shortly after receiving notice of his contract termination, both Bates and his MP, Betty Williams, wrote to Leighton explaining the branch shortfall problem and describing the Post Office's "outdated 'Stalinistic' management approach".[11] This was used "to bludgeon its will onto the poor sub-postmaster", they said, and was "an issue that could bankrupt every sub-post office in the country". Bates received a reply from a lowly official with the standard line that "there is nothing inherently wrong with the Horizon system installed at the branch".[12] Leighton didn't have time to read such letters. He was also chairing another four major corporate boards, including BHS and Lastminute.com, while sitting on four others, including those of BSkyB and Leeds United. This was one corporate fashion – "going plural", as it was called back then – that he did like, so much so that he'd also set up a consultancy company called Going Plural Ltd. (Not long after this trend attracted criticism, the UK's corporate governance code would be amended to require that directors "have enough time available to devote to the job".)[13]

Around Fujitsu Services' boardroom table over in Bracknell, meanwhile, the priority was to establish the company as the pre-eminent supplier to the New Labour government's ambitious information technology programme. The

---

10 Royal Mail Holdings plc annual report, 2002/03
11 Letter from Alan Bates to Allan Leighton, 7 August 2003, POL00107538
12 Letter from Ria MacQueen to Bates, 27 August 2003, POL00040354
13 iod.com/app/uploads/2022/02/Combined-Code-2006-46026682c2a92c78329e8616d3ea4a85.pdf

company's reputation was already taking a pasting, however. In April 2003 the Commons public accounts committee looked at an IT system, Libra, that it had been commissioned to develop for the country's magistrates courts and declared it "one of the worst PFI deals that we have seen".[14] As with Horizon, the company hadn't understood the task and "took on excessive risk and underpriced its bid". Costs more than doubled in four years and the courts still didn't have what they needed. The exposure of another major foul-up would establish an unhelpful pattern, just as Fujitsu was putting in for, and winning, a major deal on yet another ill-thought-out mega-project of the time, the NHS's £12bn National Programme for IT. Like Horizon, this was being pushed through by Tony Blair.

Despite admitting his own computer illiteracy, the prime minister was now sinking taxpayers' money into vast IT projects with the zeal of the convert. In the summer of 2003, the Parliamentary Office of Science and Technology reported: "Government departments have 100 major IT projects under way with a total value of £10bn."[15] With a target of "making all services available electronically by 2005", there was a huge amount up for grabs. The incentive to cover up faults and lie about the efficacy of Horizon – Fujitsu's flagship deal to date – was huge.

Lack of suspense

For the Post Office, supposed independence from government wasn't yet going to plan. It needed a stream of government handouts, starting with £450m in 2003 to keep its network of rural branches alive and pay compensation for closing down hundreds of urban ones.

Straitened times and bosses fixated on financial returns required even more faith in the power of the Horizon system to catalyse the Post Office business. In 2003, yet another transformation initiative, this time called Era, spawned the Impact Programme. Its aims included improving the flow of information with outside agencies such as the National Lottery operator and government bodies selling services via post office counters, combined with a push to limit how much the Post Office was owed by such clients – and, crucially, by sub-postmasters. The specific aims of Impact included "increase the amount of debt recovered" and "enable matching of cash at branches with settlement with client". Among the "business drivers" was the need to "re-focus on debt recovery (financial recovery of money), target 95 percent".[16]

For sub-postmasters, this translated into withdrawing their ability to place accounting shortfalls in a suspense account, pending resolution. The

---

14 publications.parliament.uk/pa/cm200203/cmselect/cmpubacc/434/434.pdf
15 parliament.uk/globalassets/documents/post/pr200.pdf
16 Stephen Grayston, inquiry evidence, 27 February 2023, POL00038878

mechanism had at least enabled some of them – albeit at the whim of Post Office managers – to report shortfalls and attempt to get to the bottom of them without automatically having to cough up. As Alan Bates's experience showed, they rarely got anywhere, but they could at least continue trading in the meantime.

The suspense account process had long irritated Post Office managers, who persisted in two prejudiced and mistaken views. Firstly, they believed that sub-postmasters were using the suspense account to dodge liability for dishonest discrepancies, even though it would be a stupid way for them to try to conceal fraud. The Impact programme manager, Susan Harding, later acknowledged that the suspense account was "removed, as historically it was used by sub-postmasters to 'hide' discrepancies in their accounts, rather than resolve them".[17] Secondly, they thought that the sub-postmaster contract automatically conferred liability for shortfalls, so removing the suspense account simply confirmed what was due. In truth, the frequent use of the suspense account was a flashing warning light, indicating Horizon's malfunction. But, rather than investigate the underlying problem, the Post Office acted like a dodgy used-car salesman and removed the bulb.

The pretence over Horizon that justified this change defied the Post Office's own knowledge, from the trial of the system, that the IT had a significant error rate (it had *targeted* 0.6 percent, after all) and that a significant proportion of the increasing millions sitting in suspense accounts were errors on the part of the system, not of the sub-postmasters. The same David Smith who had been in charge of "automation transformation" during Horizon's error-strewn rollout was still an IT director working on the Impact programme. He would later admit to the public inquiry that it would have been fairer to consider what the suspense account was being used for before scrapping it.[18]

By the time the Impact programme concluded in 2005, the approved options for a sub-postmaster faced with a shortfall as he or she tried to balance the weekly books were limited to either putting their own cash into the branch or "settling centrally", which meant the money would be deducted from their income from the post office. Either way, the sub-postmaster had to pay up. The other option, when faced with the financial ruin this would entail, was to claim incorrectly that the books balanced.

The commercial revolution had given the Post Office the most powerful weapon yet with which to attack its sub-postmasters.

---

17 Susan Harding, witness statement, 22 February 2023, WITN03980100
18 David Smith, inquiry evidence, 24 February 2023

5

NO CRIME AND PUNISHMENT

The Post Office coerces sub-postmasters into false confessions

HORIZON didn't just provide fake evidence of non-existent crimes. By all but forcing sub-postmasters to claim their books balanced when they didn't, it increasingly *created* them. This suited the Post Office on a couple of levels. Firstly, if shortfalls were caused by its agents' criminality, then accounting discrepancies weren't the fault of the IT system. Thus Horizon's "robustness" could be asserted, and that dealt with one risk to the financially beleaguered organisation. Secondly, at a time when every penny counted, the same criminality could be leveraged in the recovery of "lost" funds. And the Post Office could reassure itself that it was honouring its golden rule of safeguarding public money.

It was all a big lie, of course. The "false accounting" charge to which sub-postmasters were pleading guilty was part of the 1968 Theft Act and required dishonesty; they had to be hiding something. But, in almost all cases there was no evidence that did have anything to hide. They had routinely raised their problems with helplines and managers and any false balance submissions they had made were only in response to a wilfully incorrect reading of their contract (that they were responsible for all shortfalls, however caused). So they had not in fact, legally, falsely accounted. For most, this would be established in the courts many painful years down the line. But for one or two, a switched-on jury saw the obvious injustice straight away.

By early 2006, Suzanne Palmer had been running her post office branch in the Essex market town of Rayleigh for three years. She'd faced repeated "shortfalls" (and occasional "surpluses"), often relating to National Lottery scratchcard sales, that she either met from her own funds or had wiped out by "error notices" from the Post Office acknowledging accounting mistakes. Like so many others, she called the helpline repeatedly, complaining of the system's failings. That February an audit identified further deficits running to nearly £15,000.[1] Given the system's record of throwing up faulty balances, Mrs

---

[1] Duncan Atkinson KC, expert report to inquiry, 18 December 2023, EXPG0000004R

Palmer had concealed these by inflating her cash balance while keeping tabs of the deficits separately, expecting the errors to correct themselves eventually. Post Office auditors first reassured her that if she repaid the shortfalls, she wouldn't be prosecuted. She did just that. But the promise, which the auditors were in no position to make, would not be honoured.

So perfunctory were Post Office investigations that the investigator who took on the case, Lisa Allen, didn't even check the records of error notices issued to the branch and the sub-postmaster's record of calls to the helpline, never mind examine the underlying audit record. Mrs Palmer's protestations of never having taken any money didn't prompt any enquiries into her finances, either.

Such an abysmal effort might have been expected to collapse on first contact with a lawyer. But not with a Post Office lawyer. The man recommending the Post Office's charging decisions was Jarnail Singh, who had joined the Post Office in the late 1980s in its property conveyancing department before, with no obvious preparation for the role, becoming a senior criminal lawyer in the mid-1990s. In Mrs Palmer's case, he advised that no further evidence was required, failed to review what little was provided and neglected to address the important test for all prosecutors of whether the "public interest" would be served by charging a suspect – in this case a woman of good character, who denied dishonesty and who had made good the relatively small "shortfalls". The prosecution could go ahead. (All this was in breach of accepted codes and rules for prosecutors but was, as we shall see, far from Singh's most ignominious contribution to the scandal.)

Within a year, Suzanne Palmer stood in the dock at Southend Crown Court charged with three counts of false accounting. When the jury was sent out to consider the limited evidence, it quickly came back with a pertinent question for the judge: "What was Mrs Palmer supposed to do if she didn't agree with the Horizon-generated figures?" The Post Office legal team had no answer (it couldn't cite the discontinued suspense account as a possibility) and, half an hour after retiring, the jury pronounced her not guilty on all charges.[2] The familiar appalling personal postscript to the case, of bankruptcy and profound financial and personal hardship, followed anyway – as it always did, even for the vindicated.

The lesson the Post Office took from the case wasn't the obvious one: that the unfair sub-postmaster contract was combining with an errant IT system to force sub-postmasters into impossible positions, and that prosecutions

---

2 Tony Utting, inquiry evidence, 17 November 2023; and Suzanne Palmer, witness statement, 26 January 2022, WITN02240100

based on Horizon were therefore inherently flawed. Instead, it was that the IT system and its prosecutorial clown car must be kept away from juries and out of the public eye whenever possible.

Plea market

In any given shortfall case, a range of offences was available to the Post Office, with theft and false accounting the two most common charges. The former was more serious and was aggravated in a sub-postmaster's case by the inherent abuse of a position of trust. For any significant sum, a conviction was likely to entail a prison sentence. The latter charge, while technically still carrying a maximum seven-year sentence, might be punished with suspended jail time or a community sentence. And, when passing sentence, a judge was likely to give the highest level of mitigation for a guilty plea. In the case of false accounting, usually in the single or low tens of thousands of pounds, the plea could be the difference between being sent down the steps or going home that day. Sub-postmasters had little if any experience at the wrong end of the criminal justice system; they wouldn't have held their positions if they had. Nearly half were women and many were not in the first flush of youth. The prospect of going to prison was terrifying.

By charging sub-postmasters with both offences, it thus became easy to leverage the prospect of conviction for theft to secure a plea of guilty to false accounting. When the Post Office offered to drop the theft charge in return for an admission of false accounting, the sub-postmaster faced the choice of taking on a powerful state body that held most of the evidential cards in court, or pleading guilty to the lesser charge and throwing themselves on the judge's mercy. For almost all, there was only one conceivable response. They had to minimise their chances of staying out of prison. The Post Office prosecutors had no qualms about turning their fear to its advantage. It was a game of legal jeopardy in which the Post Office had a licence for legal abuse.

False confessions of a sub-postmaster

No prosecution showcased the cynicism of the Post Office's prosecutors better than that of the sub-postmaster in the village of South Warnborough in Hampshire. Jo Hamilton was resourcefulness and good humour personified, and her branch epitomised what a good post office could offer. She'd taken over the village shop in 2001, having previously run a pub and a haulage business (with her own HGV licence). She was soon managing the small post office branch within it on behalf of the existing sub-postmaster, whom she succeeded within a couple of years.

Jo's problems began with the installation of a chip-and-pin banking system towards the end of 2003. When a deficit of around £2,000 appeared from nowhere, she first used the suspense account then still available. Then, on the phone to the Post Office helpline, she attempted to shift the balance back on to her own account as instructed, in the hope the error would correct itself. But the number doubled before her eyes. She was forced to pay most of the new shortfall. As further Horizon-generated shortfalls cropped up over the following months, she had to remortgage her house and borrow from a neighbour to keep her head above water. These sources inevitably dried up and before long she was signing off accounts saying she held cash that she didn't.

By early 2006 the Post Office was expressing concern at the amount of money that Horizon was showing was in Mrs Hamilton's branch. It demanded that she return £25,000, which she didn't have. Desperately worried, she turned to the National Federation of Sub-postmasters. It requested an audit on her behalf.

Matters quickly darkened. The auditors, having identified the shortfall, immediately called in a Post Office investigator, Graham Brander, and contracts manager, Elaine Ridge. Jo could offer them no explanation for her shortfalls, beyond citing repeated Horizon problems. (These included, she later recalled, Fujitsu engineers having to replace her Horizon base unit three times because, they said, "the system was not sending them the correct information".)[3] Straight from the corrupt Post Office script, her inquisitors responded that she was the only one having trouble with Horizon. She was immediately suspended. After a further "intimidating" interview under caution, she was informed that the shortfall she had to repay was £36,000. A few days later, she was sacked. That still wasn't the worst of it. Later that year she was summonsed to Aldershot Magistrates Court to face a single charge of theft in the full amount of the shortfall. On 6 December 2006, Jo Hamilton stood in the dock and pleaded not guilty.

Given the seriousness of the charge, the case was transferred to Winchester Crown Court. Ahead of a trial there, the Post Office should have disclosed any information that might help Hamilton's defence. Instead, it suppressed compelling evidence that supported her case. "Having analysed the Horizon printouts and accounting documentation," the investigator Brander had written in the records for her case, "I was unable to find any evidence of theft or that the cash figures had been deliberately inflated."[4] This

---

3 Utting, inquiry evidence, 17 November 2023, and witness statement of Suzanne Palmer, 26 January 2022, WITN02240100
4 Second Sight evidence to Commons business select committee, 25 January 2022, committees.parliament.uk/writtenevidence/43568/pdf

should obviously have been disclosed to a defendant charged with, er, theft. But it wasn't.

The reason for this was that, like the lies about Horizon, concealing unhelpful evidence was demanded by the Post Office. Internal rules on "offender reports and discipline reports" stipulated: "Significant failures that may affect the successful likelihood of any criminal action and/or cause significant damage to the business must be confined, solely, to the confidential offender report." This, in contrast to the discipline report, was protected by legal privilege and was not shown to the sub-postmaster. Anything that didn't reflect well on Horizon was then to be omitted from the separate discipline report that was disclosed. "Care must be exercised when including failures within the discipline report," ran the policy, "as obviously this is disclosed to the suspect offender and may have ramifications on both the criminal elements of the enquiry, as well as being potentially damaging to the reputation or security of the business."[5] This was a state body perverting the course of justice as a matter of policy.

As Jo Hamilton's trial loomed, in November 2007 the Post Office offered a deal: plead guilty to 14 counts of false accounting and it would drop the theft charge. This, advised Jo's solicitor, left open the chance of avoiding prison. There was no guarantee, but it was the only realistic option, in the same way that Kafka's protagonist had been told: "Confess to them as soon as you get the chance. It's only then that they give you the chance to get away, not till then."

The offer came with a further bitter twist; Mrs Hamilton would have to agree she'd had the benefit of the money – effectively saying she *had* hidden something – and not to criticise the Horizon system. This was standard practice, designed to help the Post Office recover the "lost" money and protect the reputation of the IT at all costs. Years later, in 2013, the senior lawyer, Jarnail Singh, would put in writing that a plea of guilty to false accounting could be accepted as long as the defendant accepts "in writing, that he does not challenge the integrity or blames or criticises the Horizon system".[6] To have any chance of retaining their liberty, sub-postmasters were required, like Orwell's Winston Smith in *Nineteen Eighty-Four*, to subscribe to their master's lies.

On 4 February 2008, Jo Hamilton did her deal with the devil and pleaded guilty to false accounting. Helped by exemplary character witnesses and a couple of coachloads of supportive villagers piling into Winchester Crown Court, Jo avoided jail. But the consequences remained severe: not just financial devastation but the loss of self-esteem and reputation, despite plentiful local support early

---

5 Post Office security operations team compliance document, 7 March 2013, POL00038452
6 Email from Jarnail Singh to Rachael Panter, 21 February 2013, POL00325434

on. Then there were the many indignities, such as the loss of her role helping at a local primary school, that the Post Office caused by criminalising her.

But it also turned Jo Hamilton into a powerful campaigner for justice, one who would prove a key figure in exposing a scandal that was stretching across the country.

Wrongful imprisonment (1)

In September 2006 at Caernarfon Crown Court, former postman, county councillor, sub-postmaster and all-round community stalwart Noel Thomas made a similar choice to Jo Hamilton's. He pleaded guilty to one count of false accounting, relating to a £48,000 shortfall in his branch accounts. He, too, had a theft charge dropped as part of a plea deal that he'd been led to believe would spare him jail. It didn't. The judge sentenced him to nine months imprisonment and he was soon marking his 60th birthday in a cell in HM Prison Kirkham, in Lancashire.

Mr Thomas and his wife had been successfully running the Gaerwen post office in Anglesey since 1981, Noel taking over from her as sub-postmaster in 1994. He was also managing another post office branch in the area. But this deep experience was no match for Horizon, which began throwing up shortfalls as soon as it was installed in Gaerwen around the turn of the century. He would later recall "screen freezes, transfer interruptions and the need to remotely reboot the system", leading to "'nil transactions' [outgoings not correctly picked up] and consequently, shortfalls".[7] The Horizon hardware had to be replaced a couple of times. The helpline helped little, and Mr Thomas took the all too common initial step of putting his hand in his own pocket to make up the deficiencies. On one occasion the Post Office did chip in to meet half of a £6,000 shortfall, in an apparent acknowledgement of its own liability. (Significantly, this was agreed at a meeting with his area manager and one Angela van den Bogerd, who at the time was the head of the Post Office in Wales but would go on to play a central role in covering up the scandal.)

Noel had taken the precaution of keeping records of what he saw as Horizon's faulty operation. So when the auditors arrived in Gaerwen in early 2005, he did have something to show them. It counted for little. Once they had identified a £50,000 deficit, Post Office investigators Diane Matthews and Steve Bradshaw arrived and carted Noel off to Holyhead police station for questioning.

The ensuing investigation was as dire as Jo Hamilton's. No evidence of

---

7 Hughie Noel Thomas, witness statement, 12 January 2022, WITN01620100

stolen money was found. And it was equally mendacious. He too was told he was "the only one" (even though Bradshaw would later acknowledge at the public inquiry that his department was "drenched in information that Horizon wasn't working from the very beginning"). Matthews was a former counter clerk who had been seconded to the Horizon roll-out team between 1999 and 2003 and was well aware of the problems that had occurred in that process. But when, just a couple of years later as an investigator, she encountered Noel Thomas's complaints of similar issues, she was unmoved. She would later protest that she was unaware of Horizon's shortcomings, believing the "corporate message" that its failings had been resolved in the intervening period.[8]

Computer misuse

Noel Thomas's investigators did, unlike in Jo Hamilton's case, request a sample of the so-called ARQ audit data, but only because he had specifically raised the prospect of IT failure as a cause of his discrepancies. They didn't, however, check it for any indication of IT bugs, errors or defects. Instead, the Horizon system was dishonestly deployed to buttress the case against Thomas, with the help of the amenable Gareth Jenkins from Fujitsu.

In a first draft of what would become his formal witness statement for the prosecution, Jenkins listed a number of possible causes of the "nil transactions" that Noel Thomas had raised. Among them was the possibility of "system failure". But when this crossed the desk of Post Office investigator Graham Ward, alarm bells rang. "This is a really poor choice of words which seems to accept that failures in the system are normal," he emailed the Fujitsu security manager who was liaising with Jenkins, "and therefore may well support the postmasters' claim that the system is to blame for the losses!!!!"[9] To emphasise the point, Ward struck through the offending "system failure" wording. After several further exchanges, Jenkins's finalised witness statement indeed omitted these words. Instead, concerning possible reasons for nil transactions, it said: "All these are perfectly normal occurrences and should result in clear instructions being passed to the [post office counter] to ensure that no cash should change hands."[10] Nothing to worry about, in other words. (Among the investigators, Ward was particularly assiduous in enlisting Fujitsu's false testimony to back up prosecutions. A few months earlier, soliciting help for the Castleton case and other potential cases, he'd written to Fujitsu security manager Brian Pinder. In light of "allegations being made by the postmasters",

---
8 Diane Matthews, inquiry evidence, 24 November 2023
9 Gareth Jenkins, draft witness statement with Ward's comments, 24 March 2006, POL00047895
10 Jenkins, witness statement, 6 April 2006, FUJ00122237

Ward was "sure you'll agree that it is very much in both ourselves [sic] and Fujitsu's interests to challenge the allegations and provide evidence that the system is not to blame for the losses being reported."[11])

The Fujitsu evidence to be used against Thomas also included a line that was clearly copied and pasted from one case to another; exactly the same had appeared, complete with spelling mistake, in a witness statement by Fujitsu security analyst Penny Thomas in Jo Hamilton's case. "To the best of my knowledge and belief," it read, "at all material times the computer was operating properly, or if not, any respect in which it was not operating properly, or was out of operation was not such as to effect [sic] the information held on it." Jenkins had initially objected to the inclusion of these words when they'd been added to his draft statement. "All I've done is interpret the data in spreadsheets that you have emailed to me," he complained.[12] But, when it came to the crunch, he relented and this blanket reassurance was included.

Jenkins's statement was backed up by one from Fujitsu security analyst Andy Dunks, a former electrician with no IT training and the man who had mockingly written of wiping away tears before giving evidence against Lee Castleton. Of Noel Thomas's calls to Fujitsu's Horizon helpdesk, he testified that "none of these calls related to faults which would have had an effect on the integrity of the information held on the system".[13] This, too, was a boilerplate statement with no foundation in reality. But, following Fujitsu engineer Anne Chambers's soon regretted appearance at the Castleton trial, he was now in demand. Her boss, head of the company's service support centre Mik Peach, had decided that his people would no longer appear in court. The job would be left to the relatively new prosecution support service within the security team, with Dunks the go-to expert witness despite his total lack of expertise.

With Noel Thomas's only possible defence – computer error – squared off, the rest of the Post Office strategy could kick in. He knew that his chances of success at court against both theft and false accounting charges were slim. The Post Office had successfully suppressed news of its failures in court, such as against Suzanne Palmer, and was upping its game on getting Fujitsu to vouch for Horizon.

Thomas, too, could be coerced into agreeing that two plus two equals five. Or, as the Post Office's lawyer on the case, Juliet McFarlane, put it in

---

11 Email from Graham Ward to Brian Pinder, 10 March 2006, FUJ00152587
12 Jenkins, comments on amended witness statement, 23 March 2006, FUJ00122204
13 Andrew Dunks, inquiry evidence, 8 March 2023, POL00039193

a read-out of a call with an external solicitor, "we would proceed with false accounting providing the defendant accepts that the Horizon system was working perfectly…"[14] (and repays the non-existent losses).

Noel Thomas signed up. He still hates the sound of doors slamming.

Wrongful imprisonment (2)

The same Post Office lawyer who thought it served the interests of justice to impose such a deal on Mr Thomas was also instrumental in prosecuting Janet Skinner, a 35-year-old sub-postmaster from Hull and mother of two teenage children. The standard investigation into a £59,000 shortfall had been performed by the same hapless duo, Diane Matthews and Steve Bradshaw. As with Noel Thomas, they'd failed to find any evidence of money going missing and didn't bother to look into the 116 calls Mrs Skinner had made to the Post Office's helpline. So lacking was the evidence, with such a large sum vanishing into thin air, that even Matthews told McFarlane that she wasn't convinced Mrs Skinner had stolen the money. These qualms were ignored and the usual double charges were made against Janet – as was the inevitable offer to drop the theft in return for a false accounting guilty plea. Advised that this gave her a chance to avoid jail, she took it. Yet, at Hull Crown Court on 2 February 2007, Janet Skinner was sentenced to nine months in prison. It seemed that the relatively large size of her shortfall had, just like Noel Thomas's, tipped the balance in favour of incarceration. Given the random variation in Horizon's spurious figures, injustice at the hands of the Post Office was an evil lottery.

The following year, facing court again over recovery of money she'd never had and traumatised by the brutal experience of prison, Janet Skinner suffered an auto-immune attack that paralysed her and leaves her still unable to work. As with Jo Hamilton and Noel Thomas, however, this didn't dim her fight for justice.

Number crunching

The two-card trick of theft and false accounting charges was central to the Post Office's prosecutions strategy, as a look at the first convictions to be overturned – including Jo's, Noel's and Janet's – illustrates.

In April 2021, after the sub-postmasters' victory in the group litigation led by Alan Bates, 39 convictions, including those of Jo Hamilton, Noel Thomas and Janet Skinner, were overturned by the Court of Appeal (with three upheld).

---

14 Cited in EXPG000004R

Of these, 35 involved guilty pleas. And 20 of these were for false accounting offences alone. (Most of the other 15 cases involved guilty pleas to theft or fraud charges, again in the hope of securing a non-custodial or suspended custodial sentence.) In at least 18 of the 20 cases, based on available records, theft charges were dropped at some stage.[15] This chimed with what investigator Steve Bradshaw later told the public inquiry, that "the lawyers, nine times out of ten, would have had two charges down: theft and false accounting".[16]

In all of the cases, there was never sufficient evidence to justify the theft charge. In none had anything vaguely helpful to sub-postmasters – such as the error logs reflecting their contacts with Fujitsu's software support centre – been disclosed.

The cynical *modus operandi* was extraordinarily successful. Some 500 Post Office-led prosecutions relating to branch shortfalls following the introduction of Horizon (there were other prosecutions relying on Horizon-covered matters such as pension and benefit frauds) led to 464 convictions.[17] This 93 percent success rate compared highly favourably with overall criminal conviction rates by other prosecutors, which were more than 10 percentage points lower – and very well with the 70 percent conviction rate achieved by the Post Office from 1999 in 61 prosecutions entirely unrelated to the Horizon system. It was probably no coincidence either that, while caution has to be exercised comparing convictions and prosecutions in any year, the gap between these narrowed after 2005, in the wake of the ending of use of the suspense account for shortfalls.

It's also worth noting that, overall, the 36 prosecutions that did not lead to conviction could be a large proportion of the contested cases. Of those considered by the Court of Appeal, 90 percent involved guilty pleas. So it's likely that far fewer than 100 of the 500 prosecutions were met with not guilty pleas – making 36 quite a high rate of acquittals (or dropping cases). This could well reflect the paucity of the underlying cases, as prosecutions such as those of Maureen McKelvey and Suzanne Palmer amply demonstrate.

Making crime pay

Given its effectiveness, it's no wonder that the double charging/plea deal strategy was so prized by the Post Office. While it launched 764 prosecutions in total in the Horizon era, including non-shortfall cases (with 697 convictions), it ran 771 investigations that did not lead to prosecutions but, it

---

15 *Hamilton & Others v Post Office*
16 Stephen Bradshaw, inquiry evidence, 11 January 2024
17 Simon Recaldin, witness statement, 4 November 2024, WITN09890500

appears in most cases, other financial settlements.[18] This 50-50 split represents an extraordinary focus on prosecution for a public body, even one quite reasonably concerned with the money it's responsible for. In HM Revenue & Customs, for example, around one in every thousand investigations converts into a prosecution.[19] Counter-fraud and compliance teams in the Department for Work and Pensions, far more aggressive on benefit fraud, prosecute well below one percent of cases where claims are found to be wrong.[20]

Those ratios reflect the relative cost-effectiveness of civil over criminal action for those agencies. So why would the Post Office be so different? Part of the reason was that civil recoveries of the money it wanted "back" from sub-postmasters were difficult. The Post Office could bankrupt people like Lee Castleton, but would struggle to enforce its debts. But if it secured a conviction, to which it could attach a "loss", then, from early 2003, the new Proceeds of Crime Act came into play. As investigator Graham Ward put it in an email to colleagues, "unlike the [Proceeds of Crime Act], [civil] compensation orders have 'no teeth' and enforcing these orders is time consuming and in sum [sic] cases ineffective, ending up with defendants paying minimal monthly instalments over a prolonged period of time".[21]

The main purpose of the new legislation was to clamp down on serious organised criminals laundering their loot, but the Post Office was quick to capitalise on it, too. "By recovering the assets we send out a clear message to the criminal/potential criminal that there is little point stealing as we will endeavour to recover their ill-gotten gains," said new Post Office guidelines in 2003. "This is a message the present government wish to send out as they are in the process of setting out the National Confiscation Agency," they continued, "whose role it will be to remove assets from organised crime."[22] Sub-postmasters were nobody's idea of organised criminals, but this was the sort of macho message that investigators whose behaviour would later be likened to a "1970s television detective show" enjoyed hearing.[23]

At the suggestion of senior security manager David Pardoe, the man who a few years earlier had written an academic study of sub-postmaster prosecutions facetiously called *There Must Be Some Mistake*, in late 2005 the Post Office created a new Financial Investigations Unit to recoup "losses".

---

18 Post Office freedom of information request, FOI2024/01264
19 HMRC annual report 2023/24
20 DWP annual report 2023/24; 655 prosecutions v 184,000 claims adjusted
21 Email from Ward to colleagues, 1 November 2012, POL00121975
22 Utting and MF Matthews, Post Office Criminal Asset Recovery Security Guidelines (version 2), 2003, POL00121521
23 Julian Blake, counsel to the inquiry, questioning Bradshaw, 11 January 2024

It became one of the first non-police bodies to apply for statutory powers of recovery under the Proceeds of Crime Act.[24] Rather than chasing sub-postmasters through bankruptcy courts, it could now get its money through a confiscation order on a "guilty" sub-postmaster – and wait for them to find the money somehow, possibly on pain of jail time. It was, wrote Graham Ward, "crucial at these confiscation hearings to ensure that the Post Office are awarded compensation from the confiscation order".[25] The theft/false accounting plea two-card trick had become a lucrative three-card trick. And the more of its workers the Post Office could criminalise, the more it could squeeze out of them.

Charmless offensive

The Post Office had just the people, suitably incentivised, for this task and it gave them the right incentives to do so. The performance of investigators such as Graham Ward, Steve Bradshaw and Graham Brander was judged partly on their success in financial recovery, with a target of 40 percent of "losses".[26] Hitting the number meant a better appraisal, and probably a higher bonus. But, perhaps more important than any personal financial incentive, the targets told investigators what the purpose of their job was. It was about money, not justice.

Often the conduct of investigators seeking these results turned from forceful to hostile, and then outright bullying of people who had done nothing wrong and were already in a state of shock. One wrongfully convicted sub-postmaster, Jacqueline McDonald from Broughton in Lancashire, later said that her investigators "behaved like mafia gangsters looking to collect their bounty with the threats and lies".[27]

Steve Bradshaw, a TV licence-fee enforcer before joining the Post Office as an investigator around the time Horizon was rolled out, was particularly charmless. Rather than exploring what might have caused a £65,000 shortfall in Mrs McDonald's case after she'd said she had no idea, he accused her of telling him "a pack of lies". She would also say that he had falsely told her she was "the only one" having problems with Horizon, when he knew this was not the case. Another woman Bradshaw was investigating, Newcastle sub-postmaster Shazia Saddiq, recalled how he'd called her a "bitch" over the telephone. Yet another, Rita Threlfall, who used a wheelchair, reported that

---
24 Gerald Harbinson, witness statement, 17 October 2023, WITN08150100
25 POL00121975
26 See, for example, examination of Gary Thomas, 7 December 2023
27 Bradshaw, witness statement, 26 June 2023, WITN04450100

he made her get in a small parcel lift at Liverpool sorting office to reach the interview room. Bradshaw would later deny the allegations.[28]

Contempt for sub-postmasters and convenient incompetence pervaded the investigation branch. When a 2008 audit showed 59-year-old Worcestershire sub-postmaster Julian Wilson had a £28,000 shortfall, he was confronted by investigator Gary Thomas, assisted by Jo Hamilton's conveniently incurious interrogator Graham Brander. Thomas was another loyal Post Office man, who'd joined as a counter clerk in 1985 and progressed to become an investigator in 2000. His training over more than a decade in the role had been "very minimal", he would later admit. ("I think a lot of it would have been either email based, or I remember going on something called a defensive driving course," was the best he'd be able to tell the public inquiry.)[29]

Thomas's investigation was a typical shambles. The home of Julian and his wife Karen was searched (without a warrant), but inevitably nothing was found. The couple gave the investigators their personal financial records, but the Post Office men didn't even look at them. Transcripts of Mr Wilson's interview showed that he had repeatedly raised the question of Horizon being at fault – with auditors, Post Office managers and with the National Federation of Sub-postmasters. But Thomas wasn't interested. His report on the case to prosecution lawyers not only omitted any mention of Mr Wilson's concerns about Horizon, it went further. "There did not appear to be any further failings in security, procedures or product integrity that directly affect this case," wrote Thomas in bold.[30]

In June 2009 at Worcester Crown Court, Julian Wilson was duly forced to plead guilty to false accounting in order to have the theft charge dropped. He was sentenced to 300 hours' community service, cleaning graves while wearing a hi-vis jacket. The inevitable confiscation order followed (as it had for all those convictions mentioned in this chapter). Mr Wilson lost his place in society, resigning as chairman of the local operatic group. His wife Karen would describe how he talked of suicide while suffering a "very, very slow decline".[31] Julian Wilson died from cancer in 2016, five years before his conviction was posthumously overturned.

He was one of scores of people who didn't live to see justice. Another was Peter Holmes, a former policeman who ran a post office in the Newcastle suburb of Jesmond on behalf of the sub-postmaster. He had repeatedly blamed

---
28 Bradshaw, inquiry evidence, 11 January 2024
29 Thomas, inquiry evidence, 7 December 2023
30 Offender report, 2 December 2008, POL00044803
31 Karen Wilson, inquiry evidence, 16 February 2022

the "bloody awful" IT system for his £46,000 shortfall, but his investigator, Robert Daily, preferred his own preconceptions. Searches showed no signs of stolen wealth and a financial investigation commissioned by defence solicitors refuted Daily's theory that the money had been diverted to Mr & Mrs Holmes's joint account. (The funds in question were actually from Mrs Holmes's cake-making business.) But Daily wasn't going to let the facts get in the way of a good result. In his witness statement ahead of trial in December 2009, he wrote that "whereas the expert report views the amounts in to the [couple's] Barclays account is [sic] the takings from the [cake-making] business, my view is that the manner in which the deposits are made suggests differently".[32] His "view" was based on nothing more than a typical Post Office investigator's prejudice towards sub-postmasters.

Three days before Christmas, at Newcastle Crown Court, Peter Holmes had to do what so many had done in the few years before and pleaded guilty to false accounting. He received a community sentence and a curfew. His wife Marion would tell how he "shut down" following his conviction. Peter Holmes died from a brain tumour in 2015, at the age of 68.

Conviction politics

For those who held out and went to trial, conviction over a phantom shortfall could bring draconian punishment. In September 2008 Harjinder Butoy, a 31-year-old sub-postmaster from Nottinghamshire with three young children, received what appears to be the longest prison sentence meted out in the scandal. He had denied stealing cash that he was alleged to have generated by making false Horizon entries for cheque payments, leading to an alleged £206,000 shortfall. He refused a plea bargain.

Having made unsuccessful attempts to trace the money, the Post Office arrived at court nevertheless with the benefit of Fujitsu vouching all was well with Horizon, and of course not having considered the possibility of bugs or errors. It was a convincing enough combination to deprive a man of his liberty for a long time. Duly convicted, he would serve more than a year and a half of a 39-month sentence in prison, and suffer ruinous financial consequences. But the Post Office once again got the confiscation order it wanted.

The results that the Post Office's investigators were bringing in thanks to Horizon reinforced their own prejudices about sub-postmasters, and reassured them that they need not question the IT system or seek alternative causes of discrepancies. Conviction after conviction bred a certainty that was

---

32 Email from Robert Daily to Juliet McFarlane, 19 August 2009, UKGI00014638

best captured a few years later when dozens of their victims had already gone to the Criminal Cases Review Commission. Reflecting on their earlier days nailing sub-postmasters, in 2015 Julian Wilson's persecutor Gary Thomas would write to Graham Ward, the investigator who'd got Gareth Jenkins to change his witness statement in Noel Thomas's prosecution. As Thomas saw it, "there is FFFFiiinnn no 'Case for the Justice Of Thieving Sub Postmasters'" and "we were the best Investigators they ever had and they were all crooks!!" After prosecutions using Horizon were terminated, "we never hit our PO Profit targets anymore as we stopped getting £XX million in recoveries from bloody good financial recoveries…!!"[33]

Top dogs

Such attitudes suited those in charge of this band of brothers, for whom it also paid to keep the conviction-and-cash harvesting machine humming along.

Tony Marsh, the Post Office head of security who hadn't got "hands on in the investigations space"[34] and had dismissed earlier reports of Horizon's failings, was succeeded in early 2007 by former police sergeant and head of Post Office physical security John Scott. His MSc in security and risk management, plus a diploma in anti-money-laundering, might have been expected to impress on him the importance of following the money, but Scott signally failed to get his investigators to do so. He simply trusted those below him to get on with it, undisturbed by any scrutiny from him. He would claim to be blissfully unaware of any fault in Horizon, even though it was perhaps his most important tool, until 2010.[35]

Scott's boss would be Post Office chief operating officer Mike Young, an ex-copper who had moved into IT. Although he oversaw the Post Office security branch, and thus the investigators, he disclaimed all responsibility for criminal investigations. Accountability for this ran through Marsh, who had been promoted to run security across the whole Royal Mail group. This had the effect of cutting the Post Office senior management and board out of accountability for the rogue investigators – but in an organisation desperate to keep its tawdrier activities going but also to dodge responsibility for them, that suited executives just fine.

Leading them as Post Office managing director from early 2006 was former National Savings & Investment boss Alan Cook. Just like his predecessor David Mills, Cook wouldn't know for more than three years that

---
33 Email from Thomas to Ward, 21 April 2015, POL0017652
34 Anthony Marsh, inquiry evidence, 5 July 2023
35 John Scott, inquiry evidence, 11 October 2023

the Post Office ran its own prosecutions – and remained studiously ignorant of the problems with his organisation's IT system. His and other directors' interest in Horizon began and ended with the reassurance that the auditors from Ernst & Young were signing off the Post Office corporate accounts, based on Horizon, as free from material errors – even if "material" for a £1bn-plus turnover business was very different from "material" for a sub-postmaster, for whom small errors could spell ruin.[36]

As with his predecessor, Cook had large bonuses based on financial results dangled in front of him. In his four years as Post Office managing director, he more than doubled his £250,000-£280,000 salary with such bonuses, including £1.2m in "long-term incentive payments".[37] These were rewards for cutting the Post Office's nine-figure losses, largely by slashing the number of sub-postmaster-run branches from 13,600 in 2006 to 10,600 in 2010 – and, of course, by not acknowledging any potential consequences of the Horizon timebomb ticking away beneath the surface. Cook didn't achieve his results alone, however. Much of the "credit" could go to an ambitious retail executive he'd recruited from Whitbread in January 2007 as his network director, one Paula Vennells, whose contribution would before long be recognised by promotion to his job.

"Frankly, I'm insulted"

---

36 Alan Cook, inquiry evidence, 12 April 2024
37 Royal Mail Holdings plc annual reports, 2006/07-2009/10

6

ARTICLES OF FAITH

Resistance takes shape; the Post Office takes cover

BY THE end of 2008, the Post Office had used Horizon to convict around 450 sub-postmasters and their assistants and employees.[1] It had probably financially ruined a similar number again. But it was unlucky in the enemies it created. They were determined people with righteous anger, who weren't simply going to swallow the Post Office's foul medicine and quieten down.

Since he set up his postofficevictims.org site five years earlier, Alan Bates had been in touch with a steadily growing number of sub-postmasters. But it was a contact he'd made in 2004 that was eventually to prove most consequential. He'd written to IT trade magazine *Computer Weekly* but, with no sign of others coming forward, nothing had come of it. That changed four years later when Lee Castleton approached the magazine with his even more alarming tale.

Computer Weekly had established its credentials exposing IT failures with a groundbreaking investigation into a 1994 Chinook helicopter crash on the Mull of Kintyre that killed a couple of dozen senior police and intelligence figures. The tragedy had been blamed on pilot error, but the magazine identified the suppression of critical information about software problems which ultimately exonerated the crew. Now, with two credible and consistent sources telling a not entirely dissimilar story, its editor Tony Collins could see another potential IT scandal.

With Alan Bates acting as the focal point, sub-postmasters were also beginning to discover each other and understand that they certainly weren't "the only one". So when Collins set reporter Rebecca Thomson on the story, she soon had a burgeoning collection of case studies and began to spot the patterns in the Horizon faults and Post Office conduct that she was being told about.

"Bankruptcy, prosecutions and disrupted livelihoods – postmasters tell their story," ran *Computer Weekly*'s front-page headline on 11 May 2009.[2]

---

[1] WITN09890500
[2] computerweekly.com/news/2240089230/Bankruptcy-prosecution-and-disrupted-livelihoods-Postmasters-tell-their-story

The piece led on Lee Castleton's story and also told those of six other sub-postmasters: Alan Bates, Jo Hamilton, Noel Thomas, Amar Bajaj (a former barrister who was forced to sell his post office in Chelmsford), Alan Brown (the original victim of the Callendar Square bug) and Julie Ford (suspended from her branch in Somerset). It pointedly reported that the National Federation of Sub-postmasters had refused to help the very sub-postmasters it was supposed to represent, no doubt because it was funded by the Post Office itself.

Thomson's investigation made the compelling case that Horizon had been wrecking sub-postmasters' lives for a decade already. It was backed up by comments from a legal expert pointing out the imbalance in the sub-postmaster contract, and from an IT expert who was experienced in giving evidence in court. His view was that "almost all IT systems ever built have malfunctioned at some point" and that what mattered was "the way a business deals with those errors and gets to the bottom of what actually happened".[3]

The story came as a shock to Post Office managing director Alan Cook, despite the widespread knowledge of Horizon's faults in his organisation. When Thomson's enquiries had reached the Post Office shortly before publication, he had asked his head of "service delivery", Andy McLean, to investigate. The nature of this instruction was, however, given away by the email from Cook's assistant to McLean stating that she was "keen that we have a robust response".[4] In the event, no investigation materialised. In line with his longstanding indifference to this aspect of the business (he hadn't even been aware of the eye-wateringly expensive legal action against Lee Castleton a couple of years earlier), Cook let the matter drift. He certainly wasn't going to get the bottom of what actually happened.

That summer, one or two others also began to see that here was a serious story. In September, S4C's current-affairs show *Taro Naw* broadcast its own investigation into the scandal in Wales, highlighting Noel Thomas's story and identifying dozens more. Then the story found its way into retail trade mag *The Grocer*.

Forwarded this latest coverage, Cook shifted uneasily in his chair at the Post Office's Old Street HQ. But he still found it all more bemusing than scandalous. "For some strange reason there is a steadily building nervousness about the accuracy of the Horizon system and the press are on it as well now," he wrote in mid-October to the Royal Mail group's communications boss, Mary Fagan. It was, he said, "the more strange in that the system has been stable and reliable for many years now and there is absolutely no reason why these fears

---

3 Ibid
4 Email from Michele Graves to Andy McLean, 7 May 2009, POL00114930

should now develop".[5] The next line gave away the prejudices that might have been behind this staggering ignorance. "My instincts tell that, in a recession, subbies with their hand in the till choose to blame the technology when they are found to be short of cash." (There might have been a post-financial crash economic downturn at the time, but a moment's thought would have told him that the sub-postmasters' grievances concerned shortfalls from the pre-crisis boom years.) Cook evidently felt familiar enough with the thousands of people running the post office branches he oversaw to call them "subbies", but not familiar enough to contemplate what life was really like for them. He wasn't inclined to find out, and the Post Office clearly wasn't going to grasp the nettle that *Computer Weekly* had presented to it.

Growing campaigns

As the scandal began to get public airing, the Post Office acquired another adversary whom it would be unfortunate to have over the following years.

James Arbuthnot was a baronet's son who had been head boy at Eton and graduated from Trinity College, Cambridge, before practising at the bar for a decade and becoming a Tory MP in 1987. It's fair to say his background wasn't one to be found too often among sub-postmasters. But, by 2009, Arbuthnot's parliamentary career included ministerial office and a long spell scrutinising government as chair of the Commons defence select committee, often poring over flawed projects inflicted on the public from Whitehall. He knew that institutions of the state and their suppliers didn't always get it right. He had also, it so happened, organised parliamentary campaigning on the Chinook disaster, and had come to respect *Computer Weekly*'s coverage of the affair.

Perhaps equally importantly, Arbuthnot had first-hand knowledge of officialdom's instincts for denial and cover-up when faced with its own shortcomings. Some time before, as a defence procurement minister in the mid-1990s, he had followed MoD briefing and dismissed doubts about the Chinook's systems. But, unlike ministers and executives reacting to the Post Office scandal, he'd been prepared to look again at the evidence and before long apologised in parliament, admitting "a gross injustice has been committed and it must be put right".[6] He knew that minds could change and be changed.

One of the seven sub-postmasters spotlighted by *Computer Weekly*, Jo Hamilton was a constituent of Arbuthnot in North East Hampshire. He heard about her case a few weeks before the article came out, when he attended a coffee morning and a local councillor told him about her experience. But it was only

---
5 POL00158368
6 *Hansard*, 27 June 2000

a while later that things clicked. Another sub-postmaster constituent, David Bristow from Odiham, wrote to Arbuthnot in October about his mysteriously appearing shortfall, linking it to Jo Hamilton's in nearby South Warnborough.[7]

Arbuthnot began making enquiries and, after talking to Alan Bates's MP over in Clwyd, fellow Tory David Jones, fired off a letter to the man who was once again running the government's business department, more than a decade after prevailing on Tony Blair to go ahead with the Horizon system in the first place. There appeared, Arbuthnot told Peter Mandelson, "to be a significant number of postmasters and postmistresses accused of fraud who claim that the Horizon system is responsible, including at least two in my constituency".[8]

When Mandelson's junior minister, Pat McFadden MP, replied in early December 2009, he avoided the issue by invoking the Blair and Byers reforms of eight years before. "Under the government's postal sector reforms introduced in 2001, Royal Mail (which includes Post Office Ltd) was given greater commercial freedom," he replied, "and government has assumed an arm's-length role as a shareholder in a public limited company."[9] These were "operational and contractual matters" for the Post Office. While this was a prohibitive barrier to accountability, which would allow successive governments to wash their hands of the affair, it did serve one purpose. In offending Arbuthnot's old-fashioned idea that government should take responsibility for what it was doing to its citizens, it stiffened his resolve.

As did, that same week, his and Jones's meetings with Post Office officials, who trotted out the mantra that Horizon was "robust" and appeared totally intransigent. But it was the following day, back in Hampshire, that Arbuthnot really became convinced of the cause. When he met Jo Hamilton and David Bristow in person, he could see that these were truthful people. (It was a shame Post Office executives never tried the same thing.) He was shown the *Computer Weekly* report and was further persuaded. A few days later he was back in contact with Jones, setting up another meeting. As he put it to his fellow MP, he "felt a campaign coming on".[10]

He wasn't the only one. With at least a small part of the rest of the world catching up with him, Alan Bates decided it was time to turn his efforts helping other sub-postmasters into a more tangible movement. He invited his contacts, spread all over the country, to a meeting at a hall in the Warwickshire village of Fenny Compton, in the heart of England. On Sunday 8 November 2009, between

---

7 Lord (James) Arbuthnot, written evidence, 12 March 2024, WITN00020100
8 Letter from Arbuthnot to Peter Mandelson, 3 November 2009, UKGI00011504
9 Letter from Pat McFadden to Arbuthnot, 5 December 2009, UKGI00011506
10 WITN00020100

30 and 40 of them arrived. As they sat in a circle and listened to each other's stories, after having been shunned and isolated for so long, they each realised they were not "the only one". The Justice for Subpostmasters Alliance was born.

Machine wash

With Bates, his band of emboldened sub-postmasters and a few parliamentary allies getting the bit between their teeth, resistance was taking shape. Even the obdurate Post Office could sense the rumblings of discontent; there were also noises coming through their own people out in the network.

When a contracts adviser for the Southeast of England wrote to the Post Office's senior civil lawyer, Mandy Talbot, in February 2010 looking for advice on dealing with complaints from a female sub-postmaster on her patch, she added that there were "many cases at the moment… where there are challenges regarding the integrity of the Horizon system".[11]

Talbot forwarded the email to the Post Office's top IT man, David Smith, who didn't hide his frustration. "As yet I haven't seen a single shred of evidence to back up any of these claims," he replied.[12] To Smith it looked like sub-postmasters making excuses, even though he knew all about Horizon's faults from the early days. A "recent meeting with MPs [presumably Arbuthnot and Jones] encapsulated the issue we face very nicely," he could report. "People know that computer systems go wrong from time to time, particularly, government computer systems, and, therefore, believe that a computer system such as Horizon could have caused these discrepancies." Rather than realise that he'd pretty much put his finger on the issue, he applied classic Post Office doublethink and moved on to how to alter this truth. "Our greatest chance of winning the argument case by case is to fix the debate on what actually happened," he continued, citing by way of example the defeat of Lee Castleton (which the Post Office had won by re-inventing "what actually happened").

To deal with the case from the Southeast, Smith recommended an independent professional look at the system, under strict control, alongside a "combined Post Office/Fujitsu effort". This work would "set out how Horizon maintains integrity and illustrate how this is ensured". Talbot responded that they would need someone "expert but also quite robust so as to be capable of rebutting anything that the sub-postmistress's expert can throw at us".[13] It wasn't the most open-minded approach.

This proposal wouldn't happen, anyway. The executives quickly realised

---

11 Email from Carol Ballan to Mandy Talbot, 16 February 2010, FUJ00156120
12 Email from David Smith to Talbot, 18 February 2010, FUJ00156120
13 Ibid

that fighting specific cases wasn't enough, and that letting anybody vaguely independent investigate Horizon was inviting trouble. Something more proactive – and more deceptive – was required.

Clear Horizon

At the end of February 2010, IT boss Smith and top civil lawyer Talbot convened with the Post Office heads of security, John Scott, of product branch and accounting, Rod Ismay, and of information security, Sue Lowther. They agreed that the Post Office would conduct its own investigation into the operation of Horizon, as "we have far more expertise and knowledge than anyone else is likely to produce for this initial piece of work", and then "gain external verification to give a level of 'external gravitas' to the response to these challenges".[14] Consultants Ernst & Young were thought most suitable for this.

Even this plan was too risky for the organisation's head of criminal law, Rob Wilson, a solicitor who had joined the Post Office's prosecution team in the mid-1980s and risen to his current position eight years earlier. He had therefore presided over hundreds of convictions and had a bit of skin in this game. Declaring himself "staggered" to have been left out of the discussion, Wilson explained how such a review would stymie prosecutions. "Inevitably the defence will argue that if we are carrying out an investigation we clearly do not have confidence in Horizon," he wrote. Proceedings might have to be stalled and "the resultant adverse publicity could lead to massive difficulties for [the Post Office] as it would be seen by the press and media to vindicate the current challenges". More widely, "every office in the country will be seen to be operating a compromised system with untold damage to the Business".[15] The capitalisation of "Business" gave a clue to the criminal lawyer's priorities.

Lowther attempted to soothe his concerns. After "taking into account Rob's comments," she told colleagues, "what we are looking at is a 'general' due diligence exercise on the integrity of Horizon, to confirm our belief in the robustness of the system and thus rebutt [sic] any challenges."[16] At no point did she or any of the others wonder whether their review might consider the incidental matter of Horizon having been used to destroy innocent people's lives.

Whitewash day

It was a sign of the concern now being felt in Whitehall that when shiftless chief executive Alan Cook shifted on to pastures new (the insurance business),

---

14 Email from Andy Hayward to Talbot and others, 26 February 2010, POL00106867
15 Email from Rob Wilson to Dave Posnett, 3 March 2010, POL00106867
16 Email from Sue Lowther to Hayward and others, 8 March 2010, POL00106867

his replacement, chartered accountant and former Parcelforce director David Smith (not to be confused with head of IT David Smith), was briefed by the government's Shareholder Executive on the subject of Horizon.

"We have to date said that this is an operational matter for [the Post Office] and resisted calls to impose a review of Horizon," wrote the executive's Oliver Griffiths to Smith on 21 July 2010.[17] But he then made it clear that for arm's-length bodies separated from government, the arms were only so long when the political heat was on. "We are in theory happy to continue holding this line," he added, "but if we do so and it turns out that there have been problems with Horizon, then there will be significant political heat." Having given the not-so-coded warning, Griffiths then asked how confident the Post Office was "that there is nothing behind these claims".

The new chief executive reacted in a manner that would often be seen from new senior arrivals at the Post Office: with genuine, but all too short-lived, curiosity. He chewed the issue over with senior colleagues including finance director Mike Moores and operations director Mike Young and emailed them with pertinent but largely rhetorical questions, including "How robust is Horizon?", "How do we treat discrepancies?" and "Are we heavy handed and disproportionate in our response?"[18]

When Smith finally commissioned a now overdue review of Horizon, he conspicuously didn't write his instructions down, so the terms of reference remained helpfully unspecified. The job went to branch accounting head Rod Ismay, a chartered accountant who had joined the Post Office from its auditor Ernst & Young in 2003 and who knew little about IT. He would be guided by Mike Young and chief information officer Lesley Sewell (who had succeeded the other, recently departed David Smith as IT head).

Chief executive Smith would later say he commissioned an "honest" and not "one-sided" piece of work;[19] Ismay would acknowledge that he was asked to provide "reassurance" on Horizon and the "counterargument" to allegations, to give just "one side of the coin".[20] He certainly did that with the report that he produced in August 2010, *Horizon – Response to Challenges Concerning Systems Integrity*. When it emerged publicly years later, it would become known as the Ismay whitewash report.

The beancounter more or less wrote down what various investigators, IT people and others told him, reflecting the Post Office party lines, and reached

---
17 Email from Oliver Griffiths to David Smith, 21 July 2010, POL00417098
18 Email from Smith to Mike Young and others, 21 July 2010, POL00417100
19 Smith, inquiry evidence, 11 April 2024
20 Roderick Ismay, inquiry evidence, 10 May 2023

the conclusions required. **1.** Where branch shortfalls appeared, "we remain satisfied that this money was missing due to theft in the branch – we do not believe the account balances… were corrupt." **2.** "Horizon is robust, but like any system depends on the quality of entries by the users." **3.** "The integrity of Horizon is founded on its tamper proof logs, its real time back ups and the absence of 'backdoors' so that all data entry or acceptance is at branch level…" **4.** "Sub-postmasters are trained to use the system, they have support material in branch and there is a wealth of helpline support available." **5.** "Accounting errors do happen through user mistakes, but these can be explained and resolved case by case. Systems issues have also arisen but again [the Post Office] has been able to explain them and rectify them… they do not bring the integrity of the system into question."[21]

Each of these points was completely wrong, but a sixth really took the proverbial: "When [the Post Office] takes a sub-postmaster to court we have strong processes for the compilation of evidence, compassionate factors are borne in mind and we have a high success rate." As for any admission of fault, Ismay made some suggestions for procedural improvements. These would, he said, "not undermine [the Post Office's] assertion regarding the integrity of Horizon, but they would tackle some of the other noise which complainants feed on."

If this read more like a briefing from the Post Office's media team, it was probably meant to. Ismay dispatched his report to all the departmental big cheeses, telling them he had performed "an objective, internal review of [the Post Office's] processes and controls around branch accounting".[22] From a man who had celebrated victory over Lee Castleton as a "considerable addition to our armoury",[23] it was unlikely ever to be that.

Mismatch of the day

The deception soon deepened further. Between writing his report and the end of 2010, Ismay was copied into emails about a serious bug in the IT, known as the "receipts/payments mismatch issue" and understood to affect around 40 branches. This involved discrepancies that should have been rolled over in branch accounts for subsequent resolution, but which could disappear, causing all sorts of confusion.[24] One of the ideas for dealing with the bug (discussed at a meeting by Fujitsu staff, including Gareth Jenkins, and Post Office officials, including one of Ismay's underlings) was to alter branch accounts centrally. For

---

21 Ismay report, 2 August 2010, POL00026572
22 Ibid
23 Email from Ismay to Talbot, 9 November 2006, POL00158577
24 Ismay, inquiry evidence, 10 May 2024

this, the minutes recorded, "Fujitsu would have to manually write an entry value to the local branch account."[25] In other words, the IT company *could* tamper with branch accounts. The issue had been found in a new Horizon Online version of the system, designed to make accounting between branches, product suppliers and the Post Office itself more instantaneous – but it was obvious and widely appreciated that there were bugs, and also that there was a backdoor, or "remote access", for sub-postmasters' accounts to be altered, unknown to them.

Although this bombshell contradicted his reassurances that there were no such backdoors in the system, it didn't prompt Ismay – who had discussed it with his colleague who attended the meeting – to revisit his report, or to mention anything to Smith or any other executives. This was no great surprise. As Ismay had put it in his report, faithfully following the head of criminal law Rob Wilson's line from a few months before, "any perception that [the Post Office] doubts its own systems would mean that all criminal prosecutions would have to be stayed. It would also beg a question for the Court of Appeal over past prosecutions and imprisonments." The catastrophe of justice interfering with Post Office prosecutions and harming the Business was too awful to contemplate.[26]

---

25 Notes on receipts/payments mismatch meeting, 29 September 2010, POL00028838
26 Ismay report

7

ROUGH INJUSTICE

The defence of Horizon justifies misleading the courts and inflicting grievous harm

AMONG more than 150 people who paid the price for the protection of the Post Office brand with a conviction, even after *Computer Weekly* raised the alarm, was 28-year-old Pembrokeshire sub-postmaster Tim Brentnall. He was fed the routine "you're the only one" line over his £16,500 shortfall in late 2009, when anyone with the slightest involvement in investigations knew this was untrue, and then hit with the theft/false accounting double charge. The usual story played out at Carmarthen Crown Court in June 2010; the theft charge was dropped in return for a guilty plea on false accounting, and Tim was landed with a suspended sentence to go with his stolen livelihood and devastated family life and mental health. A member of the group of 555 sub-postmasters who took legal action in *Bates and Others v Post Office*, he would become an eloquent spokesman for sub-postmasters, powerfully reminding those tempted to see an IT scandal that "it wasn't Horizon that prosecuted us" and that what it was all about was "the people".

What Rod Ismay dismissively described as "noise" a couple of months after Tim Brentnall's conviction was the sound of 60 Horizon-based convictions in 2009 and 37 in 2010, coupled with suspensions still above 200 in 2009/10 (more than 90 percent of these over audit shortfalls, with less than a quarter of people ever reinstated).[1] Like a Ponzi scheme in which more people have to be ripped off in order to cover earlier misappropriations, the Post Office was increasingly persecuting sub-postmasters to show that it was right to have prosecuted sub-postmasters. And its stance on those prosecutions was hardening.

One of the Post Office's loyal henchmen would boast to his bosses of taking the toughest of lines possible precisely to protect Horizon. In November 2010, Jacqueline McDonald, the Lancashire sub-postmaster who would accuse her investigator Steve Bradshaw of mafia-like behaviour, was convicted of

---
1 FoI release and Ismay report

the theft of more than £90,000 – despite having repeatedly protested about Horizon's failings (including 216 calls to the Post Office's helpdesk) and there being no proof of any real losses. She had originally pleaded guilty to false accounting and it appeared that the prosecution counsel wanted to accept that and not go ahead with a trial for theft. According to Bradshaw's 2010/11 self-appraisal a few months later, however, he convinced them to push on with the theft charge. "I challenged the recommendations of the barrister and persuade[d] him that a trial would be necessary," he wrote, "as the reasons given by the defendant (Horizon integrity) would have a wider impact on the business if a trial did not go ahead." There were, he added, "current issues ongoing regarding the Horizon system".[2]

The trial didn't go ahead. Mrs McDonald had recently watched a fellow sub-postmaster convicted and imprisoned after trial (networks of mutual support were growing) and was desperate to mitigate her own sentence. She pleaded guilty to the theft charge and was given an 18-month prison sentence anyway. Bradshaw got his innocent victim and, perhaps, a decent performance appraisal.

The message had clearly got through to the frontline investigators that Horizon was under assault and they needed to plough on. As Bradshaw would ultimately explain to the public inquiry, his words reflected "the way the business wanted things doing".[3] This "way" was never more inhumanely and dishonestly pursued than in the case of the sub-postmaster from Surrey whose conviction had persuaded Jacqueline McDonald to make her own guilty plea. It proved just how far above justice the Post Office put the protection of Horizon and its cherished brand.

Three unwise men

When a judge at Guildford Crown Court summed up the case against 34-year-old sub-postmaster Seema Misra, accused of stealing £70,000 from the Post Office, he could have been describing hundreds of others that didn't go to court. "There is no direct evidence of her taking any money," he told the jury on 20 October 2010. "She adamantly denies stealing. There is no CCTV evidence. There are no fingerprints or marked bank notes or anything of that kind. There is no evidence of her accumulating cash anywhere else or spending large sums of money or paying off debts, no evidence about her bank accounts at all. Nothing incriminating was found when her home was searched."[4]

The entire case against Mrs Misra was the accounting shortfalls at her

---

2 Stephen Bradshaw, self-appraisal form 2010/11, POL00165946
3 Bradshaw, inquiry evidence, 11 January 2024
4 His Honour Judge NA Steward, judgment in *R v Seema Misra*, 19 October 2010, POL00065708

branch in West Byfleet, making the question of Horizon's accuracy decisive. "Do you accept the prosecution case that there is ample evidence before you," the judge asked the jury, "to establish that Horizon is a tried and tested system in use at thousands of post offices for several years, fundamentally robust and reliable…?" Evidently, they did. They returned a guilty verdict. Three weeks later, Seema Misra, who was eight weeks pregnant, was despatched from Guilford Crown Court in a prison van to begin a 15-month sentence for theft. It was also her son's tenth birthday.

Mrs Misra's troubles with Horizon followed a familiar pattern. Over a couple of years, shortfalls at her post office had moved into high five-figure amounts. She first suspected her staff of stealing, repaid what she could and then tried to cover up what she couldn't by declaring her accounts balanced when they didn't. Following the audit and investigation, which were only going to reach one conclusion, she was charged with theft and false accounting over a two-and-a-half-year period from June 2005 to January 2008.

Seema Misra pleaded guilty to the false accounting charges in March 2009 and had been scheduled to stand trial for theft in May. But the *Computer Weekly* article that month raised the serious prospect of a new defence – that Horizon was unreliable. For the Post Office, this meant that a new trial could attract awkward public scrutiny of Horizon. Or, to turn the problem around, it presented an opportunity to demonstrate the soundness of Horizon-based convictions and quell the rising discontent. The stakes were high: so high that they justified a conspiracy by the Post Office and Fujitsu to falsely convict a sub-postmaster.

Three men largely held Seema Misra's fate in their hands. One was an expert on the Horizon system and knew its long history of bugs and defects; the other two were lawyers whose primary professional responsibility was serving justice. This triumvirate should have been able pretty quickly to reach the conclusion that the IT was obviously flawed, so any prosecution relying exclusively on it was a non-starter. That was not, however, the Post Office or Fujitsu way.

When Mrs Misra's defence team produced a report setting out apparent problems with Horizon, both at her branch and known from earlier cases, the Post Office turned to Fujitsu to provide its rebuttal. The task was handed to the man whom ICL had honoured as a "distinguished engineer" soon after its 1990 takeover by Fujitsu, the slightly unworldly and suggestible 59-year-old Cambridge maths graduate Gareth Jenkins. For its part, the Post Office entrusted its efforts to the incompetent but faithful lawyer Jarnail Singh, working alongside the barrister it had given the brief, Warwick Tatford.

The chances of Jenkins discharging his responsibilities with an open mind were always slim. When looking at another case in January 2010, he had written to a colleague, security analyst Penny Thomas, that it was "highly political" and "we don't really want to be seen to be undermining a [Post Office] prosecution!"[5] He could be as dismissive of the sub-postmasters' cases as a typical Post Office investigator. "This is another example of postmasters trying to get away with 'Horizon has taken my money'," he wrote the following month when asked to provide his expertise.[6] And then in March, summarising a run-through of Mrs Misra's case he'd just had with Singh, the Fujitsu man concluded: "When she went to court, she saw an article in *Computer Weekly* magazine indicating that Horizon was unreliable and decided to jump on the bandwagon."[7]

Crucial to any chance of success for Seema Misra were the records from her branch for the period in which she was accused of being on the take. The Post Office resisted providing these, not wishing to incur the costs of doing so under its contract with Fujitsu. It eventually handed over audit data for less than half the period in question. But even this was meaningless without the details of errors in the system, known by Fujitsu, against which the data could be carefully compared. Jenkins failed to examine those error logs or to alert the defence to the point.

Instead, in dealing with pre-trial questions from the IT expert appointed by the defence, Professor Charles McLachlan, Jenkins limited his comments to the one bug that was known outside Fujitsu and the Post Office: the so-called Callendar Square bug that had emerged in Lee Castleton's case three years earlier. This, naturally, was played down. "As with any large system there will be occasional faults such as the one found in Callender [*sic*] Square, Falkirk," wrote Jenkins. "Any such faults… would be investigated and resolved appropriately." He wasn't aware of any at West Byfleet, but if "specific transactions can be identified [out of 500,000 in the period disclosed] where the user feels the system has caused losses then further investigation can be made".[8] This once again threw an impossible burden of proof on to the sub-postmaster. It was akin to telling Mrs Misra's team: "Here's the haystack, show us where the needle is and we'll have a look at it." Jenkins even evaded questions from the Post Office's own lawyers. His witness statement pointedly did not address Jarnail Singh's request that he "mention whether there are any known problems with the Horizon system that Fujitsu are aware of". The lawyer added: "If none could

---

5 Email from Gareth Jenkins to Penny Thomas, 27 January 2010, FUJ00152888
6 Email from Jenkins to Suzie Kirkham and Tom Lillywhite, 25 February 2010, FUJ00156122
7 Email from Jenkins to Jarnail Singh, 1 March 2010, POL00175839
8 Jenkins, witness statement in *Misra* case, 9 March 2010, POL00001643

this be clarified in the statement."⁹ These weren't questions he really wanted to answer, given the obvious implications of honest answers.

When Jenkins did display a hint of candour, he was reined in. As the trial neared and he put together his witness statement, the barrister Tatford became twitchy over parts of it. In one draft, Jenkins proposed responding to comments from Prof McLachlan about problems with the Horizon screen buttons by saying: "While I can't 10% [sic] rule out such issues as causing some issues… I can't see how this could account for anything like the full extent of the losses."¹⁰ Tatford responded: "Please rephrase. This will be taken as a damaging concession."¹¹ Jenkins complied with this and other suggestions to strengthen his statement.

Tatford, for his part, bought into the Post Office's priorities in a way that wouldn't be expected of a barrister charged with serving the interests of justice. Having been told by the Post Office of cost constraints on getting data from Fujitsu, he resisted requests by Mrs Misra's defence for all audit data over the period of the indictment, replying to McLachlan: "If one requested and received every piece of paper for West Byfleet, we would probably fill this room."¹² He also failed to ensure that requests for error logs – obviously essential information – were considered. When one legal executive suggested to him that, given that Mrs Misra's pleas to false accounting would be on the basis that she was covering up *others*' thefts, this would make it "very difficult for us later to obtain a Confiscation Order and subsequently compensation,"¹³ Tatford replied, "The case for theft is strong and we should not accept the pleas. Confiscation would also be a non-starter if we did." He would later deny that he was taking into account financial recoveries when recommending what charges should be made, which would have been an improper placing of the financial cart before the justice horse.

Trial and errors

As the trial date approached, Jenkins's witness statement had become a grossly misleading document. The failure to mention Horizon bugs, beyond addressing the "fixed" Callendar Square one, was bad enough. But, on another critical point, he actively misdirected the court. McLachlan had raised the possibility of entries appearing in branch accounts from elsewhere in the system. Jenkins responded to this by saying: "There are no cases where

9 Email from Jarnail Singh to David Jones, 5 February 2010, FUJ00122794
10 Gareth Jenkins, draft witness statement in *Misra* case, 6 October 2010, FUJ00123006
11 Warwick Tatford, comments on Jenkins statement, 7 October 2010, POL00167219
12 Tatford, inquiry evidence, 15 November 2023
13 Email from Phil Taylor to Tatford, 22 May 2009, POL00051586

external systems can manipulate the branch's account without the users in branch being aware of what is happening and authorising the transactions."[14] The distinguished engineer had in fact known since 2000 about the possibility of so-called "remote access" but failed to mention this.[15]

More remarkably, just a couple of weeks before the trial in October, Jenkins had written a four-page memo on the "receipts/payments mismatch" bug. The Post Office needed to be informed of this, he said, and agreement reached on "correcting the data". Any tweaking of branch data would "need to be carefully communicated to the branches to avoid questions about the system integrity".[16] Options outlined at a discussion between Post Office and Fujitsu officials, at which Jenkins was present, included: "Alter the Horizon branch figure at the counter to show the discrepancy." The downsides of this, the notes say, included "moral implications of Post Office changing branch data without informing the branch".[17] In other words, remote access certainly *was* possible, and it was being discussed by Jenkins just days before he was to tell a jury it wasn't.

The risks to the Post Office's prosecutions were understood. The same notes recorded five impacts of the bug. Two were technical, but three spelt out serious broader consequences: "if widely known could cause a loss of confidence in the Horizon system by branches"; "potential impact on ongoing legal cases where branches are disputing the integrity of Horizon data"; and "it could provide branches ammunition to blame Horizon for future discrepancies". Even though the bug had been found in the new Horizon Online, it evidently undermined the whole Horizon programme – the "ongoing legal cases" mentioned, such as Seema Misra's, all involved the original Horizon system. Yet still Jenkins didn't make the necessary changes to his witness statement.

When he appeared at Guildford Crown Court on 14 October 2010, Jenkins did so as an expert witness with a duty to present objective evidence on his area of expertise. But there was no sign that he'd received instructions from either of the lawyers, Tatford or Singh, on the obligations that came with the role. What he had been told informally was wildly off-beam. At one point before the originally scheduled trial, Singh had said: "Just a reminder you are an expert for Fujitsu… the judge and jury will be listening very carefully and a lot will hang on the evidence."[18] Jenkins would later admit that he saw himself as effectively part of the "prosecution team".

Having taken the oath to tell the whole truth, in the witness box Jenkins

---

14 Jenkins, fifth *Misra* witness statement, 8 October 2010, FUJ00083737
15 Jenkins, inquiry evidence, 26 June 2024
16 Jenkins, *Correcting Accounts for "Lost" Discrepancies*, 29 September 2010, POL00028838
17 Notes on receipts/payments mismatch issue meeting, undated, POL00028838
18 Email from Singh to Jenkins, 1 March 2010, POL00054267

brushed off the challenges he faced. Asked by Tatford if his analysis had found "even the slightest symptom of any computer fault", he replied that he hadn't – but that he'd only been doing "high-level rough analysis".[19] Most computer problems would be visible to users anyway, he told the court, and Prof McLachlan hadn't pointed to any fault (not mentioning that the defence hadn't been given the information that would have enabled it to do so). Asked by the judge if his evidence had been influenced by being a "Fujitsu man", Jenkins calmly rejected the suggestion.

That was, however, exactly what Jenkins was. Only a true Fujitsu or Post Office man would have concealed what he did, when doing so could wreck someone's life. But he wasn't the only Fujitsu man to give evidence. So did the dependable security analyst Andy Dunks, vouching for matters such as the operation of Fujitsu's software support centre, of which he had no knowledge.

Singh when he's winning

After the verdict demonstrated that the jury had believed the Fujitsu men and the system they defended, the mood in the Post Office returned to levels not known since the victory against Lee Castleton.

Jarnail Singh sent an email to senior colleagues with the heading "Attack on Horizon", betraying exactly how the Post Office saw the case. Thanks to the hard work of Tatford and the investigator on the case, Jon Longman, plus the "considerable expertise of Gareth Jenkins of Fujitsu", the Post Office had been "able to destroy to the criminal standard of proof (beyond all reasonable doubt) every single suggestion made by the defence". Singh "hoped the case will set a marker to dissuade other defendants from jumping on the Horizon bashing bandwagon".[20] The second Post Office show trial had achieved its purpose.

David Smith, who had just ended his short tenure as Post Office chief executive to become commercial director for the Royal Mail group (if not helped, then certainly unhindered by having kept a lid on the scandal), forwarded Singh's email to senior colleagues, including the woman who had stepped up to replace him, Paula Vennells. The win was "brilliant news", he said. Chief accountant Ismay saw vindication in the "excellent work going on in so many teams to justify the confidence that we have in Horizon".[21]

The Post Office might have been cheating, but it was still winning. Or so it thought.

---

19 *Misra* trial transcript, 14 October 2010, POL00029406
20 Email from Singh to colleagues, 21 October 2010, POL00169170
21 POL00169170

8

SECOND COMMERCIAL BREAK

A new regime promises a bright future for the Post Office, but makes protecting the brand more essential than ever

WHEN the Coalition government was formed in May 2010, and Nick Clegg's resurgent Liberal Democrats were given the business department, they acquired responsibility for a Royal Mail group that was losing around £300m a year – thanks to ever-increasing competition and the never-ending hangover of huge pension costs.

New business secretary Vince Cable asked former BT executive Richard Hooper to update a report he'd written on the Royal Mail for Peter Mandelson a couple of years earlier, titled *Modernise or Decline* (after a decade of modernisation *and* decline). In September, Hooper's *Saving the Royal Mail's Universal Services in a Digital Age* set out the situation: volumes of letters were decreasing and business practices lagged behind the proliferating rival postal operators. Urgent action was needed in the form of lighter regulation, offloading the pension liabilities and, in a critical extension of Hooper's previous ideas, the introduction of private sector capital "in the form of sale to a partner/trade investor or IPO" (initial public offering) – in other words a stock market flotation.

Cable also replaced Royal Mail chief executive Adam Crozier, who'd moved on to run ITV, with Canadian public official turned businesswoman Moya Greene. Her CV featured privatisation of the Canadian railways in the 1990s before entering the business world and a stint running her country's (publicly owned) mail company, Canada Post. There she'd pushed through an automation and cost-cutting programme that, taken with the rail sell-off experience, made her just the woman to realise Cable's vision of the Royal Mail in the second decade of the 21st century. Beside Greene, with his hand on the tiller through the choppy waters ahead, would be City grandee Donald Brydon, who'd replaced Allan Leighton as chair the year before.

Hooper's latest recommendations quickly became a new Postal Services Bill, allowing for the privatisation of Royal Mail. For the Post Office itself,

Cable and his postal services minister Ed Davey set out separate ambitions in a paper titled *Securing the Post Office Network in the Digital Age*. The network of post offices was still swallowing £150m a year in subsidies, so this was essentially a cost-cutting exercise with a "modernisation" twist. Renewed plans for technological innovation would enable more services to be offered, compensating for reduced financial support. To make it a bit more appealing, the carrot of mutualisation – handing ownership over to the sub-postmasters – was also dangled in front of them. The prospect of them taking over from their corporate masters at Post Office Ltd HQ represented, said Cable in the Cameroonian spirit of the time, "the Big Society in action".[1]

Davey stamp

The sub-postmasters' ongoing plight – Horizon-related convictions still running at around 40 a year, suspensions about 150 – wasn't serious enough to command attention against these grand plans. Alan Bates wrote to Davey a couple weeks after the general election, telling him that Horizon was being used to "intimidate and prosecute sub-postmasters", and that his group now had close to a hundred members.[2] He requested a meeting. Bates was fobbed off with the "arm's length" line and told a meeting would not "serve any useful purpose".[3] When he wrote back, calling Davey's response "offensive" and pointing out that it was the same as he'd heard seven years earlier, adding that governments had allowed "a once great institution to be asset stripped by little more than thugs in suits", the new minister relented.[4] By the time they sat down in October, Davey had received letters from numerous MPs, including Valerie Vaz, George Osborne and Alun Michael, on behalf of sub-postmaster constituents. Aspiring new Tory backbencher Priti Patel was asking some pointed parliamentary questions. The minister at least listened to Bates, but was briefed with false lines from the Ismay whitewash report and was already being dragged into the cover-up.

A couple of weeks later, Seema Misra was convicted. Before sentencing, she contacted her MP, Jonathan Lord. He then wrote to Davey, asking specifically about "remote access" to Horizon, prompting the Shareholder Executive to seek a fuller briefing from Post Office executives. They were by now aware of the possibility of remote access, following discussion of the receipts/payments mismatch bug. But when the Shareholder Executive's

---

1 gov.uk/government/news/post-office-could-be-mutualised
2 Letter from Alan Bates to Ed Davey, 20 May 2010, UKGI00016119
3 Letter from Davey to Bates, 31 May 2010, ABAT00000001
4 Letter from Bates to Davey, 8 July 2010, UKGI00000062

Michael Whitehead asked if the Post Office was "categorically stating that there is no remote access",[5] Post Office head of regulatory relations Mike Granville fudged the issue with talk of access for "technical changes".[6] Presumably relieved by the reassurance, Whitehead drastically beefed this up. The reply to Lord that Davey signed claimed that the Post Office "categorically states that there is no remote access to the system or to individual branch terminals".[7] He used exactly the same phrase in a letter to Bates.[8] Wilfully misleading advice from the Post Office had been turned into an outright lie by its shareholder, the government. The price, as ever, was justice; had Lord's question been answered accurately, Seema Misra would have had compelling grounds for appeal a decade before she was ultimately exonerated.

Davey didn't follow up on either this or his dealings with Alan Bates. The Shareholder Executive had shielded him from the aggravating sub-postmasters. Ministers could get on with their plans to flog the Royal Mail and rescue the Post Office, untroubled by any hassle over IT systems and miscarriages of justice.

Lamb chops

Under Davey's successor from February 2012, Norman Lamb, the idea of "securing the Post Office network in a digital age" became a "network transformation" programme. Although it echoed previous periodic efforts – an "urban network reinvention programme" from 2002 and a "network change programme" from 2007 – the new initiative was more drastic.

It would be overseen by the woman who had been promoted to become managing director in October 2010, Paula Vennells. The 51-year-old languages graduate had arrived at the Post Office less than four years earlier after a career in marketing at companies, including Argos, Dixons and Whitbread, for which brand was everything. Her role at the last company, putting Beefeater restaurants next to Premier Inns and peppering high streets with Costa Coffee outlets, had convinced the Post Office board that recruited her in 2007 as "network director" that she was just what they needed in their perennial efforts to make the branch network viable.

While making her enduring contributions to the British retail and hospitality scene, Vennells had also trained to become an ordained priest. She

---
5 Email from Michael Whitehead to Mike Granville, 26 November 2010, POL00417094
6 Email from Granville to Whitehead, 29 November 2010, POL00417094
7 Letter from Davey to Lord, 7 December 2010, SMIS0000268
8 Letter from Davey to Bates, 7 December 2010, POL00186759

would later tell *Sunday Times* interviewer Oliver Shah that faith "influences my values and how I approach things". Her former chairman at Whitbread told the same reporter that she was "straightforward, competent and really nice".[9] She was now in a job that would test her personal virtues against the brand instincts embedded by three decades in marketing.

The network transformation programme involved grants to larger "main" post office branches to jazz them up; in return for these, the sub-postmaster would lose fixed income payments from the Post Office but be expected to boost fee-paying business. Smaller branches would become slimmed-down "locals" offering a narrower range of Post Office services, typically across a corner shop's regular retail counter.[10] Allegations would later emerge that sub-postmasters were sometimes coerced into changes and contracts that were not, in fact, in their financial interests.[11] Whatever the truth of that, the extra services to be offered at the main branches, as well as the requirement for new IT installations at the locals, meant greater dependence on the Horizon system. And, with the plan dependent on increased sales of services in a competitive market, the Post Office brand became a more critical asset than ever.

Bonus balls

When she appeared before a committee of MPs in May 2012 to discuss the network transformation programme, Vennells drove the point home. After years of cuts in branch numbers, the Post Office had "become a victim, and that is not the place a brand as strong as the Post Office should be". She gave her own bold vision. "We should be really strong," she told them. "We should be playing to the market competitively." Expanding the business was crucial, and "that growth will come if I run a network that is sustainable, because then I can go to clients [to win more business]".[12]

Vennells had ample reasons of her own to pursue this growth. Under two incentive plans – short-term and long-term, both dominated by financial and corporate targets – she could more than double her salary. When the long-term scheme based on improved profits paid out in 2012/13 (so not *that*

---

9 *Sunday Times*, 17 August 2014
10 The transformation would be a slow and painful process for sub-postmasters. At the last count, of 9,250 standard branches, 3,266 are "main" branches, 4,201 are "locals" and 1,783 are traditional, i.e. they have not transformed. There are also 1,834 part-time or mobile "outreach" branches and 606 "drop and collect" branches. The Post Office also directly owns 115 Crown branches. See researchbriefings.files.parliament.uk/documents/SN02585/SN02585.pdf
11 House of Commons statement by postal services minister Gareth Thomas, *Hansard*, 8 April 2025
12 Paula Vennells, evidence to Commons business, innovation and skills committee, 15 May 2012

long-term), her £250,000 salary turned into a total package of £697,000.[13] At the start of that financial year, she also ceased to be managing director of the Post Office as it moved out of the control of the soon to be privatised Royal Mail. At this point, Vennells became a grander chief executive, with no superior board to answer to.

Vennells's financial incentives told her the metric by which performance at the helm of the Post Office was measured in practical terms. Doing the right thing by sub-postmasters didn't feature in this. But, since their growing complaints over Horizon could blow the whole profit-driven business model apart, keeping a lid on them certainly did.

"I believe in the Law and the Profits"

---

13 Post Office Ltd accounts 2012/13, including cash in lieu of pension contributions of £62,500

9

EYE-OPENER

Private Eye picks up the story, MPs get organised and the Post Office tries to look concerned

FOR all the horrors of the Post Office scandal, it did have its fortuitous elements. That James Arbuthnot was Jo Hamilton's MP would turn out to be one. Another materialised in late 2010, with the Post Office at its most aggressively defensive.

One Wednesday morning in November, a cab driver from Guildford tweeted to a radio presenter on BBC Radio Surrey's breakfast show, enquiring about the station's taxi account. The broadcaster was freelance journalist Nick Wallis, whose appetite for content prompted him to ask the cabbie if he would come on air and tell tales from the local taxi world. He got a swift response: "I have a story to tell you."[1]

Wallis's new social-media contact was Davinder Misra. He was the husband of Seema, who was at that moment beginning the fifth day of her prison sentence. When the journalist and the badly affected husband met the following day, the hack's reaction was similar to Arbuthnot's on meeting Jo Hamilton. The story and the righteous anger burning in Davinder appeared genuine and demanded further investigation.

The Misras had been in touch with Alan Bates through his Justice for Subpostmasters Alliance, and Davinder put Wallis on to him. The hack learned of a few more similar tales by reading the *Computer Weekly* article. Bates told him his own story and explained that the prosecutions were the tip of an iceberg. He estimated that the number of sub-postmasters sacked or suspended, and often bankrupted, probably ran into the "high hundreds, possibly more". There appeared to be enough for an investigative TV piece, which Wallis duly pitched to the BBC's *Inside Out South* editor, Jane French.

When Wallis's report aired in February the following year, it featured a tearful interview with Davinder Misra and told Jo Hamilton's and David

---

[1] For a full account, see Nick Wallis's *The Great Post Office Scandal* (Bath Publishing, 2021)

Bristow's stories from the shops they were struggling to keep afloat in South Warnborough and Odiham. Also on camera was James Arbuthnot, telling how his parliamentary work had revealed "a lot of cases which seem to be cropping up all round the country". The Post Office told Wallis that Horizon was "absolutely accurate and reliable". The lawyer who was already acting for 55 sub-postmasters whom Alan Bates had brought together, Amanda Glover from Shoosmiths, said quite the opposite. They appeared to be "very good citizens", she said, who were "very believable and when you've got such numbers it has to be more than coincidence".[2]

The Post Office tried to gloss over this regional exposé, while Fujitsu's bosses appeared indifferent. Post Office chief operating officer Mike Young emailed Fujitsu's UK chief executive, Duncan Tait, who had joined the company as managing director in 2009 overseeing the Post Office account. Young sent him a link to Wallis's film. "I need you to take a look at this if you haven't seen the programme already," he said. "Undoubtedly, Horizon integrity remains a core [sic] to our safe operation and to date, nothing has surfaced that suggests there is any evidence that the system is flawed in anyway. Can we briefly just talk through these latest developments."[3] There's no evidence they did. Questioned years later, Tait couldn't even recall having watched the programme. He'd been satisfied by Young's reassurance. His focus was the Fujitsu bottom line, to which Horizon made a major contribution. It was funding his high six-figure salary and would propel him into the global Fujitsu boardroom, its first non-Japanese member. (And when he left the group in 2020, it would generate a £2.6m payoff.)

Disappointingly for Wallis, his story gained little public traction, even though he was inundated with contacts from more sub-postmasters sharing their experiences. This changed a few months later, however, when *Private Eye* acted on an approach from him. I spoke to a handful of sub-postmasters and wrote the magazine's first report in September 2011.[4] "Computer says no," ran the headline, picking up on a long history of government IT cock-ups covered by the *Eye*, including the delays and cost overruns on Horizon itself more than a decade previously. "As Britain's multi-million-pound public IT programmes hit the next stage in the lifecycle of botched computer projects – malfunction – alarming repercussions are being felt in Britain's post offices," the piece began. These included the Hamilton, Misra and other anonymised cases. Arbuthnot commented to the *Eye* that he couldn't believe there was such widespread

---
2 Most of Wallis's *One Show* films are available on YouTube
3 Email from Mike Young to Duncan Tait, 8 February 2011, FUJ00174417
4 *Eye* 1298, September 2011

dishonesty when "the alternative is… a public sector computer system which has gone wrong. We've heard of that before."

The Post Office's insistence about the infallibility of its IT system had become yet less credible since Wallis's film, the *Eye* reported, not least because "in July the entire Post Office banking system was shut down by a 'Horizon online issue'". And if the system wasn't infallible when it was assumed to be, it could be causing miscarriages of justice.

Board games

Donald Brydon, the chairman of the Royal Mail group – of which the Post Office was still a part – read the *Eye*'s coverage. A couple of days after the piece was published, he emailed Vennells, copying in Royal Mail CEO Moya Greene and new Post Office chair Alice Perkins. The latter had just been brought in as a safe pair of hands after a long career as a senior civil servant, followed by a number of non-executive positions, and had a sideline as an executive coach. "I was a bit surprised to see the article in *Private Eye* this week about a class action by sub-postmasters," said Brydon – indicating, if nothing else, that the Post Office had kept its parent company's board in the dark for at least two and a half years. "The article raises some questions about Horizon," he added. "Have we ever had an independent audit of Horizon?"[5]

The problem had "reared its head before", replied Vennells. "In summary, each time any cases have gone to court, [the Post Office's] position has been upheld. And from memory, in at least two cases fraud was proven with subsequent imprisonment."[6] Two was of course a ridiculous understatement, and the first point about 100 percent success in court was also plain wrong. In the Post Office's newspeak, however, it had by now become a truth just like Horizon's infallibility. And it was clear which version of Vennells – virtuous priest or corporate brand protector – was going to prevail.

Perkins remained silent – which was odd, as the role of chair was to remain alive to serious risks and challenge executives. It was all the more remarkable given that, just two days before, she'd had an introductory meeting with the Post Office's lead auditor, Angus Grant from Ernst & Young (now EY). He had told her, she'd noted, that Horizon was a "real risk". Her jottings from the encounter also asked "does it capture data accurately" and noted "cases of fraud – suspects suggest it's a systems problem". Perkins heard from Grant that the problems were deep-seated, and wrote that the Post Office had driven "a v hard bargain on price but they [Fujitsu] took back

---
5 Email from Donald Brydon to Paula Vennells, 29 September 2011, POL00405910
6 Email from Vennells to Brydon, 29 September 2011, POL00405910

on quality/assurance".[7] (It was now 12 years since Ernst & Young had first expressed concerns about Horizon impairing the production of accounts "to a suitable degree of integrity",[8] giving a long period in which the accountants could have spoken up publicly.)

This wasn't the new chair's first warning, either. In the summer of 2011, after being chosen for the Post Office job but before taking it up, Perkins had bumped into James Arbuthnot at a conference. The pair knew each other from the Ministry of Defence in the 1990s. He'd raised his concerns over the sub-postmasters and she'd assured him she'd like to help. Sitting in the boardroom, she appeared less keen.

Elsewhere in the Post Office, a co-ordinated response to the publicity and the Shoosmiths action was organised through a "responses to challenges regarding Horizon system" steering group. This was chaired by the accountant and safe pair of hands Rod Ismay. In a note setting out the group's first actions sent to the head of network services, Angela van den Bogerd, and the heads of all the major functions including legal, security and IT, Ismay wrote: "Reactive statement stance should *Private Eye* style coverage continue".[9] Sure enough, as and when reports appeared elsewhere, the same fact-free response given to the *Eye* would be churned out.

It was time to batten down the hatches. That summer, along with auditor Angus Grant's informal warnings to Perkins, Ernst & Young had delivered its private "management letter" for 2010/11. Horizon, it said, was the "main issue" that the Post Office board needed to focus on. One of the problems was inadequate monitoring of who within Fujitsu could access the system, which "may lead to the processing of erroneous or unauthorised transactions".[10] It was not a good time to hear such a message. So when a report on the auditor's views went up to the Post Office audit and risk committee that considered these things, Rod Ismay ensured it was neutered. "The IT control issues identified during the audit did not question the integrity of accounting data in the system," he added to the report. His reason for this, he admitted candidly to colleagues, was that "for purposes of ongoing… prosecution activity, Rob Wilson [head of criminal law] has advised that were that not the case the current prosecutions would have to be stayed".[11] The consequences, not the truth, determined what was to be said about Horizon.

The directors sitting around the Post Office boardroom table were similarly misled. Minutes of the January 2012 board meeting record that non-

---
7 Alice Perkins, hand-written note, 27 September 2001, WITN00740122
8 POL00090839
9 Rod Ismay, note, 12 October 2011, POL00294879
10 Letter from Ernst & Young to Post Office management, 27 March 2011, FUJ00086945
11 Email from Ismay to Sarah Hall and others, 30 November 2011, POL00295091

executive director (and old colleague of Donald Brydon's from the insurance business) Les Owen shared his concerns. He wanted "assurance that there was no substance to the claims bought [sic] by the sub-postmasters which had featured in *Private Eye*".[12] A Post Office board meeting might have been the time for some realism, but Owen was also fobbed off with the impeccable prosecutions canard. The Post Office's general counsel, Susan Crichton, an experienced corporate lawyer who had joined the organisation in 2010, informed Owen that "the system had been audited by [Royal Mail group] internal audit with the reports reviewed by Deloittes" and that the "audit report was very positive".[13] This was untrue. Deloitte hadn't looked at the internal auditors' work – a Deloitte secondee had worked on the internal report.[14] And the internal auditors hadn't reviewed Horizon in any case. What the internal auditors *had* said, about poor progress on external auditor Ernst & Young's recommendations from the previous year, was far from positive.

Crichton's false reassurance typified a strategy of keeping as much from the board as possible. This gave Vennells and Perkins every mediocre boss's dream of plausible deniability, which could be used whenever they had to answer to the press, sub-postmasters (whose letters were by now flooding into Vennells's office) or even parliamentarians.

Commons touch

Brydon and the other Royal Mail directors may have been placated, but James Arbuthnot was less receptive to stonewalling and obfuscation. He had been busily corralling members of parliament who also had constituents afflicted by Horizon. In December, he wrote to Royal Mail CEO Moya Greene and postal services minister Ed Davey, telling them of 34 sub-postmasters suffering the consequences of the system's faults that he was aware of – including the successor sub-postmaster to his constituent David Bristow (a coincidence that further convinced him something was wrong). Both Greene and Vennells replied, separately, with the standard claims of "robustness".

Unimpressed, Arbuthnot chased up his old contact Alice Perkins directly, fixing up a meeting a few weeks later in the Commons with her and company secretary Alwen Lyons, a Post Office lifer whose father had been a sub-postmaster and general secretary of the NFSP. At the meeting, Perkins trotted out the same false assurance about Deloitte and the internal auditors that Crichton had fed to the board. Arbuthnot was far from convinced. So

---

12 Post Office board meeting, 12 January 2012, POL00021503
13 Ibid
14 Cited by barrister Flora Page during Susan Crichton's inquiry evidence, 24 April 2024

Perkins, apparently (at this moment) concerned, invited him and fellow Tory MP Oliver Letwin – who also had a constituent affected by the scandal and, helpfully, a position in David Cameron's government – over to Old Street to talk to her executives. There appeared to be a glimmer of hope. (Arbuthnot wouldn't know that a couple of days later Perkins told her board that she "hoped that she could find a way to convince him and the other MPs that the system was not at fault".)[15]

When Perkins, Vennells, Arbuthnot and Letwin sat down on 17 May, along with Post Office officials Susan Crichton, Lesley Sewell (who had replaced one of the David Smiths as head of IT), Rod Ismay and Angela van den Bogerd, things got off to a cagey start. "Although we recognise that Horizon is not perfect, no computer system is, it has been audited by internal and external teams," read the briefing for Sewell to deliver. The system had "also been tested in the courts and no evidence of problems found (of the nature suggested by JFSA [Bates's campaign group])".[16] Vennells and Perkins explained how struck they had been on visits to post office branches by just how much cash there was on hand, with the implication that for some this would be too tempting. But with several parliamentarians and their own directors now asking questions, they knew they had to make some sort of concession and wanted to look like they were on the front foot. As the meeting closed, Vennells agreed that forensic accountants should conduct a Post Office-funded investigation into the use of Horizon in cases against sub-postmasters. A delighted Arbuthnot took the news back to his fellow MPs.

His joy was soon tempered at a follow-up meeting, bringing the Post Office top two together with half a dozen MPs including staunch campaigners Andrew Bridgen (Conservative) and Mike Wood (Labour). Perkins and Vennells can't have failed to feel the intensity of interest. But they parroted the false lines about Horizon never having been found at fault and underscored the narrative with suggestions that cash "put temptation in people's way" and of sub-postmasters "borrowing" Post Office money to support their other businesses.[17] Perkins told Wood that she, like the MPs, had initially been sceptical of the system's infallibility but, the minutes noted, "had seen that in each case that had arisen, there was always another explanation than a systems explanation".[18]

The Post Office hadn't opened its collective mind. But it had at least been forced to let a chink of light in on its treatment of sub-postmasters.

---

15 Post Office board meeting, 15 March 2012, POL00021505
16 Post Office briefing document, 17 May 2012, POL00029492
17 Alice Perkins, inquiry evidence, 5 June 2024
18 Minutes of meeting between MPs and Post Office, 18 June 2012, JARB0000001

Sight screen

The forensic accountants selected for the investigation were a couple of old corporate-fraud hands who had come together as Second Sight. Ron Warmington was a bluff chartered accountant and certified fraud examiner who had run financial security and investigation divisions in heavyweight financial institutions such as Citibank. His colleague Ian Henderson had also spent a career ferreting out misfeasance in the City and, as a certified information systems auditor who had given expert computer evidence in a number of trials, had the IT systems expertise the pair would need.

Second Sight was brought in on the recommendation of Post Office general counsel Susan Crichton, who had worked with Warmington several years earlier on fraud investigations at GE Capital. The firm's proposal, which would involve looking at the performance of Horizon in cases where complaints had been made about it, was preferred to a pitch from Deloitte for a detailed forensic audit of the system – which would have been more expensive, and also looked riskier for the Post Office than confining the review to specific cases.

Campaigners and MPs were sceptical. Andrew Bridgen worried that anything funded by the Post Office was undermined on the "he who pays the piper" principle. His constituent Michael Rudkin was a NFSP official who four years earlier had witnessed Fujitsu staff remotely accessing branch accounts at its Bracknell HQ. Rudkin's account of the episode had been dismissed, while his sub-postmaster wife Susan was investigated and then wrongly convicted. His MP wasn't going to underestimate the organisation's cynicism. Arbuthnot was more pragmatic, pointing out that the only money available for the review was in the Post Office's coffers.[19]

Alan Bates, whose efforts for a resolution through the legal action he had undertaken with Shoosmiths had reached a stalemate, also wanted to be sure that the Second Sight duo were the right men for a task in which they would inevitably encounter resistance from the secretive Post Office. He'd recently recruited to the cause his own forensic accountant, Kay Linnell (another helpfully located neighbour of Jo Hamilton in South Warnborough). Her formidable CV included a spell as chief investigating accountant at the Inland Revenue, pinning down the most complex tax frauds. When, in June 2012, she and Bates gave the Second Sight men a grilling, she left them in no doubt about what the Justice for Subpostmasters Alliance expected. But Warmington and Henderson met Linnell's exacting standards, and that

---

19 Lord (James) Arbuthnot, witness statement, 10 April 2024, WITN00020100

summer Second Sight was formally tasked with assessing "whether there are any systemic issues and/or concerns with the 'Horizon' system, including training and support processes".[20]

Generic response

Even before Second Sight opened its first case file, those running the Post Office's prosecutions – whose actions were being implicitly called into question – struck a defiant posture.

In early June, Susan Crichton – who, significantly, had no criminal law experience before her arrival as Post Office general counsel two years earlier – emailed senior criminal lawyer Jarnail Singh in light of the impending review. About to make a charging decision in a case against sub-postmaster Tracey Merritt from Yetminster in Dorset, she wanted to know "if we decide not to go ahead with prosecution are there any risks for [the Post Office]?"[21] Singh fired back a panicky response. Any change of tack, he worried, might lead to a "third party examination of our cases by say Director of Public Prosecution [which] may result in withdrawal of our ability to prosecute". In trademark style, he pointed out: "Decision not to prosecute can not be kept secret 'everybody will find out what we are doing' this may open Post Office to criticism and undermine faith in Horizon."[22]

The Horizon-protection tail still wagged the prosecution dog. A "U-turn will be exploited by potential third party sub-postmaster's alliance," warned Singh, and "may send a green light for defendants to get hold of their member of parliament and result in copulation." ("Presumably you meant *capitulation*," a smirking counsel would point out at the public inquiry 12 years later.) Singh was adamant: "We hold a robust stance, any wrongdoing will be investigated, prosecuted and money recovered."[23] (The charges against Tracey Merritt were eventually dropped, but she still lost her livelihood.)

The arrival of Second Sight was also giving the Post Office's external lawyers kittens. Harry Bowyer, a barrister working with the solicitors Cartwright King (which took on the Post Office's prosecutions following the split from Royal Mail in April 2012), worried that "we have now given ammunition to those attempting to discredit the Horizon system".[24] This shouldn't have been his concern. "The argument will be that there is no

---

20 Second Sight interim report, 8 July 2013, POL00029650
21 Email from Susan Crichton to Jarnail Singh, 7 June 2012, POL00180229
22 Email from Singh to Crichton, 7 June 2012, POL00180229
23 Ibid
24 Harry Bowyer, advice in *R v Wylie*, 11 July 2012, POL00180894

smoke without fire," he went on, "and we would not have needed to audit a bomb proof system." He advised the Post Office to "defend [Horizon] aggressively", and warned in apocalyptic terms: "If the integrity of the system is compromised then the consequences will be catastrophic for all of us including [Fujitsu]. The financial consequences of convictions and confiscation orders being overturned and confidence in the Post Office book keeping being restored for future prosecutions will be astronomical." Fujitsu "should be made to understand that this is a firefighting situation and it's not just our house that would be burned down if the system were compromised".

This Cassandra's prognosis was close to the mark. But then he suggested a response to the crisis that would ultimately just compound it. "An expert should be identified and instructed to prepare a generic statement which confirms the integrity of the system and why the attacks so far have been unfounded," advised Bowyer. And this expert "should be deployed in all cases where the Horizon system is challenged".[25]

The expert identified was, once again, distinguished engineer Gareth Jenkins. His colleague Kevin Burgess hadn't been wrong when, after a report of the Seema Misra trial appeared in a local paper, he'd emailed him: "Nice one Gareth. Looks like you now have a side line of resident expert witness in future Post Office fraud cases."[26] It was about to become more of a production line deployed in frantic defence of Horizon.

As a new batch of prosecutions approached in the autumn of 2012, Jarnail Singh, following Bowyer's advice, asked Jenkins directly for "an experts report from Fujitsu UK, the Horizon system developers, confirming the system is robust".[27] Jenkins provided a couple of reports he'd written back in 2009, which Bowyer saw as a "good base" that "can be tweaked to cover [any specific challenges]". The barrister confidently told his Cartwright King colleague, solicitor Martin Smith, that "most challenges to the Horizon system should now vanish away before the trial".[28]

Jenkins's reports duly became the requested generic witness statement. "In summary," it read, "I fully believe that Horizon will accurately record all data that is submitted to it and correctly account for it. However, it cannot compensate for any data that is incorrectly input into it as a result of human error, lack of training or fraud (and nor can any other system)."[29] The statement contained no mention of the bugs or errors of which Jenkins was aware.

---

25 Ibid
26 Email from Kevin Burgess to Gareth Jenkins, 22 October 2010, FUJ00225196
27 Email from Singh to Jenkins, 1 October 2012, POL00096997
28 Email from Bowyer to Martin Smith, 2 October 2012, POL00096997
29 Jenkins, inquiry witness statement, 21 March 2024, WITN00460300

Jenkins's IT expertise wasn't matched by awareness of how it was being exploited. When he learned, later that month, that his generic witness statement had just been used directly in a prosecution, he was taken aback. He pointed out that he really ought to see "more background on the specific case and exactly what is being alleged" before offering his expert view, as experience in the cases of Seema Misra and Noel Thomas would have shown him.[30] But there was good reason why he was in such demand: he quickly relented. Within weeks he was despatching signed generic statements to Cartwright King for use in several further prosecutions.

Story time

Prosecutions had been performative for some time now. Following Second Sight's arrival on the scene, they all but merged with the public relations campaign as the Post Office's lawyers and media team came together to create their "story" about Horizon.[31] This might have been a familiar corporate crisis comms response, but the Post Office went way beyond this, feeding the PR guff directly into legal documents forming the basis of prosecutions and convictions.

Jarnail Singh was, for some reason, tasked by a senior group including Susan Crichton and her number two, Hugh Flemington, with drafting the story. His effort was passed to the Post Office's interim head of communications Ronan Kelleher, a recent arrival from a career spinning for banks including Royal Bank of Scotland. He massaged Singh's prose into the kind of statement that might be issued to a journalist preparing a critical piece on the scandal. "As the Post Office continues to have absolute confidence in the robustness and integrity of its Horizon system and its branch accounting processes," he spun, "it had no hesitation in agreeing to an external review of these few individual cases." This was "in no way an acknowledgement by the Post Office that there is an issue with the Horizon". In summary, wrote Kelleher: "Over the past ten years, many millions of branch reconciliations have been carried out with transactions and balances accurately recorded by more than 25,000 different sub-postmasters and the Horizon system continues to work properly in post offices across the length and breadth of the UK. When the system has been challenged in the criminal courts, it has been successfully defended."[32]

It was a fairly routine, if polished, Post Office deception. But the next

---

30 Email from Jenkins to Sharron Jennings, 19 October 2012, POL00097061
31 Email from Singh to Hugh Flemington and others, 31 July 2012, POL00058155
32 Email from Ronan Kelleher to Simon Baker, 27 July 2012, POL00051855

step was extraordinary. Kelleher's version of the "story" was used word-for-word by Cartwright King in drafting witness statements for use in criminal cases. Often these would be signed by investigators such as Steve Bradshaw, who would later admit he had given no thought to what he was putting his name to.

The generic IT evidence from Fujitsu plus the PR-driven testimony from the Post Office worked, and the conviction sausage machine kept churning out its grim product. Khayyam Ishaq, a sub-postmaster from Birkenshaw in West Yorkshire, was forced to plead guilty to stealing £18,000 after the Post Office countered his defence with the generic nonsense. It refused more meaningful disclosure requests concerning Horizon and failed to look for evidence of bugs affecting his branch, despite his claims of Horizon malfunction and the absence of evidence of missing money. Convicted in March 2013, Mr Ishaq would spend three months of a one-year prison sentence alongside serious offenders in HM Prison Leeds, and face financial ruin, depression and stigmatisation. He would tell the public inquiry how he prayed only at home and not at his mosque. For the Post Office, his shattered life was another victory in the campaign to protect Horizon as it fell under the gaze of Second Sight.

Paradise lost

Although the Post Office had separated from the Royal Mail in April 2012, the latter's delayed privatisation now loomed over everything. The last thing ministers needed to hear was what the barrister Bowyer had predicted to be "astronomical" costs of exposing Horizon's failings, which dated almost entirely from Royal Mail's ownership of the Post Office. Thankfully, a board overseen by the politically savvy Alice Perkins and led by the ambitious Paula Vennells, below a Shareholder Executive providing a further buffer, ensured that such a terrifying prospect wouldn't reach the attention of ministers.

The business secretary pushing through the privatisation, Vince Cable, and postal services minister Norman Lamb could remain with their heads in the clouds. Around the same time that Second Sight was invited in, Lamb had published *Building a Mutual Post Office*. The policy paper was full of hope for the financial stabilisation of the company and promised "clear progress… towards mutualisation of the Post Office by the end of this parliament [in 2015]". Lamb invoked the words of the patron saint of liberalism, John Stuart Mill, about "the civilising and improving influences of association, and the efficiency and economy of production on a large scale, [that] may be obtained without dividing the producers into two parties with hostile interests and feelings". In time, "the relation of masters and work-people will be gradually superseded by partnership".[33]

The following years didn't *quite* bring this utopia. The divisions would widen, the hostility would intensify and the masters would become crueller. Thanks to its belligerence in the face of scrutiny, the only mutual thing between the Post Office and the sub-postmasters would be loathing.

"They love to roleplay, as they make sense of the wider world through re-enacting everyday scenarios"

"If you don't cover this nine-grand shortfall now, I will have to prosecute you and put you in jail..."

---

33 *Building a Mutual Post Office: The Government's Response*, July 2012

10

BRAVE REVIEW

The independent experts prove a little too independent

WHEN Alice Perkins and Paula Vennells updated the Post Office board after agreeing to appoint forensic accountants, the minutes recorded that the Post Office would use them "to investigate the system, and give further comfort to those concerned about these cases". This gave the game away almost immediately. A few weeks later, ahead of the review becoming public knowledge, Vennells warned the board that the exercise was "a deliberate decision by us to be utterly transparent and hopefully to close down what has become a bandwagon based on no fact".[1]

Such doublethink was a hallmark of Vennells's communications and instructions: profess an honourable but abstract intention, like being "utterly transparent", then lace it with an opposite meaning that loyal staff and directors were to get, in this case that concerns over Horizon should be squashed.

At least Second Sight was able to get to work. The firm appeared to have some carefully hedged support from Post Office chair Alice Perkins. In early June, executives were arguing over whether cases on a list presented by MPs should come within Second Sight's review if the sub-postmaster in question had been convicted. One case was Seema Misra's. General counsel Susan Crichton thought that including it would be a "red rag to a bull", inviting further challenge to the conviction.[2] Perkins demurred, suggesting that "if (which we don't believe) there were new evidence in a case which had been decided, we would want to do, and be seen to do, the right thing by that."[3] Company secretary Alwen Lyons wrote to Vennells that "Alice feels this is the business pushing back unnecessarily and she feels this has happened throughout the process and she is having to keep pushing us!"[4]

James Arbuthnot remained in contact with Second Sight's Warmington

---

1 Email from Vennells to board and colleagues, 21 June 2012, POL00295355
2 Email from Vennells to Alwen Lyons, 9 June 2012, POL00096606
3 Email from Alice Perkins to Vennells, 9 June 2012, POL00096606
4 Email from Lyons to Vennells, 9 June 2012, POL00096606

and Henderson, and soon knew that they would be challenging the Post Office's stance on Horizon when they produced a scheduled interim report. Preparing the ground in March 2013, Arbuthnot wrote to his old contact Alice Perkins. "In my discussions with Ron and Ian," he told her, "I gather that questions have been raised over the absolute integrity of Horizon, though without their being so fundamental as to say that the system is not fit for purpose."[5] It was clear that Second Sight was not simply going to offer the "comfort" that Vennells expected.[6]

Arbuthnot's questioning of Horizon's "integrity", along with a payoff to the letter saying that he could not "recall a more important campaign", set alarm bells ringing in Old Street. Even signing off with a touch of Old Etonian charm – "You have my gratitude and admiration for how the Post Office is handling this" – didn't placate Vennells when she saw the letter. She got on to Alwen Lyons, affecting concern before betraying her true priority. "I don't want us being defensive as I am pleased to find these things out (sort of!)," she said, "but goodness, this is very very serious if either true and/or leaked." (Translation: I *do* want us to be defensive.) That the potential fallout, rather than the continuing questions over Horizon, was the most important consequence was clear from her next comment. "Who is now working up the comms…?"[7]

Bug out

Vennells and Perkins, less comfortable now that Second Sight was unearthing trouble, were kicking themselves (and, before too long, others) for having let the firm get so far. Vennells emailed Perkins with ideas for reining in Second Sight, and was told in response: "I do hope you can retrieve this as we are running out of lives on this issue and as Neil [McCausland, non-executive director] said, quite coincidentally yesterday, the timing would be terrible if this were to go wrong."[8]

Indeed it would have been. The privatisation of Royal Mail was to be announced at any time. Although the Post Office wasn't a part of this, any threat to the sell-off posed by controversy over Horizon during their years of common ownership could spell trouble for its own financial future. It wasn't unthinkable that the austerity chancellor George Osborne might have second thoughts about the pencilled-in "network transformation" subsidies if he didn't get his billions from the Royal Mail sell-off. And queering the privatisation pitch

---

5 Letter from James Arbuthnot MP to Perkins, 7 March 2013, POL00097588
6 Arbuthnot, witness statement, 10 April 2024, WITN00020100
7 Email from Vennells to Lyons, 11 March 2013, POL00097592
8 Email from Perkins to Vennells, 22 May 2013, POL00098336

certainly wouldn't help Paula Vennells's CV, or the standing of an establishment non-executive like Alice Perkins (who within months would become a non-executive director at the BBC on the back of her "experience of organisations going through change").[9] The objective now was to contain and delay any controversy over Horizon. For Perkins and Vennells, this meant keeping the rest of the board in the dark while readying that all-important comms strategy ahead of anything emerging publicly from Second Sight's work. This became critical towards the end of May 2013 when the Post Office's head of programmes and planning, Simon Baker, gave Second Sight's Ron Warmington some game-changing information. There were two "bugs" that he knew of in the system.

When the Post Office leadership got wind of this, rather than demand further information and deeper enquiries, they chose to wish away the problem with some Orwellian newspeak. IT boss Lesley Sewell reacted to an account of one of the "bugs", the receipts and payments mismatch, by suggesting replacing the word *bug*, synonymous with an IT failing, with the more general *fault*. Even this was too strong for Vennells. She told her senior colleagues that she'd asked her "engineer/computer literate husband" for a "non-emotive word for computer bugs, glitches, defects…" He recommended "exception or anomaly". "I like exception v much," said Vennells's PR adviser Mark Davies.[10]

By the end of June, however, with Second Sight preparing to deliver an interim report on the Horizon system and sub-postmasters' experiences of it, the Old Street HQ was in a state of anguish. Vennells's chief of staff Martin Edwards wrote to his boss, advising her that Second Sight "could turn out to be quite dangerous" if threatened with legal action or sacked – showing the lengths that the Post Office was already contemplating going to in order to frustrate the firm. He preferred a "Plan B", which would involve "explaining to [James Arbuthnot] calmly but firmly" that Second Sight's interim report needed to be "delayed or repositioned as a very neutral update".[11]

A few days later the Post Office board was told of the two "anomalies" (© Mr Paula Vennells). But, the minutes record Vennells saying, the business "has dealt with these anomalies to ensure no sub-postmaster was out of pocket". She was more concerned that what she had seen of the forthcoming Second Sight interim report "was not as factual as expected and could lead to loose language at the MP meeting" – at which, a week later on 8 July 2013, Second Sight's report would be released.[12]

---

9 Tony Hall, BBC director-general, quoted in press release, 28 March 2014
10 Email from Mark Davies to Vennells, 2 July 2013, POL00380985
11 Email from Martin Edwards to Paula Vennells, 27 June 2013 POL00098777
12 Post Office board minutes, 1 July 2013, POL00021515

The board, led by Perkins and with retail executive Neil McCausland as its senior independent director, responded to the heads-up by keeping their heads down. The non-executives, whose job it was to keep the company honest, chose not to demand the Post Office come clean or redouble investigations into the threat that IT defects posed to an organisation whose accounting depended on the Horizon system. They took the easier option of asking Vennells and PR man Mark Davies to "ensure changes were made to the [Second Sight] report where possible and… to prepare their communication to combat any inaccuracies".[13]

The sanitised minutes of the board meeting masked harder feelings at the top towards the Second Sight duo. One of the Post Office's civil lawyers, Simon Richardson of Bond Dickinson (as Bond Pearce had become that year), recorded after talking to Susan Crichton and her number two Hugh Flemington that "the board want to sack SS [Second Sight] and of course are now not coping well with the fact that they are independent".[14] Perkins wrote to Vennells three days after the board meeting: "If we have to continue with SS, my firm belief is that we need a totally different approach to managing and rewarding them."[15]

The stance to take on the forthcoming report, Vennells told Perkins, "is about no systems issues, some improvements to be made, and keeping perspective so that our brand reputation is protected".[16] Not much to see here, was to be the message.

Top spin

For Paula Vennells, Mark Davies was more guru than press man. The former hack had arrived as the Post Office's head of communications just a couple of months before. He'd been recommended by Alice Perkins after spending several years in the Noughties as special adviser to her husband, Labour cabinet minister Jack Straw. He was the politically attuned and faithful spin doctor that the Post Office thought it needed, putting its reputation above all else, and quickly became a prop for the flailing Vennells. A few years later, when she was awarded a CBE, Vennells would gush to Davies: "I have lost count of the number of times I have relied on your judgement, listened to your wisdom and taken your advice over the last few years. Your call was always the right one: guiding us through stormy waters of all kinds."[17]

In the same way that advice from his predecessor Kelleher had been taken beyond the world of news management to become misleading evidence

---

13 Ibid
14 Note by Simon Richardson, 10 July 2013, POL00407582
15 Email from Perkins to Vennells, 4 July 2013, POL00098990
16 Email from Vennells to Perkins, 3 July 2013, POL00098921
17 Information obtained by Tim Bush under FoI, shared with *Private Eye*. See *Eye* 1623

in court, Davies's counsel would shape the Post Office's real-world response to Second Sight's findings. The amorality of a spin doctor would be deployed to answer questions with deeply moral implications.

Ahead of the 8 July unveiling of the report to Arbuthnot and other MPs, Vennells emailed Davies and her chief of staff Martin Edwards with ideas for what to offer by way of response. She floated the option of a joint Post Office/Justice for Subpostmasters Alliance group reviewing "all prosecutions in the past 12/18 months since [the Post Office] has been independent of [Royal Mail]". But in what looked like a rare flash of interest in doing the right thing, she added in brackets: "Why would they not review all cases of false accounting [the charge which Arbuthnot was said to be most concerned about], e.g. over the last 5-10 years…?"[18]

The seasoned operator Davies knew a hostage to fortune when he saw one. He expressed his concern that "there is real danger in going too far in commitments about past cases". He didn't think Second Sight's report warranted the idea, and risked drawing unwelcome attention. While the "current media strategy would mean there would be some coverage, but not very much (the usual suspects)", any commitment to looking at past cases "will open this up very significantly, into front page news… it becomes mainstream, very high profile".[19]

Vennells's reaction revealed her order of priorities. "You are right to call this out," she replied. "And I will take your steer. No issue." There were, she said, "two objectives, the most urgent being to manage the media." The other – "to make sure we do address the concerns of [Arbuthnot] and Alan Bates, mainly looking forwards" – came second to this.[20]

Report stage

The report that Second Sight presented to MPs revealed the existence of a couple of software bugs. These had led to "76 branches being affected by incorrect balances or transactions, which took some time to identify and correct".[21] Against this, the forensic accountants also said that they had "so far found no evidence of system wide (systemic) problems with the Horizon software". There were plenty of other criticisms, though – which one of the "usual suspects", *Private Eye*, summed up as "the brutal way the Post Office investigated financial errors; unreliable hardware; the absence of training or

---
18 Email from Vennells to Davies and others, 6 July 2013, POL00099055
19 Email from Davies to Vennells, 7 July 2013, POL00099055
20 Email from Vennells to Davies, 7 July 2013, POL00099055
21 Second Sight interim report, 8 July 2013, POL00099063

support for sub-postmasters… and an unfair business model that automatically makes sub-postmasters responsible for any discrepancy".[22]

Even so, Warmington and Henderson had been relatively conservative. They had not mentioned Fujitsu's ability to access branch accounts remotely, which they had been told about by Gareth Jenkins.[23] Alan Bates was disappointed by their comment about not finding systemic problems, of which he thought there was ample evidence. But the qualification "so far" on this point showed that they were playing a longer game; this was, after all, just an "interim" report.

They were also too polite (publicly) to mention the obstructiveness of the Post Office, which had denied them files they needed while swamping them with unnecessary information – the archetypal tactic of an organisation with something to hide. As Ron Warmington put it in an email to James Arbuthnot, "What we are getting are highly technical, multi-page, responses that will appear to many to have been crafted so as to avoid actually giving any answers to [the] assertions and allegations at all." He enclosed an example that "shows my exasperation in trying to get them to ANSWER THE BLASTED QUESTIONS."[24] Although 47 cases had been sent to Second Sight for review, it had been able to reach conclusions on just four "spot reviews", i.e. particular issues.[25] From such limited evidence, the findings were remarkable; "so far" was not all that far.

When postal services minister Jo Swinson stood up in the House of Commons to answer MPs' questions on the report, she clung to the "systemic" point. She'd been fed the usual lines from the Post Office, via the government's Shareholder Executive, and regurgitated the platitudes about tens of thousands of people using the system successfully every day. She then sweetened the message with a couple of positive-sounding announcements about a working party to continue the review of cases, bringing in Alan Bates's JFSA and retaining Second Sight.[26]

Arbuthnot was wary. He questioned whether the ongoing review could be sufficiently independent and pointed out that "some sub-postmasters would never have been prosecuted, sued or disciplined" had it not been for the Post Office's failings. Wouldn't the minister agree that "we must look after them and try to provide them with redress, perhaps through the Criminal Cases Review Commission?" Swinson saw "no evidence to suggest that any

---

22 *Eye* 1344, July 2013
23 Ian Henderson, witness statement, 18 June 2024, WITN00420100
24 Email from Ron Warmington to Arbuthnot, 12 June 2013, JARB0000053
25 Warmington, inquiry evidence, 18 June 2024
26 *Hansard*, 9 July 2013

convictions would have been different", adding that it was "difficult to second guess when somebody has entered a guilty plea".[27] Except, she didn't add, when it was a coerced one.

Strong advice

As if the heat from the Second Sight investigation weren't enough, a couple of days later, on 12 July, a letter from the country's official second-guesser of convictions landed on Paula Vennells's desk. "For obvious reasons, we have read the recent media coverage concerning the Post Office Horizon computer system with interest," wrote an official from the Criminal Cases Review Commission (CCRC), the statutory investigator of potential miscarriages of justice set up in the 1990s after the overturning of the Birmingham Six terrorism convictions. "Clearly, it would be very useful for us to have more information directly from the Post Office," she continued, "especially accurate information as to [the] number of convictions that might be impacted by the issue and what action is proposed…"[28] Here was another opportunity – or, more accurately, obligation – to come clean. By now, Vennells knew about bugs and, she would later admit, had heard concerns about the reliability of Gareth Jenkins as a witness during a corridor chat with IT boss Lesley Sewell. But, once again, the chief executive failed to grasp the nettle and palmed it off on her general counsel Susan Crichton.

It was an inauspicious time to have a miscarriage of justice watchdog sniffing around. A couple of weeks earlier, on 28 June, Crichton's deputy Hugh Flemington had written to senior lawyer Jarnail Singh concerning the imminent prosecution of a Birmingham sub-postmaster, asking Singh to get the prosecution lawyers from Cartwright King "up to speed" on Second Sight's as yet unpublished interim findings. They needed to "say something to [the] judge re bugs PO have found… to offer the judge the chance to postpone the case".[29] Two lawyers from Cartwright King – Martin Smith and the barrister Simon Clarke – then made a recorded telephone call to the man who knew all about these bugs, Gareth Jenkins.

Jenkins's admissions to Smith and Clarke, in comments such as "you can never say there are no more bugs in the system, so we've got to be careful about trying to say anything like that", flatly contradicted statements he had given for prosecutions. Clarke asked the Fujitsu man to confirm what appeared to be his position: "if the defence were to suggest erm there is a problem with

---
27 Ibid
28 Letter from CCRC to Vennells, 12 July 2013, POL00039994
29 Email from Hugh Flemington to Singh, 28 June 2013, POL00060572

Horizon and therefore we can't rule out that there might be other problems with Horizon, what you say is as far as you're concerned the integrity of the system is intact". Jenkins replied "Yes", exposing the deceptiveness of his past testimony.[30]

Clarke followed up with some advice for the Post Office ten days later. Firstly, it should stop using Gareth Jenkins as a witness. Secondly, it should tell Royal Mail that Cartwright King was going to conduct a review of prosecutions, since many would pre-date the April 2012 separation. A few days after this, when the CCRC letter landed, Clarke's stance on Jenkins hardened further still. Now, after a careful look at many of Jenkins's witness statements, both specific and generic, Clarke advised that the Fujitsu man had been implying that "there must be no bugs" and was "attesting… there is nothing wrong with the system".[31] With a certain understatement, the barrister noted: "Unfortunately, that was not the case…" The corollaries of this were damning: Jenkins "has not complied with his duties to the court, the prosecution or the defence"; he was "in plain breach of his duty"; and his "credibility as an expert witness is fatally undermined". The IT man's failure to disclose relevant material about bugs had a "profound effect" and placed the Post Office "in breach of their duty as a prosecutor". Disclosure in current cases was essential. And anyone already convicted who thought the disclosure failures were material (and was lucky enough to find out about them) "may seek the leave of the Court of Appeal to challenge his conviction".

There could hardly have been a clearer argument for opening up to the CCRC. Indeed, when Clarke suggested some wording for the Post Office's response to the commission, he made it clear that in prosecutions Jenkins had vouched for the robustness and accuracy of Horizon – and that the Second Sight interim report "demonstrates that this was not the case".[32]

Clarke's opinions did not go down well at the Post Office. General counsel Susan Crichton turned to Andy Parsons of Bond Dickinson – a firm that was becoming increasingly important in the Post Office's defensive operation, despite the obvious conflict of interest because it had its own reasons to keep the Horizon scandal covered up. The firm had acted for the Post Office in civil cases, such as that against Lee Castleton, for years. Clarke's "advice feels odd to me", Crichton told Parsons, and "somehow it feels as if there is a conflict here which I am not sure I understand".[33] (There was in one sense: Clarke's

---

30 Transcript of call between Simon Clarke, Martin Smith and Jenkins, early July 2013, POL00142322
31 Clarke, *Advice on the Use of Expert Evidence Relating to the Integrity of the Fujitsu Services Ltd Horizon System*, 15 July 2013, POL00006357
32 Clarke, draft paragraphs for reply to CCRC, 12 July 2013, POL00039995
33 Email from Crichton to Andy Parsons, 16 July 2013, POL00039996

employer Cartwright King had acted in prosecutions using Jenkins, and was about to mark its own homework with its review of past convictions. But his proposed honest response to the CCRC, and the essence of his advice, were obviously right.) Parsons's senior partner Gavin Matthews then weighed in, arguing that Clarke's account was "unhelpful given that the [Second Sight] report found there to be no systemic problems with Horizon".[34] This was neither true nor relevant – it hadn't found systemic problems "so far". Besides, Jenkins's evidence as a witness had gone much further.

Hugh Flemington – who, like his boss Crichton, had no experience of criminal law to draw on – caught the mood. "Presumably we need to give off the signals that we are proactive," he wrote to her and others, "doing all the right things re writing to people to keep the [Attorney General] and CCRC calm." If they saw this happening, "they may leave it to us for the moment".[35] The reply to the CCRC later that month, drafted by the conflicted Bond Dickinson, duly offered reassurance that "an external firm of criminal specialist solicitors" was on the case.[36] For added comfort, the work was being given the once-over by Brian Altman QC, an eminent "former First Treasury Counsel" – that is to say, a senior government advocate. There was no mention of the embarrassing Mr Jenkins. The miscarriage of justice body duly backed off, leaving Altman and the lawyers from Cartwright King to get on with it. "That's an ideal response from the CCRC," wrote Gavin Matthews of Bond Dickinson. "They don't look like they want to get involved."[37] Mission accomplished.

Shred of evidence

Simon Clarke, meanwhile, was being kept busy by the Post Office's disregard for the rules that constrained it. No sooner had he fired off his advice about Jenkins and disclosure than he was pointing out more legal truths the Post Office shouldn't have needed to be told.

During a call at the end of July, Post Office head of criminal law Jarnail Singh told Cartwright King solicitor Martin Smith about a group that had been set up, on Clarke's recommendation, to collate details of challenges – the so-called "Horizon Issues" group. Smith had been driving at the time and pulled over to write down what he had been told: "JScott [John Scott, head of Post Office security] has instructed that typed minutes be scrapped."[38] Singh

---

34 Email from Gavin Matthews to Crichton and others, 16 July 2013, POL00407546
35 Email from Flemington to Smith, 15 July 2013, POL00122552
36 Letter from Crichton to CCRC, 26 July 2013, POL00297983
37 Email from Matthews, POL00458652
38 Martin Smith, note, 1 August 2013, 1 August 2013, POL00139745

emailed Smith the following day, possibly covering his own backside, asking him to get Clarke to look into what Singh's keyboard-hammering rendered as "the common myth that emails, written communications etc.. meetings. If its produced its then available for disclosure. If it?s [sic] not then technically it isn?t? [sic] Possible true of civil cases NOT CRIMINAL CASES?"[39]

Clarke got the gist. A couple of days later he produced what became known as his "shredding advice". He revealed the existence of an internal instruction that minutes of a previous conference call of the Horizon Issues group "should be, and have been, destroyed".[40] He added that "the word 'shredded' was conveyed to me". It had also been agreed, said Clarke, that "handwritten minutes were not to be typed and should be forwarded to [Scott]". But the barrister set out in no uncertain terms the Post Office's duties to "record and retain material". He emphasised that even information that hadn't been committed to writing would be disclosable in a trial. To believe otherwise "represents a failing to fully appreciate the duties of fairness and integrity placed upon a prosecutor's shoulders".

When Susan Crichton expressed concern over the handling of the Horizon Issues group, her head of security shot back, effectively blaming her. According to Scott, Crichton had said the group should "provide in effect an under the radar escalation point from across the business of issues that may impact the integrity of the Horizon system".[41] He claimed she had been "frustrated" by the circulation of a security analyst's report in June about a specific Horizon failure in a Yorkshire post office, and that she "therefore did not want any electronic communication which may be subject to [freedom of information requests] or disclosure". The unjustly maligned Scott had merely followed this steer. "[Hand] Written notes [which would not turn up on electronic searches] have been taken for each call and activity has been driven behind the scenes," he told his boss. Crichton didn't respond. But it was clear, in line with the need to cover up at all costs, that the decision to make unhelpful Horizon-related information untraceable was made at a senior level.

Not all of Simon Clarke's notes of advice were as inconvenient as those covering Jenkins and shredding. In September, he delivered a much more accommodating one stating that, were sub-postmasters ever to make claims of malicious prosecution, it would be his firm and not the Post Office in the firing line.[42] This would later prompt the accusation – strongly resisted – that

---

39 Email from Singh to Smith, 1 August 2013, POL00139746
40 Clarke, *Advice on Disclosure and the Duty to Record and Retain Material*, 2 August 2013, POL00006799
41 Email from John Scott to Crichton, 14 August 2013, POL00139690
42 Clarke, Post Office advice note, 12 September 2013, POL00114253

Cartwright King was offering to throw itself under the bus for the Post Office, as well as the suspicion that, when the organisation ceased to be under the auspices of the Royal Mail, Cartwright King – which had previously provided some services in the East Midlands area – had been brought in to provide legal cover.[43]

Chair women

There was another possible avenue of enquiry into the Post Office's little local difficulty that needed to be closed off ASAP: questions from its own board.

The Second Sight report was up for discussion at a board meeting the day after Clarke delivered his bombshell advice about Jenkins and disclosure. It should have been the occasion for the directors of this public company to be left under no illusions about the findings and their implications. Ahead of the meeting, Susan Crichton, who had commissioned the Second Sight report that led to all this, prepared a paper on the forensic accountants' work. It made no mention of the problem with Gareth Jenkins and downplayed the likely impact of Second Sight's findings, suggesting that additional disclosures would need to be made in just five percent of past prosecution cases.

Even this pale reflection of the state of play was too much for Alice Perkins and Paula Vennells to allow their general counsel to present to the board. So, while Vennells took the directors through their general counsel's paper, the woman who had written it was left outside the room, waiting to be summoned in. The board minutes recorded a trademark Vennells performance: "The CEO explained that although the Second Sight report had been challenging it had highlighted some positive things as well as improvement opportunities."[44] The non-executive directors were left grumbling about the handling of Second Sight's work – but blind to its significance, and ignorant that the Post Office's key prosecution witness was a legal pariah. The woman who would surely have felt compelled to mention this, Susan Crichton, was left sitting on a chair in the corridor.

A working lifetime in the Whitehall corridors of power had not made Perkins a fan of airing controversies. So the fact that Ron Warmington and Ian Henderson had been allowed to show some independence and talk about things like bugs seemed to irritate her. Crichton was the main object of her annoyance, over her handling of what had "been potentially very serious indeed for the [Post Office] in terms of our national reputation and the effect it could have on our funding negotiations with the government." Having given

---

[43] See, for example, examination of Clarke at inquiry, 9 May 2024. Ed Henry KC: "You, on behalf of your firm, were basically saying, 'We will take the rap for malicious prosecution…'"
[44] Post Office board meeting, 16 July 2013, POL00021516

the lawyer a dressing-down a couple of weeks later, Perkins wrote that she "understood that SS's investigation had to be independent, but in the civil service there would have been someone marking it who was close to all the key people [Second Sight, James Arbuthnot, Bates's JFSA] and knew what was going on between them".[45] Crichton replied that, as a lawyer, it would have been "inappropriate for her to influence the key stakeholders". That didn't impress the former mandarin, who wrote that "she should have flagged that up and someone else could have been brought in". She professed to be "astonished" by Crichton's position.

After angry meetings of her own with a humiliated Crichton, Paula Vennells followed up with a "reflection on what happened with SS". It seemed to her that "Susan was possibly more loyal to her professional conduct requirements and put her integrity as a lawyer above the interests of the business."[46] Crichton – who, Vennells noted, felt that the Post Office leadership "had ruined her reputation and compromised her" – had in fact made numerous compromises with those professional standards, and often bent to the will of the Post Office corporate interest. Nevertheless she still wasn't as on-message as a Post Office lawyer was expected to be. Susan Crichton would resign within a couple of months, to be replaced with a more aggressive lawyer who agonised a bit less about his "professional conduct requirements".

Alice Perkins proposed a "lessons learned" review in light of what she saw as the mismanagement of Second Sight, under an independent chair. Bond Dickinson's Andy Parsons advised against it. If such a review addressed problems with Horizon, as it would surely have to, "then Post Office may be obliged... to pro-actively pass this information to sub-postmasters involved in criminal prosecutions (both on-going and historic)."[47] Vennells duly shelved the review. Lessons were not for learning.

False prospectus

Hovering behind the Second Sight drama in the blistering summer of 2013 was the privatisation of the Post Office's former parent company, Royal Mail. The last thing anybody in Whitehall wanted was controversy over the persecution of sub-postmasters before the 2012 split.

The institutional nervousness was clear from a briefing for government whips ahead of two potential banana-skin moments. On 9 July, business minister Jo Swinson had been due in the Commons to answer questions on the Second

---
45 Perkins, note on meeting with Crichton, 31 July 2013, POL00381455
46 Vennells, file notes on meeting with Crichton at Costa Coffee, 30 September 2013, POL00381629
47 Email from Parsons to Simon Richardson, 2 September 2013, POL00146243

Sight report. The following day business secretary Vince Cable was to make a statement formally adopting the recommendation for Royal Mail privatisation.[48] "In the eyes of many MPs, the media and the public at large, Royal Mail and the Post Office are the same entity," wrote government officials, and "the adverse coverage that [James] Arbuthnot is seeking to attract is likely to have a significant and diversionary impact on the messaging of the Royal Mail statement."[49]

Should past Horizon troubles emerge as a potential difficulty for the Royal Mail flotation, there would certainly be blowback for the Post Office – just at the point that it was handling the Second Sight fallout and in need of financial help of its own from government. So, when drafts of the Royal Mail flotation prospectus included Horizon in the "IT risks" section, Alice Perkins and Paula Vennells had both political and financial reasons to resist.

Vennells deputed her PR man Mark Davies to negotiate some finessing of the document. He reassured his chief executive that, although the "section on risk is very problematic for [the Post Office]", his "PR team are across it".[50] By the end of August he could report that the prospectus had "improved greatly but may still require some tinkering to be politically acceptable".[51] This was not the generally accepted benchmark for market-sensitive information.

Royal Mail itself, not wanting to be challenged on mis-statements or omissions some time down the line, was less cavalier. One director, who knew something of the Horizon backstory, was particularly cautious. Les Owen had been a Post Office non-executive director before the April 2012 split and was the one who'd asked for "reassurance that there was no substance to the claims… featured in *Private Eye*".[52] He remained alive to the dangers posed by Horizon and, according to Royal Mail's lawyers, was "adamant that a reference to this must appear in the prospectus".[53]

The government's Shareholder Executive wasn't keen, but the full force of opposition came from the top of the Post Office. As the leading Shareholder Executive official on the Post Office, Will Gibson, told his colleague Tim McInnes, "Alice [Perkins] is properly up for a fight."[54] McInnes responded: "Apparently her line is 'how can they expect us to distribute prospectuses with this wording in…'"[55] The chair and former mandarin was now obviously "marking" this one herself.

---

48 *Hansard*, 10 July 2013
49 Whips briefing on Horizon system, 4 July 2013, UKGI00001679
50 Email from Davies to Vennells, 16 August 2013, POL00381531
51 Davies, "holiday notes", 30 August 2013, UKGI00017369
52 POL00021503
53 Email from Alex Dunn to Jonathan Lewis, 18 September 2013, UKGI00002057
54 Email from Tim McInnes to Will Gibson, 18 September 2013, UKGI00002057
55 Email from Gibson to McInnes, 18 September 2013, UKGI00002057

Paula Vennells got the message and, as the 23 September deadline for finalising the prospectus loomed, intervened directly. By this time, the proposed wording on Horizon was quite anodyne, not mentioning the bugs, and merely stating that Second Sight's report "confirmed that no system wide problems had been found in relation to the 'Horizon' software, but suggests that [the Post Office] should examine its support and training processes for sub-postmasters".[56] But, for Vennells, even the watered-down take on Second Sight's work was laundering too much dirty linen in public. Thankfully, the wording presented her with a neat opportunity.

The reference to Horizon was, she told Royal Mail's company secretary, "particularly misleading in the IT risks section", because "the findings of the interim report related to [sub-postmaster] training and support not IT faults".[57] (This was incorrect, but the truth had long lost any importance.) In other words, the mention of Horizon was in the wrong part of the prospectus. As well as arguing on this technicality, Vennells pointed out that including Horizon at all "potentially opens up a sensitive and politically high profile situation". If not exactly threatening the Royal Mail man, she was certainly choosing her words for maximum effect on the brink of a politically charged, national transaction. The offending section should be removed, she said, adding ominously that her chair Alice Perkins would contact Royal Mail chairman Donald Brydon "if necessary".

Vennells's intervention succeeded, and Royal Mail dropped Horizon altogether from what it told investors about the company they were buying. It was another victory in the long war to protect the brand and the IT system – and a triumph, as she saw it anyway, for Vennells. "I have earned my keep on this one," she emailed Perkins, forwarding the email chain that showed Royal Mail's capitulation.[58] Months later, the episode would feature as a key achievement in Vennells' 2013/14 performance self-appraisal.

Fitness test

A couple of weeks after Vennells secured the don't-mention-Horizon prospectus, yet another damning verdict on the Post Office's IT arrived. It was the culmination of months of work by Detica, the IT specialist arm of BAE Systems, which Post Office security boss John Scott had commissioned a few months earlier with a view to tightening up fraud prevention generally.

The advisers came back with a devastating picture of Horizon's

---
56 Email from Vennells to Jon Millidge, 20 September 2013, POL00146462
57 Ibid
58 Email from Vennells to Perkins, 22 September 2013, POL00146462

flaws and the "complex and fragmented" IT's failure to cope with myriad other systems that fed into the Horizon system, such as those tracking cash-machine transactions in post offices. "Post Office systems are not fit for purpose in a modern retail and financial environment," was one conclusion.[59] Given that Horizon had been bought on the promise of facilitating a range of products and services in a brave new commercial world, this was pretty damning.

No less serious were conclusions on the Post Office's methods that would have explained a great deal to sub-postmasters on the wrong end of false allegations: "progress [against fraud] is only measured by the number of audits raised by the team resulting in suspension; there is no incentive to operate preventatively". It was thus in auditors' and investigators' interests for there to be more (assumed) fraud. More depressingly still, "Team success is measured by the number of failed audits out of the number raised". As the Detica analysts put it, "rewarding interventions solely based on the failure of a [sub-postmaster's] career, home and livelihood is likely to be a contributory factor behind the blame culture identified by Second Sight". Henderson and Warmington's "observations resonate strongly", they said, "notably the disjointed response by the Post Office and the habitual desire to assign responsibility to an individual rather than to conduct root cause analysis". The awkward forensic accountants had been right about the use of Horizon and the unfair sub-postmaster contract to blame individuals for shortfalls automatically.

Within the Post Office, the report was buried. Not one of the major players who saw it – including IT boss Lesley Sewell and Angela van den Bogerd, now leading a branch support programme intended to address the lack of training and help for sub-postmasters – bothered to pass it on to Vennells. Bad news was not to go up the chain at the Post Office.

Exit strategy

By now Second Sight's review had, as promised by minister Jo Swinson, become a scheme to which more sub-postmasters would be invited to present their cases. These would be investigated by the Post Office, then reviewed by Second Sight and, if eligible, put into a mediation process.

While this was welcomed by James Arbuthnot and others at the time, it was never really going to be sufficient. The Post Office had consistently resisted Second Sight's requests for the files it needed to examine the limited number of cases it was given ahead of the interim report. Arbuthnot and Alan Bates

---

59 Detica NetReveal, *Fraud and Non-Conformance in the Post Office; Challenges and Recommendations*, 1 October 2013, POL00029677

had ensured that Second Sight was kept on, but the chances of the Post Office co-operating any better now looked slim.

In fact, as cases poured into the new scheme, the Post Office was already planning on giving Warmington and Henderson the elbow. Paula Vennells had told Fujitsu UK chairman Simon Blagden at the end of July that she was "planning carefully how we bring the independent review to completion: it needs to progress at pace but not so quickly that we fail to close it down".[60] (Blagden, incidentally, was something of a confidant of Vennells, assuring her of Horizon's reliability, yet he would later bag a government job by falsely claiming to have had nothing to do with Horizon and to have never met Post Office officials. He lost the job when *Private Eye* exposed his porkies.)[61]

Then in November, Angela van den Bogerd wrote to Post Office head of retail Kevin Gilliland asking for more auditors and investigators for the mediation work. They would be "highly credible with Second Sight as we start to initiate their exit from the scheme," she said.[62]

The Post Office's real imperatives remained financial. At the same time as Van den Bogerd was talking of pushing out Second Sight, Vennells was launching a "Post Office 2020 Strategy", with the promise of a "modern, digital and thriving business" (in other words, free of government subsidy) by the end of the decade.[63] This would never be achieved if Second Sight's discoveries, Simon Clarke's damning advice and the consequent review of convictions turned into anything remotely resembling accountability or justice. All such challenges had to be defeated.

---

60 Email from Vennells to Simon Blagden, 25 July 2013, POL00108049
61 *Eye* 1629, August 2024
62 Email from Angela van den Bogerd to Kevin Gilliland, 13 November 2013, POL00027684
63 Post Office press release, 27 November 2013

11

SEE NO EVIL

Hopes for the independent review turn to ashes, and keeping a lid on the scandal becomes a conspiracy to cover up

CORPORATE risk-management reports tend to hide as much as they reveal, but the one presented to the Post Office board on 20 November 2013 spoke volumes.

One of the critical risks was "reputational damage following allegations relating to the integrity of the Horizon system". Among the impacts were "long term brand damage" and "political impact". There was no mention of people wrongly going to jail. The first "controls and assurance" measure against this reputational damage was called a "containment project".[1]

A key priority was containing the fallout from Simon Clarke's legal advice and the interest from the Criminal Cases Review Commission. The mechanism for this was the review of past prosecutions by the legal firm Cartwright King, with a view to further disclosures in relevant cases, as vouched for by eminent public prosecutor Brian Altman QC. There was a distinct whiff of "containment" in selecting him. Discussing a shortlist of possibles, Bond Dickinson senior partner Gavin Matthews had pointed to Altman's "possible attraction politically" and remarked that "he has the ear of the [Director of Public Prosecutions]/[Attorney General]'s Office".[2] The Post Office's number-two lawyer, Hugh Flemington, had chipped in: "his connections sound useful."[3] Bond Dickinson's Andy Parsons agreed that Altman was "very live to the political dimension".[4]

The "containment" tone could also be sensed in the terms of Cartwright King's review, which had been limited to post-January 2010 shortfall cases. It thus ruled out the vast majority of convictions (since they often took a couple of years to end up in court, it really meant around 2012, so less than 10 percent of

---
1 Quarterly risk review, 19 November 2013, POL00197997
2 Email from Gavin Matthews to Susan Crichton, 18 July 2013, POL00192287
3 Email from Hugh Flemington to Matthews, 18 July 2013, POL00192287
4 Email from Andy Parsons to Rodric Williams, 18 July 2013, POL00297951

Horizon-related convictions would be covered). This was the point from which Horizon Online was rolled out and was appropriate, Clarke had said, based on "proportionality; resourcing; transparency; and [Post Office] reputation".[5]

When the Post Office's top legal brass sat down at Brian Altman's Bedford Square chambers on 9 September to discuss the review with him and Clarke, there was decades of legal experience around the table. Along with the two barristers were the Post Office's outgoing general counsel Susan Crichton, senior criminal lawyer Jarnail Singh and litigation lawyer Rodric Williams, plus Gavin Matthews and Andy Parsons from Bond Dickinson and Harry Bowyer and Martin Smith from Cartwright King. All were professionally obliged to put the service of justice above all else.

Somehow, though, one of the most elementary points of criminal justice escaped this august gathering. Every trainee lawyer knows that even after a conviction, material that has any bearing on its safety has to be disclosed to the defendant. Yet, discussing the most prominent case that would *not* be within the Cartwright King review, Seema Misra's, the lawyers decided to abrogate this responsibility. Notes of the meeting recorded Altman saying: "She went to prison. Jenkins gave evidence."[6] He then raised the question: "What disclose?" After this, the notes show a "provisional view" that the cut-off date for the Cartwright King review was "sensible". But this might not prevent others from coming forward – a prospect insensitively recorded as "cant [sic] avoid possibility Misras may crawl out of woodwork".

Altman also advised of the threat from the mediation scheme that had been announced after Second Sight's interim review, to which Seema Misra was expected to apply. "The concern is that lawyers acting for those individuals may be using the scheme to obtain information... in order to pursue an appeal."[7] A couple of weeks later, Smith told Crichton that Altman "was concerned that Misra would use the mediation scheme to obtain some sort of concession to allow her to appeal".[8]

Of the many astonishing episodes in the Post Office scandal, this was one of the more jaw-dropping. In a high-profile case, a woman had been convicted and imprisoned based on the evidence of a man whom these senior lawyers knew to have no credibility and to have misled courts. The professional duty, never mind the moral one, to disclose Jenkins's unreliability to Seema Misra's team was glaringly obvious. But, such was the identification of the lawyers

---

5 Simon Clarke, advice to Post Office, 8 July 2013, POL00006365
6 Notes of meeting with Brian Altman QC, 9 September 2013, POL00139866
7 Notes of meeting with Altman, 9 September 2013, POL00006485
8 Email from Martin Smith to Crichton, 26 September 2013, POL00066817

with the Post Office's corporate interests and perhaps the wider "political interests" – not to mention the fees coming out of this rich seam of work – that they could all disregard their principal responsibility to serve justice. If only by omission, they were collectively perverting it. A few weeks later, Clarke would explicitly advise, for reasons even he couldn't later fathom, that information including the Second Sight interim report and Jenkins's unreliability should not be disclosed to Seema Misra's lawyers.

When Altman produced his appraisal of the Cartwright King review on 15 October, he said plainly that Gareth Jenkins was "tainted". Nevertheless, he found that the review, which by that point had advised disclosure in nine cases out of 197 initially sifted, was "fundamentally sound". And Clarke's 2010 cut-off date, which was based on the introduction of the Horizon Online system and excluded many Jenkins-assisted convictions, was "logical, proportionate and practicable in light of all the known circumstances".[9] The essential boxes – or containers – were ticked.

New broom

As Altman delivered his stamp of approval, Susan Crichton's replacement as general counsel arrived in the person of Chris Aujard, a hard-nosed Australian mergers and acquisitions lawyer whose CV talked about "adding value" for his clients. Here was the tougher, uncompromising new broom the Post Office wanted to sweep up the mess left by the brow-beaten Crichton and her imperfect commitment to professional integrity.

Aujard immediately received a briefing from Simon Clarke on his devastating findings of a few months earlier. The barrister explained the background to the Post Office's prosecutions and how, when it was "necessary to provide evidence and testimony dealing with the integrity of [Horizon Online]... we have relied upon Dr [sic] Gareth Jenkins, an expert witness provided by Fujitsu".[10] Jenkins's failure to mention Horizon defects in evidence, added Clarke, "was an important and far-reaching failure the consequences of which are only now beginning to crystallise". Had the material been known during "any particular prosecution, it would undoubtedly have been disclosable to the defence". It wasn't exactly what a new head lawyer would want in his in-tray, although it was also something that a responsible one wouldn't ignore. But as the scandal rolled on over the couple of years that Aujard remained at the Post Office, knowledge of this serious failing merely led to a greater determination to bury it. Anything else would not "add value".

9 Altman, review of Post Office prosecutions, 15 October 2013, POL00006581
10 Briefing note from Clarke to Chris Aujard, 15 October 2013, POL00108136

A few days after Aujard's arrival and his briefing from Clarke, Paula Vennells emailed her chair Alice Perkins late at night with some updates, ahead of going on holiday the next day. "My concern," she said, "currently is our obligations of disclosure re., [*sic*] an unsafe witness."[11] Fujitsu's witness, she said, had "made statements about no bugs, which later could be seen to have been undermined by the [Second Sight] report". Having raised such an obviously important matter, she then undercut it. "We do not think it material but it could be high profile." The idea that an "unsafe witness" was not legally significant was barely credible, and appeared to be more ill-considered justification for concealment. Either way, this fundamental flaw in Post Office prosecutions and its ramifications were demonstrably now understood at the top of the Post Office: by its chief executive, its chair and its chief lawyer. They would be complicit in any further concealment, however they dressed it up.

For the present, however, with their main plan of action given the Altman seal of approval, they had "contained" the threats from the CCRC and Seema Misra. They just had to pull off the same trick with some other awkward customers.

Sparrow hawks

Unaware of the machinations inside the Post Office, James Arbuthnot's faith that it would do something approaching the right thing remained just about intact. When the mediation scheme was unveiled at the end of August 2013, he declared it "fair, thorough and independent".[12] The doubts he'd expressed in the Commons the previous month, immediately after Second Sight's interim report, appeared to have been assuaged. Alan Bates was less sanguine, but this was the only show in town.

Arbuthnot had been given grounds for trusting Vennells. That summer he'd been talking to Fujitsu UK chairman Simon Blagden about defence matters, in his other role as chair of the Commons defence select committee, and had raised Horizon. Blagden, who happened to be a significant Tory party donor and schmoozer, recommended "a continued open and inclusive dialogue with Paula Vennells would be the best way forward". As other captains of industry had before, he vouched for her effusively. She was "without doubt the most morally and socially aware CEO that I deal with".[13] Once again, the virtuous persona of the ordained priest convinced.

The working group overseeing the mediation scheme was made up of

---
11 Email from Paula Vennells to Perkins, 21 October 2013, POL00372551
12 Post Office press release, 26 August 2013
13 Email from Simon Blagden to James Arbuthnot, 18 July 2013, JARB0000068

the Second Sight duo, along with Alan Bates and Kay Linnell representing JFSA, and a group of senior Post Office executives and lawyers, including Chris Aujard and Angela van den Bogerd, with one Belinda Crowe acting as the secretariat. They were joined by the ubiquitous Andy Parsons from Bond Dickinson. From November, the group would be chaired by retired Court of Appeal judge Sir Anthony Hooper, whom Bates and Arbuthnot rated.

The presence of the previously unheard of Belinda Crowe belied the superficial balance of the working group. She was a 30-year career civil servant brought in a couple of years earlier ostensibly to handle the Post Office's work on mutualisation, for which appetite had since waned. Crowe had also been chosen by Vennells as programme director for Project Sparrow. This was the shadowy name for the "containment project" identified in the risk management report, designed to run Second Sight's work and other challenges into the sand. The board sub-committee running it included Vennells, Aujard, Perkins and, tellingly for a supposedly "arm's-length body" whose executives were normally expected to get on with things themselves, Richard Callard, a non-executive director from the government's Shareholder Executive. This group of course put the mission more euphemistically – "resolve matters as quickly as possible whilst limiting adverse publicity" – but the intention was clear.[14]

As early as 22 October 2013, Belinda Crowe wrote to Van den Bogerd, nominally responsible for branch improvement following the Second Sight interim report but now assuming greater authority. "I said I would do a note about how to move to a place where Second Sight are able to leave the working group and allow Post Office to take over sole responsibility for the investigations? [sic]" Crowe wrote.[15] She was following up a message from Andy Parsons the day before, drafting some lines to give Paula Vennells. "Work is continuing on managing SS out of the scheme," Parsons had written. Second Sight's role was "gradually being reduced until they can be removed entirely. This work has already begun."[16]

While Warmington, Henderson and the JFSA knew nothing of the plot to spike their guns, they could feel that the mediation scheme was already being slowly strangled. Despite a commitment that it would be an open process without any "no-go" areas for Second Sight, the Post Office was refusing to discuss criminal cases, even though those with convictions had originally been admitted into the scheme. Ideas about what might be reasonable sums

---
14 Briefing for Project Sparrow sub-committee, 9 April 2014, POL00138251
15 Email from Belinda Crowe to Angela van den Bogerd, 22 October 2013, POL00300442
16 Email from Parsons to Andy Holt, 21 October 2013, POL00123004

in cases where the Post Office was found at fault differed wildly. Lawyers from Linklaters had advised that the Post Office shouldn't pay out more than three months' salary in cases of wrongful contract termination. Sub-postmasters pointed out that destroyed futures might be worth a bit more. Vennells was recorded as telling Second Sight that payments would be "more of the nature of a 'token' with an apology".[17] There was what Aujard called an "expectation gap",[18] which was in reality a growing chasm between what the sub-postmasters deserved and what the Post Office was prepared to give them.

Zebra crossing

Towards the end of 2013, Post Office prosecutions had all but ended. New top lawyer Chris Aujard took the pragmatic view that there were better ways to deal with losses from the business. While Vennells didn't want to cease the activity, the numbers show his view prevailed. In 2014 there would be just two Horizon-related convictions, and none in later years.

The move didn't, however, signal a softening of attitude. The campaign against Second Sight was becoming attritional. Documents that Henderson and Warmington needed for their reviews of cases ahead of any decision to mediate weren't provided, frustrating them even more. At one point, Aujard, suspecting Henderson of leaking to James Arbuthnot, threatened the Second Sight man with legal action if he said anything that harmed the Post Office.[19]

Alan Bates reported to Arbuthnot the growing pressure on the forensic accountants and the distinct possibility of the firm walking away. By the spring of 2014, it had been able to complete only a single case review.[20] Other MPs who had constituents hoping for some justice were also running out of patience. Arbuthnot tried to re-apply some pressure on Vennells and Perkins, but at further meetings in his House of Commons office it became clear they were less interested in progress and more in stifling a further report that Second Sight was scheduled to produce, pulling together themes from its investigations over the previous months. Vennells wrote to Arbuthnot claiming that such a report would "damage the integrity of the [mediation] scheme".[21] The real reason, however, was obviously to suppress any more findings from the firm that had gone only "so far" last time.

Against this bleak outlook, the Post Office board decided it needed to present a more positive vision of its own. It would commission consultants "to

---

17 Aujard, notes on meeting with Vennells and Second Sight, 24 February 2014, POL00100336
18 Aujard, inquiry evidence, 2 May 2024
19 Ian Henderson, witness statement, 20 May 2024, WITN00420100
20 Arbuthnot, WITN00020100
21 Letter from Vennells to Arbuthnot, 11 April 2014, POL00100671

give them and those outside the Business comfort about the Horizon system". As usual, it wanted a review to be about "comfort" or "reassurance" and not actually finding anything out. A potentially amenable firm, Deloitte, was selected for the task under yet another codename, Project Zebra.

No consultants could turn the Horizon sow's ear into a silk purse, however. The Deloitte crew even showed an annoying objectivity, Second Sight-style. When they reported in June 2014, they addressed the crucial matter of access by Fujitsu staff to branch accounts. The system, they said, "allows for posting of additional transactions centrally without the requirement for these transactions to be accepted by sub-postmasters", recommending action on "communications with the relevant sub-postmaster prior to any adjustment being made to their ledgers".[22] The "remote access" that the Post Office had long denied, even while knowing about it, was both possible and, indeed, routine. And now it was in black and white, from a major independent consultancy. This was definitely not part of the containment plan; it needed to be swept under the nearest carpet as soon as possible.

The Project Zebra report had been due to go to the board's Project Sparrow sub-committee (featuring Vennells, Aujard and Perkins), but it didn't. It wasn't even discussed there. Instead, Aujard presented a lesser "summary" of the report to the Post Office's June board meeting. He omitted anything to do with remote access. And, while pointing out that Deloitte would not "publicly assert that the system is working with integrity unless they undertake specific testing", the general counsel told the board that "the report does give some comfort for the board on the design for processing and storing transaction data with integrity".[23] Any "further comfort or assurance" would require more work from Deloitte, which wouldn't be commissioned. The Zebra slipped silently back into the bush.

Battle of denial

The report that Second Sight produced in August 2014, a first version of its snappily titled *Initial Complaint Review and Mediation Scheme Briefing Report Part 2*, was strictly confidential, but the *Eye* and others were able to report leaked extracts.[24] One was the answer to the question of whether the Horizon system was fit for purpose. It was a simple one: no.

But Warmington and Henderson had seen more than just a poor IT system causing grief, and were able to go much further than they had the previous year. "Post Office's investigation team has, in many cases, failed to

---

22 Deloitte, Project Zebra report, 23 May 2014, POL00107160
23 Aujard and Mark Davies, report for Post Office board, 6 June 2014, POL00027153
24 *Eye* 1375, September 2014

identify the underlying root cause of shortfalls prior to initiating civil recovery action or criminal proceedings," they found.[25] This was the case even when sub-postmasters "brought to the auditors' or investigators' attention their own suspicions as to the underlying root causes". Investigators then "seem to default to seeking evidence that will support a charge of false accounting – rather than an open minded investigation into the root cause". This was partly because training for investigators "seems to have disregarded the possibility that the Horizon system could be in any way relevant to their investigations". The Post Office plods had found that "recording these admissions of false accounting… was the key to achieving relatively rapid, and (to Post Office) inexpensive, asset recovery". If sub-postmasters requested help getting to the cause of a shortfall, "this has often been refused… in line with the standard contract".

Second Sight had rumbled the Post Office's methods: the convenient failure to consider whether money had actually been lost; ignoring Horizon flaws; the cynical false accounting trick; the refusal to help; and the exploitation of the one-sided sub-postmaster contract. The Post Office's response was, predictably, denial: repeating the out-of-date mantra of no systemic issues and asinine statistics about millions of successful transactions, while privately dismissing Second Sight's criticisms as beyond the firm's remit. In more than five years since *Computer Weekly* first reported the sub-postmasters' plight, it had done no more than stick its head deeper in the sand.

Paula Vennells and her PR machine had tried to pre-empt the latest revelations. "Part time curate ordained to deliver salvation for the Post Office", ran the headline on a *Sunday Times* profile four days before Second Sight's report. (It followed "The female curate offering salvation to the Post Office" on a BBC puff piece earlier in the year;[26] a cynic might suspect a certain PR man's hand at work.) The profile covered her handling of commercial challenges but didn't mention the Horizon word. Vennells, snapped for the occasion in red jacket, red shoes and perched on a red leather armchair, painted the now standard self-portrait. Her faith "influences my values and how I approach things", but at the same time, "I'm quite calm and resilient and you have to have those sorts of qualities, as well as ambition and commercial drive, to be successful in a business like this."[27]

Networking seemed to help, too. A couple of months later, Vennells would be one of Fujitsu UK chairman Simon Blagden's guests at a Tory party

---

25 *Initial Complaint Review and Mediation Scheme Briefing Report Part 2*, 5 August 2014, POL00021819
26 bbc.co.uk/news/business-25965476
27 *Sunday Times*, 17 August 2014. Nearly ten years later, the interviewer, Oliver Shah, admitted "it was not my finest moment (*Sunday Times*, 28 January 2024)

fundraising dinner, sharing a table with a handful of up-and-coming Tory parliamentarians and wannabe MPs. A political shindig wasn't quite the place for a paragon of virtue who, as a senior public official, should have been challenging the IT supplier who was paying for the event.

Back in the mediation working group meetings, the mood was less convivial. The Post Office was arriving more lawyered up than ever, prompting James Arbuthnot to tell Alice Perkins that her organisation was turning the process into a "legal battlefield". As 2014 drew to a close, with Arbuthnot having decided not to stand in the 2015 general election and his patience now wearing thin, it was time for one last effort to make the mediation scheme work. On 17 November, the Post Office A-team of Vennells (plus Mark Davies), Perkins, Van den Bogerd and Aujard arrived at Arbuthnot's office to face him, Bates and three other unimpressed MPs: Oliver Letwin, Andrew Bridgen and Mike Wood. It didn't go well. Aujard and Van den Bogerd, dominating a cowed Vennells, refused to shift on the MPs' demands for a swifter, more open, process.

The Post Office was now querying around 90 percent of cases proposed for the mediation process. The chances of justice on any scale in any reasonable time frame were non-existent. The final straw for Arbuthnot was the Post Office's refusal to allow mediation for his constituent Jo Hamilton, the woman whose transparent innocence had first rallied him to the cause. After years of campaigning largely behind the scenes, he was going to put the issue centre-stage.

Show time

"MPs lose faith in Post Office mediation scheme", ran the heading on Arbuthnot's press release on 8 December 2014. Other members of a 140-strong group of MPs now seeking action also chimed in. "Either the Post Office is awash with criminals… or something has gone terribly wrong," said Batley and Spen MP Mike Wood, whose constituent Alison Hall had been convicted of false accounting in 2011. "MPs are inclined to believe the latter and we are all shocked that the Post Office seems not to want to get to the bottom of all this."[28]

The no-more-Mr-Nice-Guy strategy immediately brought renewed attention to the cause. The following morning, Arbuthnot repeated the message on Radio 4's *Today* programme. Vennells sent Davies out to put the Post Office's side, but he fluffed it with the revealing gaffe that sub-postmasters had "lifestyle problems as a result of their having been working in Post Office branches".[29] That evening, journalist Nick Wallis fronted another report on the BBC, in

---
28 Arbuthnot, press release, 8 December 2014, POL00101690
29 *Hansard*, 17 December 2014

which Arbuthnot accused the Post Office of setting up an expensive scheme and then denying its use to sub-postmasters. It was "an awful way of behaving".[30]

Inside the Post Office bunker, the mood was becoming fevered. Ahead of a follow-up item from Wallis a few days later, Project Sparrow director Belinda Crowe responded to some agonising by spin doctor Mark Davies over how to handle the exposure. She admitted that "we are on really dodgy ground if we get into the detail of case" but insisted they had some good general points.[31] "I am trying to keep thinking of Kipling," she told him – a reference to the poem *If*. Davies could do better than that, replying with Theodore Roosevelt's "Man in the Arena" speech from 1910: "It is not the critic who counts… The credit belongs to the man who is actually in the arena, whose face is marred by dust and sweat and blood…"[32] Crowe appreciated it. "Brought a lump to my throat," she replied. "Covered in blood as I am. Thanks. Great words."[33]

There were more blows for the Post Office gladiators to take, starting with a debate that Arbuthnot led in Westminster Hall on 17 December on what he called the "sham" mediation scheme. MP after MP stood up to denounce the Post Office. Labour's Kevan Jones, set to take over leading the campaign and MP of Durham sub-postmaster Tom Brown (wrongly accused of stealing £83,000), called it a "national scandal". Jo Swinson had little to offer in reply and, when she bleated about the complexity of cases as an excuse for the torpor, Jones could bear it no longer. "You're the minister, do something!" he cried – cutting through the legal but politically illiterate nicety that ministers could remain at "arm's length".[34]

That evening, the *One Show* covered the debate and the story of another sub-postmaster, Steve Phillips from Nelson in south Wales, who'd been improperly forced to repay £18,000. He told Wallis that sub-postmasters were all saying the same thing: "Do not trust the Horizon system."[35] Other campaigning sub-postmasters sketched the familiar nightmares. Julian Wilson explained the impossibility of admitting a shortfall and opening up after accounting day. Jo Hamilton told the nation why she had been compelled to plead guilty to false accounting. Noel Thomas recounted his 42 years with the Post Office ending in a prison cell.

In the face of this onslaught, even Vennells's caring chief executive mask slipped. That evening she turned TV critic, emailing Davies, Perkins and

---

30 *One Show*, BBC1, 9 December 2014
31 Email from Crowe to Davies, 14 December 2014, POL00101860
32 Email from Davies to Crowe, 14 December 2014, POL00101860
33 Email from Crowe to Davies, 14 December 2014, POL00101860
34 *Hansard*, BBC1, 17 December 2014
35 *One Show*, BBC1, 17 December 2014

others with her review of the film. While the Post Office statements had come across well ("Mark has achieved a balance of reporting beyond anything I could have hoped for"), she thought the rest "was hype and human interest". She was "more bored than outraged". Then came the sneering. "The MP quoted (who?) was full of bluster, and inaccurate. Jo Hamilton lacked passion and admitted false accounting on TV. [Arbuthnot] was nowhere to be seen. And the bulletin was too long." Sub-postmasters' complaints about struggling with the IT, "in my eyes made [them] look inadequate".[36]

The arrogance and wilful misreading of the report spoke volumes. Jo Hamilton had indeed looked weary of still having to tell her story, but had accurately summarised the false-accounting bind. Arbuthnot wasn't on because he'd been used on the show the week before. The "blustering" MP was staunch campaigner Kevan Jones, whom she should have known. And if eight minutes was too long, perhaps it was Vennells's attention span for unwelcome information that was the problem.

The following day, Vennells addressed the contribution of Steve Phillips, still a serving sub-postmaster. Asking Chris Aujard to watch the film, she vented: "Steve Phillips is completely out of order, inaccurate at best, lying at worst. And has wilfully collaborated to [bringing] us into disrepute."[37] A touch menacingly, she asked the lawyer: "Any views?" Speaking up was not the Post Office way. Loyalty to the brand was expected from all, including the sub-postmasters whom the chief executive was now treating with barely disguised contempt.

Silence please

This attitude could plumb dark depths. In the autumn of 2013 a sub-postmaster from Cheshire, Martin Griffiths, had taken his own life after years of torment at the hands of the Post Office. He'd been suspended and reinstated following shortfalls, then earlier that year told his contract would be terminated. On top of which, he was held liable for tens of thousands of pounds stolen from his branch in an armed robbery a few months earlier. One morning, he stepped in front of a bus, leaving a note of apology to his family.

When Mr Griffiths died after three weeks on life support, Vennells reacted with concern but, as ever, a concern that was circumscribed by the need to protect the Post Office. As well as offering condolences and concern for her team, she told colleagues, "we need to look to the business: to help me brief this properly to the board, can you let me know what background we

---
36 Email from Vennells to Davies and others, 17 December 2014, POL00109806
37 Email from Vennells to Aujard and others, 18 December 2014, POL00150352

have on Martin and how/why this might have happened."[38] She had heard "that there were previous mental health issues and potential family issues". (Asked about this several years later at the public inquiry, she had no idea where she'd heard it from, but denied fishing for personal information that might limit the Post Office's blame.)[39]

Over the following year, the Post Office would do everything it could to keep this tragedy quiet, culminating in a compensation deal linked to a non-disclosure agreement with Martin's widow, Gina, in January 2015. Payments would be staggered, Post Office lawyer Rodric Williams told Angela van den Bogerd, "as an incentive to Mrs Griffiths maintaining confidentiality". If she "were to breach confidentiality, we could stop any further payments".[40] Even a widow of a sub-postmaster driven to take his own life had to fall in line with the Post Office imperative to protect its brand.

The two faces of Paula Vennells's approach to sub-postmasters were also on display when, in the same month that Gina Griffiths was being silenced, she was contacted by Derbyshire sub-postmaster Michael Crocker. He told her of repeated Horizon statements showing that his village post office was holding a hundred more Lottery scratchcards than it actually was, and that the Post Office helpline had told him the cause must be theft. He was having to make the books balance with his own cash. It didn't matter whether the theft was by him or a real crook; he had to cough up either way.

"Thank you very much for taking the trouble to let me know," Vennells replied unctuously. "It's only when colleagues do that I can help." She would "do my best to sort this out for you".[41] Thirty minutes later, she tetchily forwarded the message to Van den Bogerd, branch accounting head Rod Ismay and others. "This complaint simply shouldn't have reached me," she said. The support centre was supposed to be "on the alert for any calls that relate to missing money and especially any that relate to the Sparrow themes". They should have been dealt with "so that we avoided any unnecessary additional noise or references to Horizon".[42] The likes of Mr Crocker were to be contained, not allowed to give her the bad news that she must not hear.

Committee stage

The other tool in Arbuthnot's escalation kit was the Commons business select committee that scrutinised Vince Cable's Department for Business, Innovation

---

38 Email from Vennells to Van den Bogerd and others, 11 October 2013, POL00027757
39 Vennells, inquiry evidence, 22 May 2024
40 Email from Williams to Van den Bogerd, 22 January 2015, POL00219796
41 Email from Vennells to Michael Crocker, 1 March 2015, POL00102381
42 Email from Vennells to Van den Bogerd and others, 1 March 2015, POL00102381

and Skills. Arbuthnot needed to persuade its Labour chair, Adrian Bailey, to turn his committee's attention to the affair. With the current parliament drawing to a close, it wasn't the ideal time for a new inquiry but, as Arbuthnot put it to Bailey, "a sub-postmaster who is having a house repossessed, or who is in danger of losing the right to sue the Post Office through lapse of time, cannot worry about our election timetable".[43] The chair agreed and, when the select committee convened on the morning of 3 February 2015 to examine the Post Office mediation scheme, Paula Vennells faced some long overdue public scrutiny.

Her preparation for the hearing revealed as much as her evidence itself. A few days beforehand, she'd asked her PR man Mark Davies and IT boss Lesley Sewell for briefing on the likely question: "Is it possible to access the system remotely?" In trademark Vennells style, she asked the conscientious question: "What is the true answer?" But next came the cynical kicker, with the implicit instruction. "I need to say no it is not possible and that we are sure of this because of xxx [sic] and that we know this because we have had the system assured."[44] She wanted the information from Sewell and Davies to "phrase the facts into answers, plus a line to take the conversation back up a level – i.e., to one of our narrative boxes/rocks". In plain English: give me the answer I need, then a way out of the awkward questions and on to the general flannel we're comfortable with. Her helpers duly complied: not with the "truth" bit of the request, of course, but with what they knew the boss really wanted. Vennells should say (incorrectly) that remote access was impossible, and then, "if pushed", that it was possible but only with the sub-postmaster's knowledge (also wrong).[45]

Before Vennells gave evidence, a warm-up panel including Alan Bates, forensic accountant Kay Linnell and George Thomson from the Post Office-funded National Federation of Sub-postmasters shuffled into their places. As soon as Bailey asked his general opener about what the big issues were, Thomson, primed to seize the agenda, barked: "May I start?" He launched into a vociferous defence of Horizon. "I think that, over that 13 or 14 years, it has performed exceptionally robustly," he told the MPs.[46] Hitting another of the Post Office's favourite buzzwords, he added: "Systemically, it is very strong." He'd brought with him a 500-page manual, "full of training materials", which he seemed to think would impress. Alan Bates, sitting next to Thomson shaking his head, pointed out that he'd set up the Justice for Subpostmasters Alliance precisely because of the absence of support from the NFSP. It was,

---

43 Letter from Arbuthnot to Adrian Bailey MP, 8 December 2014, JARB0000098
44 Email from Vennells to Davies and Lesley Sewell, 30 January 2015, POL00029812
45 Addendum to briefing pack for Vennells, 2 February 2015, POL00117097
46 Commons business, innovation and skills committee, 3 February 2015. See committees.parliament.uk/oralevidence/4526/html

he said sardonically, "like they are in a paid position in the Post Office". Thomson's body *was* in its pay and he didn't hesitate to put his paymasters' case in the kind of offensive terms that Post Office people usually reserved for private exchanges. The growing controversy, said Thomson, was in danger of "creating a cottage industry that damages the brand".

The MPs weren't having that, and began to understand the central issue when Kay Linnell answered questions from Conservative MP Brian Binley. He used the analogy of money going missing in the pubs he'd once managed, and wanted to know the difference. Linnell explained how in a pub the landlord could see the accounting records and investigate a loss, whereas in a post office the "accounting is outside the [sub-postmasters'] control". Nevertheless, under the sub-postmaster contract they remained liable. "How can they be expected to be responsible when in fact they do not have the tools to carry through that responsibility?" asked Binley rhetorically. "Is that the nub of it?" Indeed it was, which is where Alan Bates had come in a decade and a half earlier.

False witness

After an hour, it was time for Vennells, along with Van den Bogerd and – catastrophically for them – Second Sight's unbiddable Ian Henderson, to move into the witness seats.

The Post Office chief executive was wearing the mask of the deeply concerned corporate leader. She "could not put this [mediation] scheme in place and not do it properly".[47] The "people who work in our branches are too important for that". She had never "worked for a company that could have done this as well as we have". This misrepresented the picture enough, but one further saccharine sentiment was followed by a more serious untruth. "We are a business that genuinely cares about the people who work for us," she simpered. "If there had been any miscarriages of justice, it would have been really important to me and the Post Office that we surfaced those." But "so far we have no evidence of that". It was less than 18 months after Simon Clarke's advice about Gareth Jenkins and her own comments to Perkins about the "unsafe witness". She knew that convictions had been secured using his evidence, so to say that the Post Office had found no evidence of miscarriages of justice was grossly misleading.

Henderson succinctly described the methods being deployed by the Post Office to frustrate his investigations and deny anything resembling redress through the mediation scheme. He'd been trying to examine Horizon access by

---

47 Ibid

Fujitsu from its Bracknell HQ. "We first requested documents relating to that in February 2013 – almost two years ago. We have still not been provided with those documents."[48] On the vexed operation of the suspense account, through which funds were being funnelled from sub-postmasters with shortfalls and becoming profits for the Post Office, he had "been asking for that information since July last year". But "the most important failure to disclose to us is the full access to the legal and prosecution files". Second Sight had been given some in the early phase of its work, but the axe had come down on this. The change of stance was "a very severe constraint on our ability to conduct an independent investigation into what has happened". Questioned on this, Vennells claimed it was the first she'd heard of the problem and asked Henderson: "Who told you that, Ian?" Henderson replied, deadpan: "It came up at one of the working group meetings, at which you and I were present."

Van den Bogerd droned sullenly on about data protection. She refused to answer whether the Post Office's lack of co-operation with Second Sight was based on legal advice, forcing Henderson to reveal that it was the general counsel, Chris Aujard, who had "said that he is not prepared to disclose to us the full legal files". When exasperated committee member Nadhim Zahawi pressured Van den Bogerd to start handing over the files, she protested: "We have been providing that over the last few weeks." Turning to the Second Sight man, Zahawi asked: "Is that right, Mr Henderson?" "No, it is not," he calmly replied. "I am sorry to say." Zahawi pleaded with Vennells to step in, since "the buck stops with you". The chief executive latched on to this as a lifeboat back to one of her narrative rocks. "It does stop with me," she agreed. "Also, therefore, as chief executive, I am responsible for the reputation of and for what happens for the Post Office."

This, and her final comment, revealed what really mattered to Vennells. "I have reduced our dependence on subsidy from £210m to £130m this year," she told the MPs. "We have an ambition to break even in three to four years. We are in financial services… It is critical to me that we keep trust in the Post Office as high as it is." On the evidence of the previous hour, it was a trust she thought would be helped by deceiving parliament.

Second's out

This public display of true priorities and denial of reality demonstrated that nothing approaching justice for the sub-postmasters could be achieved through co-operation with the Post Office.

As he prepared to stand down as an MP, James Arbuthnot met the

---

48 Ibid

Criminal Cases Review Commission's chairman, Richard Foster, convincing him this really was something for the miscarriage body. Foster followed up with a note explaining that – 18 months after being fobbed off with the reassurance of the Cartwright King review, as vouched for by Brian Altman QC – the CCRC was establishing a unit dedicated to looking at sub-postmasters' cases.[49]

The Post Office couldn't cope with the public scrutiny or the peek behind the curtain of the mediation process that Ian Henderson had given in parliament, any more than it could with a south Wales sub-postmaster telling a TV reporter that Horizon wasn't to be trusted. Somebody had to pay. So just over a month after Vennells and Van den Bogerd had been mauled by MPs, the Post Office sacked Second Sight and disbanded the working group.

The media and parliamentary furore had given Vennells the spurious justification that Warmington and Henderson had been "captured" by Bates's JFSA and were breaking their contract by criticising the Post Office. The firm's *Part 2* report would not be published or even shown to postal services minister Jo Swinson. Second Sight had finally been "managed out".

The engagement with Second Sight and the sham mediation scheme had been little more than a badly managed three-year exercise in "containment". The Post Office had been able to point to these things, as cover for delays, concealment and deception. The trick was no longer working and, by doing what they thought they'd been brought in for and getting towards the truth, Ron Warmington and Ian Henderson had signed their own termination notice. The mediation scheme's pitiful output – of 150 applicants, 20 cases resolved, four after mediation, with total payouts £60,000[50] – served only to betray the ruse.

Alan Bates knew that something much more direct was required. A new phase in the fight for justice was beginning.

---

49 Arbuthnot, witness statement, 10 April 2024, WITN00020100
50 Aujard, witness statement, 24 April 2024, WITN00030100

12

INSIDE JOB

A Fujitsu whistleblower breaks cover; new brooms keep sweeping under the carpet; and Alan Bates finds backers to put their money where his mouth is…

THE English legal system doesn't exist to help the little people. Using it to right wrongs requires money and, when the opponent is a state-backed company with effectively limitless resources, lots of it. Having decided that the only way to hold the Post Office to account was to sue it, Alan Bates was having trouble finding the huge amount he needed.

By 2015, however, an industry in funding litigation and insuring against opponents' costs in the event of defeat was fairly well-developed. It had grown rapidly after a ban on lawyers taking a cut of a client's winnings had been lifted in 2011. The theory had been that financially incentivised lawyers might lose impartiality, but this had long denied access to justice to anyone but the wealthy.

The new market was built on the gamble by specialist litigation funders that they would back enough winners and take a large enough share of payouts to cover the costs they paid when they lost. In this brutal calculus, Bates and the other hundred or so sub-postmasters he'd assembled by now – some with convictions for dishonesty – were not the most attractive prospect in which to invest a probable ten-figure sum. But they weren't a completely hopeless cause, either.

This was where James Arbuthnot's recent, profile-raising campaign began to pay off. On the morning of 4 February 2015, James Hartley, a partner with Leeds-based solicitors Freeths, heard a report of the previous day's select committee hearing on Radio 4's *Today* programme as he drove to work. As he listened to the summary of the sub-postmasters' complaints and their impossible – and perhaps unlawful – position under their contract with the Post Office, he began to wonder if this might be one for his practice in commercially funded and insured disputes. When he arrived at the office, he called Bates, only to learn that the JFSA was already talking to other lawyers. Hartley would leave him to it for the time being.

Roll's voice

The stronger the evidence for the injustice, and the more people signing up to fight it, the greater would be the chances of getting litigation off the ground. So when Bates, who brought a certain guile as well as persistence to his campaign, acquired a whistleblower with blockbuster revelations, he decided to deploy him to maximum effect.

A Fujitsu IT engineer from the early 2000s called Richard Roll had contacted Bates and told him all about the bugs and errors in Horizon from the outset. Even more significantly at this stage, he also explained how Fujitsu was routinely altering sub-postmasters' branch accounts without their knowledge.

Bates decided to save his special source for the big occasion. He told journalist Nick Wallis that he would put him in touch with the Fujitsu whistleblower only if the hack secured coverage in the BBC's flagship investigative *Panorama* slot. A serious, more extended exposure of the scandal would, he thought, move the story on significantly. The plan worked. In the spring of 2015, Wallis persuaded the programme's editors to commission just such a film. Critically, and courageously, Roll agreed to talk on camera.

As soon as the programme's producer, Matt Bardo, put to the Post Office what reporter John Sweeney would present on screen, it was clear that the "containment" strategy was under serious assault. This was the more "mainstream" coverage that communications boss Mark Davies had feared a couple of years earlier. And it would publicly expose one of the big lies at the heart of the affair. The reaction inside Post Office HQ was correspondingly fierce. Davies lobbied all the way up the BBC hierarchy, claiming "overwhelming evidence that the losses complained of were caused by user actions, including deliberate dishonest conduct".[1] Those lined up to appear on the film received threatening legal letters. "If your statements go as far as to harm Post Office's reputation," lawyers told Second Sight's Ian Henderson, "then we may have to take even more serious action in order to protect our brand."

Alice Perkins, by now a member of the BBC executive board but oblivious to the conflict of interest, suggested to Davies that he contact a former civil servant she knew from her time in the Cabinet Office and who was now BBC director-general Tony Hall's chief of staff. Davies replied that he did indeed know her and "might drop her a line", adding "I always worry about going too nuclear too early but this is now getting to that point I think."[2]

Whether the Post Office considered lying to journalists to be "going

---

1 Report on the affair by Andrew Head (*Panorama* editor in 2015) and producer Tim Robinson, 12 January 2024, bbc.co.uk/news/uk-67884743
2 Email from Mark Davies to Alice Perkins, 23 June 2015, POL00317714

nuclear" or not, it was certainly prepared to do so. Although unwilling to put anybody up for interview in the film, it did invite Bardo and his colleague Tim Robinson into its new HQ at Finsbury Dials, just north of the City of London, for an on-the-record discussion with Angela van den Bogerd and Patrick Bourke, a lawyer who at the time was programme manager for the mediation scheme – but whose brief seemed to range much wider.

Addressing the killer allegation from Richard Roll about remote access, Bardo asked formally: "So in sum, it is not now and never has been possible for anybody from Post Office or Fujitsu to interfere with transactions, without the clear knowledge of the sub-postmaster?" Bourke, who had been sent the briefing on Deloitte's Project Zebra report the previous year which acknowledged the possibility of remote access, replied: "It is 100 percent true to say we can't change, alter, modify, existing transaction data, so the integrity is 100 percent preserved." Asked if that had been the case "for the duration of the system", Van den Bogerd said "Yeah."[3] By this time, she too knew this to be untrue. She'd received emails that explicitly referred to remote access. In 2010, following the discussions on how to deal with the "receipts/payments mismatch" bug, she had been forwarded a message from a colleague saying "I found out this week that Fujitsu can actually put an entry into a branch account remotely."[4] In 2011, another had told her that Fujitsu "do this on numerous occasions on a network wide basis in order to remedy glitches in the system".[5]

The threats and the deception, however, just delayed rather than spiked the programme. When *Trouble at the Post Office* aired, Roll told a prime-time audience that he and colleagues "went in through the back door [to branch accounts] and made changes".[6] Sometimes, he said, "you'd be putting several lines of code in at a time". Henderson told of the bugs Second Sight had reported, of "institutional blindness" to Horizon faults and the use of theft charges to secure pleas of guilty to false accounting. Jo Hamilton, Noel Thomas and Seema Misra told the country what these things meant in the real world.

So deep was the institutional self-delusion now that no amount of serious first-hand evidence exposing the Horizon system could shift it. The Post Office would, said the official response, be complaining to the BBC about the "unsubstantiated allegations". Vennells briefed the Post Office board,

---
3 BBC report, op cit
4 Email from Lynn Hobbs to John Breeden, 3 December 2010, forwarded to Van den Bogerd on 5 December, POL00088956
5 Email from Tracy Marshall to Van den Bogerd and others, 5 January 2011, POL00294728
6 *Panorama*, BBC1, 17 August 2015

thanking "the Sparrow team" and claiming that the programme "contained no new information".[7] Remote access might not have been new to her, but it was to the British public – and to some viewers in the legal profession, which before long would prove transformational.

No, minister

The May 2015 general election dispensed with the Lib Dems as coalition partners and providers of hapless postal services ministers. From now on, the wool would have to be pulled over a series of Conservative ministers' eyes.

The first was former mandarin, ex-Tesco director, Tory peer and junior minister Baroness (Lucy) Neville-Rolfe, whom the Shareholder Executive swiftly set about getting onside. Senior Shareholder Executive official Laura Thompson briefed her in strident terms. "There is *no evidence* of systemic flaws in Horizon," she wrote. Any issues were "contractual disputes between two independent businesses ([Post Office] and agent)".[8] There was "*no evidence* that any of [the Post Office]'s prosecutions against sub-postmasters for either false accounting or theft are unsafe" (emphasis her own). The new minister should not correspond with Bates's Justice for Subpostmasters Alliance as this would "serve to prolong their campaign". The sub-postmasters' own federation, the NFSP, "does *not* support JFSA's arguments" (which was about the only true point in the briefing) and "the complaints of JFSA have borne no fruit" despite having been "comprehensively investigated over several years". It was the Shareholder Executive's "*strong recommendation that government should maintain the position that this is not a matter for government, and increase our distance from this matter*" (again, Thompson's emphasis). The new minister should "resist calls for further independent investigation".

Neville-Rolfe wasn't convinced. The categorical denials didn't tally with what she already knew, partly from having seen Second Sight's final report. She was less willing than her predecessors to accept that the "arm's-length" relationship meant disavowal of responsibility. And the parliamentary furore to which she was going to have to respond showed no sign of abating post-election. At the end of June, Andrew Bridgen led another adjournment debate in the Commons. Not for the first time, he told the tale of his constituent Michael Rudkin, the former sub-postmaster and senior NFSP official who had witnessed remote access at Fujitsu's Bracknell HQ seven years before.

The minister responding in the Commons, George Freeman, wasn't going to agree to the judicial inquiry that Bridgen called for and trotted out

---

7 BBC report, op cit
8 Briefing by Laura Thompson for Baroness (Lucy) Neville-Rolfe, 2 June 2015, UKGI00004453

the usual defensive lines about Horizon. But he did concede, in a change of ministerial tone, that sub-postmasters "should not be made the victim of criminal judgments when their crime is nothing more than being unable to cope with a new IT system".[9] He would convene a meeting between MPs and the new team.

Freeman and Neville-Rolfe wanted Second Sight to attend this, but the Shareholder Executive and Paula Vennells vehemently, and effectively, resisted. Nevertheless, when Bridgen and Kevan Jones met the minister a couple of weeks later, she still heard some of the difficult truths. Notes recorded by PR man Mark Davies summarised the well-rehearsed allegations against the Post Office: "Abusing its prosecution powers and using plea bargaining to 'cajole' people into accepting guilty pleas"; "curtailing Second Sight's work and the mediation scheme"; "forcing [Second Sight] to moderate its reports"; and "'Dickensian' contract arrangements with postmasters", to give just four.[10]

Neville-Rolfe would later describe this meeting as "my sort of road to Damascus". She had been surprised from the start "that so many people from normally reliable sections of the community were being convicted of dishonesty". A touch of snobbishness helped. "Lord Arbuthnot's constituency," she would tell the public inquiry years later, "I think is in Hampshire, you know, leafy, middle-class people, who suddenly, out of the blue… [end] up in court and being convicted."[11] Many, perhaps most, victims were in fact honest working-class people from leafy and non-leafy parts of the country doing a valuable job. But, however Neville-Rolfe arrived at her view, it marked a refreshing shift in political thinking on the scandal and one which, against officials' and executives' advice, she made some attempt to transform into action.

Green light

Heading into the second half of 2015, Alan Bates had still not been able to secure litigation funding so, months after their first contact, he gave commercial disputes lawyer James Hartley from Freeths a call.

Bates's and Kay Linnell's herculean efforts had brought about 100 sub-postmasters together by this stage, but Hartley knew he needed more to be able to win the scale of damages that would get the funders interested. So over the following months, with the help of a PR agency, he ran an advertising

---

9 *Hansard*, 29 June 2015
10 Email from Mark Davies to Vennells and others, 15 July 2015, POL00027729
11 Neville-Rolfe, inquiry evidence, 23 July 2024

campaign and a host of town-hall meetings at which sub-postmasters could sign up to the cause. By November, there was enough interest for the JFSA to issue a press release headlined "JFSA prepares for group litigation against Post Office". [12] This was met with derision within the government's Shareholder Executive. Its man on the Post Office board, former Deloitte accountant Richard Callard, commented to Mark Davies and others: "Seriously though, do you know how many legal firms they have had – would be good to take the lines with ministers that this is yet another sabre rattle, and that once legal firms get into the evidence they pull away."[13] The comment gave away how much officials were underestimating Bates – but also hinted at the scale of the task that he, Linnell and Hartley were taking on.

Freeths wasn't pulling away, but it still needed to find a courtroom legal team persuaded of the cause and braced for a long haul. For this, Hartley turned to experienced commercial and civil fraud silk Patrick Green QC from Henderson Chambers. When, some years later, Nick Wallis asked Green what had persuaded him to take up the case, he gave a two-word answer: "Richard Roll".[14] The *Panorama* film, and the efforts of Bates, Wallis and others in getting it out, had pushed the battle on to the next stage.

The case was still fraught with difficulties: many of the sub-postmasters might be barred from making civil claims, given statutory time limitations; they had willingly signed up to their contracts; some had pleaded guilty to offences; and the forensic evidence was relatively sparse at this stage. But what Roll had revealed about remote tampering with accounts, coupled with Second Sight's findings about the Post Office's treatment of sub-postmasters, gave enough for Hartley and Green to get a case off the ground.

With a high-powered legal team in place and the line of sub-postmasters behind the pied piper Bates getting longer, Hartley persuaded a litigation funding outfit called Therium to put up the cash. When papers were filed at the High Court in April 2016, *Alan Bates & Others v Post Office Ltd* was born.[15]

Bluffer's guide

Alice Perkins's four-year term as chair had ended the previous July, and she'd been in no mood to seek an extension. To replace her, Neville-Rolfe picked the lusciously bouffant-haired captain of industry Tim Parker. He was a serial chief executive favoured by private equity owners for cost-cutting

---

[12] Justice for Subpostmasters Alliance press release, November 2015, jfsa.org.uk/archive1.html
[13] Email from Richard Callard to Davies and others, November 2015, POL00162786
[14] Wallis, *The Great Post Office Scandal*
[15] Adam Mawardi in *The Lawyer* magazine provides a good account of the lead-up to the group litigation: thelawyer.com/how-justice-done-in-post-office-scandal/

ruthlessness that earned him the nickname "the prince of darkness". He'd also had a short spell several years before as a deputy London mayor under Boris Johnson. At 60, he was picking up a string of prestigious chairmanships, including the National Trust, to go with a longstanding similar position at suitcase company Samsonite. He appeared to be the "strong" chair Neville-Rolfe wanted on this troublesome bit of her patch. He could certainly talk a good chairmanship game, later describing the role as being a "guarantor of good behaviour, transparent management".[16]

Even before Parker arrived at Finsbury Dials in October 2015, he was warned of the Horizon problem. On a call with Neville-Rolfe that summer, she'd asked him to "look at things with fresh eyes" when he arrived,[17] and followed up with an instruction that "on assuming your role as chair, you give this matter your earliest attention".[18] Around the same time, a new Post Office general counsel wrote to Neville-Rolfe proving just what an incalcitrant organisation Parker was expected to bring to heel.

Headhunted to replace Chris Aujard a few months earlier, Jane MacLeod was another Australian financial services lawyer. Vennells clearly liked the sort (having boasted of bringing a "more commercial focus to legal issues" with the recruitment of Aujard).[19] The recent *Panorama* film, MacLeod told the minister, contained "inaccurate statements, drawn selectively from limited information, to create a misleading and damaging impression of how and why Post Office undertook prosecutions".[20] It didn't take the right sort of lawyer long to adopt the Post Office's mantras.

The public evidence against Horizon was, however, mounting. In October, a former sub-postmaster and regular thorn in the Post Office's side called Tim McCormack, who had a blog called *Problems with POL* [Post Office Ltd], received evidence that a glitch known as the "Dalmellington bug", discovered at a branch in Ayrshire, was causing intermittent problems in many others. This belied the official line that, after the couple picked up by Second Sight had been sorted, the system was now bug-free. McCormack wrote to Vennells in strong but prescient terms, informing her of the bug and inviting her to "accept that many of the claimants in the JFSA sage [*sic*] are honest and decent citizens whose lives were destroyed by your organisation... or await the inevitable judicial review where you

---

16 Business West/University of the West of England interview with Parker, 3 May 2018, businesswest.co.uk/blog/qa-tim-parker-chairman-post-office
17 Email from Thompson to Lyons, 6 August 2015, UKGI00005361
18 Letter from Neville-Rolfe to Tim Parker, 10 September 2015, POL00102551
19 Vennells, review of achievements against 2013/14 personal objectives, POL00158149
20 Letter from Jane MacLeod to Neville-Rolfe, 7 September 2015, SUBS0000006

will personally be exposed and perhaps leave yourself open to criminal charges".[21]

Computer Weekly's Karl Flinders then publicly revealed the Dalmellington bug the following month, while the Post Office continued to brush off the impertinent former sub-postmaster. Litigation lawyer Rodric Williams told Van den Bogerd and Davies that McCormack was "a bluffer, who keeps expecting us to march to his tune".[22]

Dozy Parker

Despite his executives' dismissiveness, Tim Parker took business minister Lucy Neville-Rolfe's cue and commissioned yet another review. It would consider "the steps taken in response to various complaints made by sub-postmasters", covering prosecutions, the Horizon system and the support provided by the Post Office. The man for the job was another establishment silk – former Treasury first counsel, or top government civil law adviser, Jonathan Swift QC.

The barrister spent a few weeks surveying the gruesome history, largely informed by the Post Office, and in February 2016 was due to present his findings to Parker. Neville-Rolfe was briefed, misleadingly, that things were looking good. A minute of a meeting between Parker and Neville-Rolfe recorded the chairman telling her that Swift "had found no systemic problem". Parker – with all the foresight of Richard Callard pooh-poohing Alan Bates's legal action – was also said to have "thought the issue might have passed it [*sic*] peak interest".[23]

Within Swift's report itself, however, were some damning conclusions. On the Post Office's prosecutorial tactics, he said: "The allegation that [the Post Office] has effectively bullied [sub-postmasters] into pleading guilty to offences by unjustifiably overloading the charge sheet is a stain on the character of the business."[24] He called for a legal review to determine whether this tactic undermined convictions and, if it did, for all the relevant cases to be re-examined. The eminent silk was getting dangerously close to the dark heart of the matter.

On the Horizon IT system, Swift had picked up on *Computer Weekly's* report of the Dalmellington bug and found that it was a "generic" defect that had cropped up at 112 branches over five years. Then he had comments on

---

21 Email from Tim McCormack to Vennells, 14 October 2015, POL00117614
22 Email from Rodric Williams to Van den Bogerd and others, 15 October 2015, POL00117614
23 Note of meeting with Parker, 26 January 2016, UKGI00006482
24 Jonathan Swift, *Concerning the Steps Taken in Response to Various Complaints Made by Sub-postmasters*, 8 February 2016, POL00030452

the matter of remote access to branch accounts. This clearly could occur "without the need for acceptance by the [sub-postmaster]", if only for balancing transactions aimed at correcting errors. Deloitte's Project Zebra findings on this point and findings it had made in 2014 on the use of "fake" digital signatures "pose real issues" for the Post Office, said Swift. It was "incumbent" on the Post Office to commission further research on the use of this facility.[25]

This wasn't the anodyne result that the minister had been told to expect, which made the next phase of the ongoing cover-up all the more shocking. Post Office lawyer Jane MacLeod had previously written to Parker that "we propose that Jonathan [Swift] will provide you with a legally privileged report... It is not our intention that this report would be made public."[26] Marking anything contentious as "legally privileged" – even when it wasn't – was a time-honoured Post Office trick, dating back to some 2011 legal advice that Angela van den Bogerd had misconstrued. It had become a widespread understanding that calling a document "legally privileged" was more or less self-fulfilling. Swift's report, which wasn't legal advice on proceedings, did not necessarily have this status. But calling it "legally privileged" provided the perfect excuse for Parker not to share it with Neville-Rolfe.

Instead of sending the report, Parker signed off a bland letter to Neville-Rolfe at the ministry, drafted by MacLeod and rubber-stamped by Swift himself. The chair said he would get another barrister to look into the charging practices (but made no mention of the "stain" on the Post Office's record). On the all-important question of remote access, Parker told Neville-Rolfe that further work was under way "to address suggestions that branch accounts might have been remotely altered without complainants' knowledge".[27] Again, though, no mention about this presenting "real issues" for the Post Office – which a minister responsible for the Post Office might have wanted to know about.

Parker didn't even share Swift's review with his own board, again taking MacLeod's erroneous advice that legal privilege prevented this. At the January 2016 board meeting, Paula Vennells would merely tell directors, according to her speaking notes, that Swift's report "sets out a limited number of recommendations and [the Post Office] will, where possible, take these forward".[28] As ever, though, the purpose would not be to get to the truth

---
25 Ibid
26 Email from MacLeod to Tim Parker, 30 October 2015, POL00102649
27 Letter from Parker to Neville-Rolfe, 4 March 2016, POL00024913
28 Vennells, speaking notes for board meeting, 22 January 2016, POL00158304

but "to demonstrate the highest possible standards of rigour and fairness in the handling of the Horizon related complaints". Vennells hadn't seen the report either, but was still happy to present the distorted summary. It was on-message, which was all that really mattered.

The supposedly strong new chairman hadn't questioned any of the substandard advice he was given, or sought other ways to ensure that those who needed to know Swift's serious findings did so. Far from guaranteeing good behaviour, he'd been complicit in yet more dire corporate conduct.

Privileged position

Once Alan Bates had filed his High Court claim in April 2016, the Post Office could conveniently deploy his legal action to its own advantage.

Bond Dickinson's Andy Parsons wrote to the barrister brought in to lead the fight against Bates, Anthony de Garr Robinson QC, telling him that "the Post Office are looking to us (and quite frankly you with your magic QC seal!) to give them some reasons for why Tim [Parker] completing the [Swift] recommendations would be ill advised". Robinson initially gave him short shrift. "I'm not here to provide political cover," he replied, before adding more helpfully, "but I am concerned that the client should protect its interests as a defendant to this substantial piece of litigation."[29] He suggested that the investigations recommended by Swift continue under the aegis of the litigation against Bates. Parsons thought that the "critical point is preserving privilege and the risk of TP [Parker] doing further potentially unprivileged work".[30] This, he believed, gave "a good enough reason to shut TP down". The Post Office's legal adviser clearly thought the law could be used to prevent the Post Office chairman from doing his job.

A couple of weeks later Parsons over-egged this discussion and told the Post Office that the QC's *"very strong advice"* was that "Mr Parker's review should cease immediately". Ongoing investigations should be "overseen exclusively by Post Office's legal team… so to maximise the prospect of asserting privilege over this work and protect[ing] against the risk that material related to these actions could be disclosed".[31] Information about the subjects that should have been investigated – the remote access and the doubled-up charges of theft/false accounting – would in fact have been disclosable. But by placing it all in the litigation lawyers' hands, the Post Office would be able to pretend that it wasn't. A report later produced by the Deloitte consultants,

---
29 Email from Anthony de Garr Robinson to Parsons, 8 June 2016, POL00242402
30 Email from Parsons to Robinson, 8 June 2016, POL00242402
31 Letter from Bond Dickinson to Post Office, 21 June 2016, POL00006601

titled "Bramble" and giving documentary proof of remote access without sub-postmaster knowledge, was accordingly hidden while the Post Office continued to deny this was possible.³²

The "fresh eyes" that Baroness Neville-Rolfe had asked for a year earlier had turned into blind ones. The Post Office's special blend of wilful incuriosity, cynicism and indifference to the sub-postmasters' plight had produced yet another entry in the long annals marked "cover-up".

32 Deloitte, Bramble draft report, 3 October 2017, POL00028070

13

ALL OUT LAW

Alan Bates gets his day in court, while the Post Office and Fujitsu plumb new depths to deny justice

IF Alan Bates's legal claims could be neutralised, the Post Office's containment strategy might still just about work. The mediation scheme had been killed. Those who had been prosecuted would have to persuade a Criminal Cases Review Commission with a dispiriting track record, and then the Court of Appeal, that their convictions after guilty pleas should be re-opened. Dozens had already registered with the CCRC, but the Post Office still held most of the cards and it would be a tough game to win. The hundreds of miscarriages of justice inflicted on others who had not come forward and the thousands of unfair civil and disciplinary actions would get lost in the mists of time.

The further Bates made it along the tortuous litigation road, the more this picture might change in the sub-postmasters' favour. So, from the moment he filed the claim in April 2016, the Post Office began using all its powers to frustrate him. It would rely heavily on its lawyers Bond Dickinson, led by Andy Parsons and in the conflicted position of defending its own conduct over more than a decade. (The firm, then called Bond Pearce, had, for example, been instrumental in ruining Lee Castleton, one of the claimants.)

After months of bad-tempered correspondence between Bond Dickinson and Bates's lawyers, Freeths, the High Court convened in January 2017 to consider the case for a "group litigation order" (GLO). The legal mechanism, which allowed multiple claimants with similar interests to pursue their cause through a single action, had been available since the turn of the century. It had previously been used by litigants ranging from victims of asbestos poisoning to multinational companies seeking to overturn tax avoidance laws. Signatories to GLO number 97, The Post Office Group Litigation, were seeking redress for "shortfalls in branch accounts" being "inappropriately attributed to them", and for the ensuing consequences.[1]

---

1 gov.uk/government/publications/group-litigation-orders/list-of-group-litigation-orders

The hearing didn't start well for the Post Office. Written skirmishing had unearthed the hitherto denied possibility of remote access (regardless of what Richard Roll had said on television). Patrick Green QC read out correspondence from the Post Office that acknowledged Fujitsu's ability to access branches, "principally designed to allow errors caused by a technical issue in Horizon to be corrected".[2] He pointed out the transparent inconsistency with previous statements. When the group litigation order was formally granted in March, Team Bates was one-nil up.

The plan from there was to break the case down into manageable chunks, with a series of separate trials. The first would be on certain issues that were common to the eventual 555 claimants. These centred on their contract and treatment by the Post Office. That trial would be followed by one about the Horizon IT system, and then further trials, as necessary, to deal with any damages and other issues.

GLO in the dark

What was always going to be a long slog got ground down almost immediately, as the lawyers racked up chargeable hours on unproductive arguments. When the judge presiding over the case, Mr Justice Fraser, surveyed progress in November 2017, the ex-Royal Marine gave m'learned friends a thorough dressing-down. He reeled off a litany of failings, "more or less equally on both sides", including "refusing to disclose obviously relevant documents".[3] In an especially tawdry episode, which emerged only a few years later, a Bond Dickinson lawyer sent an email, approved by Andy Parsons, to the Post Office about disclosing its investigations guidelines. "Although we may face some criticism later on," she said, "we are proposing to try and suppress the guidelines for as long as possible."[4]

This was attritional warfare, which suited a state-backed institution in a fight against claimants whose commercial funders, like a poker player with a limited kitty, would not be able to up the stakes forever. In fact, this style of combat appeared to be central to the Post Office's strategy. Shortly before Fraser's ticking-off, Bond Dickinson had prepared a paper for a "litigation steering group", chaired by Post Office group strategy director Tom Moran and including lawyer Rodric Williams (by now promoted to the revealingly titled role of head of legal, dispute resolution and brand), his boss Jane MacLeod and Andy Parsons. "We believe the better solution is to try to force the claimants into a collective position where they will either abandon the claims

---

2 Bond Dickinson, note on remote access, 21 July 2016, POL00243366
3 Mr Justice Fraser, *Bates v Post Office* Judgment No.1, 10 November 2017
4 Email from Amy Prime to Rodric Williams, 10 May 2016, POL00038852

or seek a reasonable settlement," wrote the law firm. The sub-postmasters were "financially supported by Freeths (whose fees are at least partially conditional on winning), a third party funder and insurers". All of these would "adopt a cold, logical assessment of whether they will get a pay-out".[5] One strategic option was to "stretch out the litigation process so to increase costs in the hope that the claimants, and more particularly their litigation funder, decide that it is too costly… and give up".[6] This last one was not recommended in the paper – but it gave an insight into the thinking in the Post Office legal war room. As did an email from Andy Parsons to Rodric Williams around the same time. "My witness statement has really annoyed them," he wrote – no doubt because it was 237 pages long. "This is good – the more time they waste on side correspondence the less time they are spending on important matters!"[7]

Thanks to such attitudes, another year rolled by before the first trial could begin. Ahead of this, Mr Justice Fraser read the riot act once again. "I have now had a total of 10 separate interlocutory [procedural] hearings with these parties in a 12 month period prior to the trial of even the first issues," he told the lawyers. "The legal advisers for the parties regularly give the appearance of taking turns to outdo their opponents in terms of lack of cooperation". It was "behaviour from an earlier era".[8] The lowest games were being played by the Post Office's side. It was seeking to have swathes of evidence thrown out, including 160 paragraphs of written testimony from the "lead claimants" whose experiences were to be considered in the first trial. Much was Alan Bates's own evidence. Fraser suspected that the Post Office was "simply attempting to restrict evidence for public relations reasons" and rejected the ploy. Its approach – which went as far as failing to disclose what it knew about something as important as the "known error logs" maintained by Fujitsu – was "aggressive and, literally, dismissive". The court, said Fraser, was "not a marketing or PR department for any litigant, and the principle of open justice is an important one". Not to the Post Office, it wasn't.

Common people

The threat to the Post Office from the litigation was so severe – or was cynically claimed to be so severe – that, in his opening submission for the "Common Issues" trial, its new lead counsel, David Cavender QC, painted an apocalyptic picture in the event of defeat. "If [the claimants] were right in the broad thrust of their case," he said, "this would represent an existential threat to Post Office's

---

5 Bond Dickinson, note for steering group meeting on Post Office group litigation, 11 September 2017, POL00006380
6 Bond Dickinson, litigation strategy options, 11 September 2017, POL00006379
7 Email from Andy Parsons to Williams, 16 October 2017, POL00041509
8 Fraser, *Bates v Post Office* Judgment No.2, 17 October 2018

ability to continue to carry on its business throughout the UK in the way it presently does."⁹ A 360-year-old national institution was, possibly, at stake.

In the Rolls Building outpost of the High Court, over 15 days in November and December 2018, the litigation became, for the sub-postmasters, a fight to expose the realities of dealing with the Horizon system and their Post Office masters. For the Post Office, it was an exercise in denying it. But the six sub-postmasters who entered the witness box as test cases – three chosen by the claimants, three by the Post Office – proved to be exactly what it had long refused to accept they were: straightforward business people who had been appallingly treated. Witnesses for the Post Office, by contrast, were as obstructive and evasive as their lawyers had already been.

At the heart of the trial was the sub-postmaster contract and whether it was being respected, which brought in matters including: the adequacy of their training; how they were treated when they experienced shortfalls; the help they received when they faced difficulties; and the consequences of shortfalls. Such matters underpinned the complaints of all the 555 claimants, whether they went on to be prosecuted, suspended, sacked or just pursued for supposed debts.

Cavender and his team sought to discredit the sub-postmasters. Bates, for example, wasn't to be trusted because he was a "campaigner" who had "convinced himself no doubt that what he is saying is true". Parts of his evidence, said the silk, were "nonsensical".[10] But Bates and the other sub-postmaster witnesses had carefully set out their cases, making it abundantly clear how they had all been ruined by an unfair contract, cruelly and incorrectly interpreted by the Post Office. Its witnesses affected ignorance of this. The most senior, Paula Vennells's henchwoman Angela van den Bogerd, could find no space in her lengthy written evidence for information about problems experienced with Horizon. She had to be presented with multiple documents she had herself written that acknowledged the sub-postmasters' difficulties.

When Mr Justice Fraser came to weigh up the credibility of the trial's witnesses for his judgment, he had no difficulty deciding whom to believe. For the Post Office, Van den Bogerd had been "extraordinarily conscious of the need to protect the Post Office's position in the case generally, which given her very close involvement in the Horizon problems with [sub-postmasters] over the years, effectively meant protecting her own position too, which led to a disregard for factual accuracy".[11] She had "sought to obfuscate matters,

---

9 *Bates v Post Office*, Post Office written closing submissions, 25 October 2017, WBON0001366
10 Transcripts of hearings in the Common Issues trial, archived on Nick Wallis's Post Office Trial website: postofficetrial.com/2019/03/common-issues-trial-transcript-day-14.html
11 Fraser, *Bates v Post Office* Judgment No.3, "Common Issues", 15 March 2019

and mislead me". Another senior Post Office official, contracts manager John Breeden, gave "inaccurate factual evidence" delivered "through a PR-prism". Down the pecking order, a more junior officer was "extremely nervous about giving evidence" unhelpful to his employer – again hinting at the Orwellian internal culture. The Post Office's witnesses, in general, "remained steadfastly committed, in their collective psyche, to the Post Office party view". They gave Fraser "the impression that they simply cannot allow themselves to consider the possibility that the Post Office may be wrong, as the consequences of doing so are too significant to contemplate".

The sub-postmasters had less to fear from the truth coming out and their testimonies were correspondingly more believable. Fraser's endorsement of the "honest, thorough and reliable" Alan Bates in particular, who had been "subjected to a sustained attack" by the Post Office, couldn't have been more ringing. It also captured *why* the Post Office had fought him tooth and claw for so long, and bears repeating:

> *The Post Office subjectively might view him as unreasonable or stubborn, as he simply refuses to let this matter drop… Mr Bates has, from about December 2000 onwards, proved himself to be a considerable irritant to the Post Office so far as the Horizon affair is concerned. He was an irritant to them in 2001 when he simply refused, point blank, to pay the £1,000 odd demanded of him (that sum ultimately being written off by the Post Office the following year). He had undoubtedly continued to be an irritant to the Post Office from then on… He is persistent and no doubt possesses what might be termed staying power. There was nothing unreasonable or stubborn in his evidence before me, and none of the pejorative terms deployed by the Post Office to describe his evidence are justified, in my judgment. The Post Office must have decided to attack him because the whole case of the Post Office requires an assumption or acceptance that the predominant, or only, cause of shortfalls is fault (or worse) on the part of [sub-postmasters]… If it were otherwise, the Post Office edifice would run the risk of collapse.*[12]

Oppressive conditions

Two decades after the scandal had begun, Mr Justice Fraser's judgment on 15 March 2019 showed why Alan Bates had been right to think the only way to get near the truth would be through the courts.

---

12 Ibid

The Post Office's contracts with sub-postmasters were "relational", decided Fraser, as opposed to just business deals between entirely independent parties, and therefore demanded each work with the other in good faith. (Given how Vennells and others routinely talked about valuing sub-postmasters as "our people", it was ironic that the Post Office had contested this.) But consistently the Post Office had not dealt fairly. One of the test claimants, Mohammad Sabir – sacked from running his branch in Cottingley, West Yorkshire, over a £5,000 scratchcard deficiency in 2009 – stood out as an example. The Post Office had told him that "under the contract for services you are responsible for all losses occurring as a result of the acts or omissions of yourself [sic] or your assistants". This was wrong, since negligence or error on the part of the sub-postmaster needed to be shown. There could be "no excuse, in my judgment", said Fraser, "for an entity such as the Post Office, to mis-state, in such clearly express terms, in letters that threaten legal action, the extent of the contractual obligation". The reason it did so, he judged, "must have been to lead the recipients to believe that they had absolutely no option but to pay the sums demanded". This was "oppressive behaviour".[13]

A sample of such oppressive actions to emerge from just six test cases also included: not allowing sub-postmasters legal representation in meetings at which they were suspended; instructions to temporary sub-postmasters, brought in to replace suspended ones, that they should destroy documents; and threatening friends of sub-postmasters providing support at interviews with prosecution under the Official Secrets Act.

To the vindictiveness was added absurdity. Another trick was for the Post Office to remove a sub-postmaster's records while investigating, then refuse to return them. The Post Office's defence to this was that "there is no evidence produced or referenced by the report [in the sample case] to support the position that data being withheld has prejudiced a [sub-postmaster] in any way". The sub-postmaster couldn't look at the records, in other words, so couldn't know if the details would have helped them. The reasoning was, said Fraser, "more akin to that in a nonsense rhyme by Lewis Carroll".

For all her disingenuousness, Van den Bogerd did make one important admission with far-reaching legal consequences. She accepted that, when a sub-postmaster with a branch shortfall "settled centrally" – acknowledged the shortfall without funding it directly from his or her own pocket – this was treated as a debt owed to the Post Office (triggering the ordeal to come). Invariably, however, shortfalls had either been disputed or simply not

---
13 Ibid

understood by the sub-postmaster, who had generally queried them with the hopeless helpline. These were thus not, judged Fraser, "settled accounts". The Post Office had been chasing debts that it wasn't owed.

This, concluded Fraser, meant that the question of a sub-postmaster "deliberately rendering a false account… in relation to any such branch trading statement for such a period therefore simply does not, in my judgment, arise". The Post Office's false-accounting prosecution strategy, the foundation for its criminal war on sub-postmasters, was built on sand.

It was beginning to look like Cavender might not have been entirely wrong when he'd called the case an "existential threat" to the Post Office. Invoking it did not impress Fraser, who thought that conjuring "dire consequences to national business should their case *not* be preferred is not helpful". It looked to him like "an attempt to put the court *in terrorem*" – scared of doing its job.[14] The Post Office legal team didn't appreciate the Latin bollocking, and would soon be out for revenge on the forthright judge.

Orders of the Brown Nose

Away from the courtroom, the groupthink that Fraser was picking up on had blinded executives and officials to how the trial was going. At the end of 2018, with the first trial having aired their malpractice but before the judgment, they were given a cause for celebration. The courtroom revelations weren't going to depress the mood.

On the recommendation of business department officials and signed off by permanent secretary Alex Chisholm, Paula Vennells was awarded a CBE in the New Year's honours list "for services to the Post Office and to charity"[15] (she was also a trustee of the charity that owned the *Church Times*). It wasn't just routine recognition for running a national institution; it was also testament to how the scandal had been "contained" to date.

When news of the CBE broke, the gushing began. No sooner had Vennells sent her effusive email to her PR man Mark Davies – "your call was always the right one: guiding us through stormy waters" – than her colleagues were lathering on the praise. Chair Tim Parker waxed about how "she cares deeply about the business, its people".[16] Tom Cooper, a former investment banker who had replaced Richard Callard as the government's man on the Post Office board in March 2018, must have been in on the award. "Great news isn't it," he agreed. "I'm glad it has been confirmed. Paula thoroughly deserves

---
14 Ibid
15 New Year Honours List, *London Gazette*, 29 December 2018
16 Post Office press release, 28 December 2018

the recognition." Angela van den Bogerd's contribution was perhaps most revealing of the Post Office culture. After one unidentified official emailed the "truly inspirational woman" being gonged, Van den Bogerd followed up with a note saying this was "a clear indication of how much [the colleague in question] has grown in recent years". Sycophancy, like toeing the party line, was a mark of ability in the Post Office.

One man who didn't share in the well-wishing was the reliably difficult campaigner and part-time Nostradamus, Tim McCormack. The former sub-postmaster wrote to Vennells again, pointing out her "total lack of effort in trying to personally understand and investigate the most alarming issues". If she accepted the award, she would "ultimately have to embarrass the Queen and probably more importantly your family when it is taken from you or you feel humbled enough to return it". Mark Davies, the PR polar opposite of the blunt but on-the-money McCormack, told Vennells that "media sentiment" was still fine, which was what mattered. McCormack was "really representing a very small minority".[17]

Mind the accountability gap

Fraser's eviscerating Common Issues judgment posed the question of how a major public body could have incurred such a humiliation.

A large part of the answer lay in the structures used to shield those in power, who might be held democratically accountable, from the truth – and exclude them from decision-making. Shortly before the Common Issues trial, the business department permanent secretary Alex Chisholm had (perhaps belatedly, given that he'd been in the job for two years) argued for settling the case. But he was fobbed off and had no position in the boardroom from which to shape decisions.

Above him, the postal services brief had passed through two pairs of junior ministerial hands since Baroness Neville-Rolfe had moved on at the end of 2016. In the summer of 2018, it ended up with Kelly Tolhurst MP. She was consistently told there was nothing to worry about and that *Alan Bates & Others v Post Office Ltd* was an entirely operational matter for the Post Office.

The buffer between the ministers and the Post Office, the Shareholder Executive, meanwhile, did little more than impede the flow of information in both directions. Its latest representative on the Post Office board, Tom Cooper, had voiced some government qualms about the handling of the *Bates*

---

17 Information obtained under FoI by Tim Bush, provided to *Private Eye*

litigation. But his influence was limited to getting his red felt-tip out to colour in "risk registers" held by UK Government Investments (as the Shareholder Executive had become in 2016), which nobody paid any attention to. Such was the resistance in the Post Office to the government learning anything about the *Bates* litigation that briefings to the main board (on which Cooper sat) from the litigation committee shaping the strategy (on which he didn't) were kept verbal. This decision, taken on advice from the now renamed Womble Bond Dickinson, left Cooper with little to pass on to his ministerial masters.[18]

The case had also given a more rarefied, if exaggerated, excuse for the government to be kept away from the scandal: the constitutional principle that the executive shouldn't interfere in the judicial process. So Greg Clark, the business secretary with ultimate responsibility for the Post Office since 2016, had next to no involvement in the scandal. He already had a dim view of the Post Office, and of the "impudent" Angela van den Bogerd in particular, from previous experience helping a sub-postmaster in his Tunbridge Wells constituency.[19] But still, as secretary of state, he followed orders not to interfere.

When the Common Issues judgment came in, showing serious misconduct from an arm of the state, this political and operational separation had to be bridged. Clark was briefed by Kelly Tolhurst and Tom Cooper on a result that the junior minister called "close to the worst-case scenario".[20] Cooper, according to Clark's notes, "indicated that there are both legal and tactical reasons for the Post Office to appeal and that it is most likely they will do so". This incensed the secretary of state, who made it plain to Cooper that "his primary objective is to see justice done".

The Post Office, however, was on a different track entirely. It was acting as an aggressive litigator in a commercial dispute, not as a public body with the fates of hundreds of citizens in its hands. General counsel Jane MacLeod had confided in Cooper before the judgment that any reversal would automatically be appealed.[21] As Fraser remarked in his judgment, it was trying to make "this intractable dispute, as difficult and expensive as it can".[22] Against opponents with limited funds, that's what tactics demanded.

Whether or not the government of the day wanted to see justice done was irrelevant. "Arm's length" meant "law unto itself".

---

18 Tom Cooper, inquiry evidence, 10 July 2024
19 Greg Clark, inquiry evidence, 25 July 2024
20 Email from Clark to Cooper and others, 16 March 2019, UKGI00009213
21 Cooper, inquiry evidence, 10 July 2024
22 Fraser, *Bates v Post Office* Judgment No.3

Bad losers

The Post Office legal team, smarting from Fraser's judgment, decided that the judge had overstepped the mark, especially on the central question of the "relational contract". Some of his harsher criticisms of the organisation's conduct they found unduly emotive. This could, they speculated, give grounds for an appeal on the basis of unfairness and bias (as well as on drier legal points). The Post Office lawyers had in fact misjudged the legal question, focusing narrowly on the terms of the contract and missing the all-important context. But it was more comforting to blame the judge.

If they were to go down this highly controversial route, effectively questioning a judge's integrity, they would have no option but to make the point that he was not fit to hear the subsequent stages of the case on the same grounds. This in turn meant trying to get the judge thrown off the case, or "recused". To test whether this was feasible, the Post Office turned to a couple of the legal establishment's grander figures, who happened to be found at the same 1 Essex Court chambers as its counsel David Cavender QC.

First, Lord (David) Neuberger, recent former president of the Supreme Court, no less, opined that there were reasonable grounds for a recusal application and that it was necessary if the Post Office was to claim that Fraser had been unfair. But, as a former judge, Neuberger couldn't act in such a case. Jane MacLeod turned to Lord (Anthony) Grabiner QC, whom she'd dealt with in a previous job and thought would be "robust".[23] (He wasn't held in universal regard. A committee of MPs looking at his conduct as chairman of the holding company of the collapsed BHS retail group not long beforehand had said his performance "represented the apogee of weak corporate governance" and that he had been "content to provide a veneer of establishment credibility to the group".)[24]

Grabiner keenly agreed with Neuberger, going as far as saying that the Post Office had a "duty" to make the recusal application.[25] The decision, however, was one for the Post Office board. This now had a different look about it. Vennells, who had just hit 60, had decided to get out while she was still, just about, ahead – to move on to the non-executive circuit, starting with positions at the Cabinet Office and Imperial College Healthcare Trust. Finance director Alisdair Cameron, who had been signing the ever-larger cheques for the fight against the sub-postmasters (£23m by March 2019), was standing in for her.

When the board met to vote on Neuberger's and Grabiner's views, the men whose job it was to bring the broader perspective to key decisions – chairman

---

23 Jane MacLeod, witness statement, 24 May 2024, WITN10010100
24 Commons work and pensions select committee, 22 July 2016
25 Note of conference with Post Office legal team and Grabiner QC, 18 March 2019, POL00006792

Tim Parker and government representative Tom Cooper – ducked out. Parker, whose relevance was dimming just as his role became more important (he'd reduced his input from six to two days per month), recused himself on the tenuous grounds that he was also chairman of the Courts and Tribunals Service, a body that administers the courts but isn't part of the judicial process. Cooper dropped out because the government that he represented should not interfere in the justice system. This looked to be another overstretch of the constitutional principle; deciding whether to launch a legal case was in a different category from influencing the judicial process. But it meant that the views of ministers Clark and Tolhurst, both opposed to the idea of claiming the judge was biased, were ignored. With not much more than the esteemed counsels' views and their lawyers' injured pride to go on, the board duly approved the operation to de-bench Fraser.

Fraser had already been presiding over the next stage of *Bates v Post Office* for a couple of weeks when Cavender casually dropped the recusal application into his court on 21 March 2019. The "Horizon Issues" trial was immediately suspended and the judge went away to consider whether he'd been biased in the previous one. After a fractious hearing a couple of weeks later, he returned to explain, over 302 paragraphs, why he had not.[26]

The next inevitable step for the Post Office, with taxpayers' money no object, was to appeal this decision. But not before a touch of lawyerly bitching suggesting it was all getting a bit personal. Grabiner remarked to Neuberger that Fraser was showing "Smith characteristics" – a reference to a judge accused of bias in a case involving British Airways, during which the beak had moaned about his luggage going missing.[27] Cavender, meanwhile, chose to cast aspersions on Fraser's relationship with the judge who would decide if the appeal could proceed, Lord Justice (Peter) Coulson. Fraser and Coulson were respectively head and past head of the specialist Technology and Construction Court (TCC). "It looks very much like this is what [Mr Justice Fraser] set up in advance", Cavender wrote, "with his mate the former head of the TCC – unless you believe in co-incidences."[28] At one point, Alisdair Cameron had to tell Cavender to tone down his language about "this awful judge".[29] Neuberger poured cold water on Cavender's conspiracy theory, but it said much about the paranoia in Team Post Office that senior legal figures were venturing such allegations against respected judges.

On 9 May 2019, Lord Justice Coulson refused permission for the appeal.

---

26 Fraser, *Bates v Post Office* Judgment No. 4, "Recusal Application", 9 April 2019
27 Lord (Anthony) Grabiner, inquiry evidence, 11 June 2024
28 Email from David Cavender QC to Parsons, 12 April 2019, WBON0000172
29 Alisdair Cameron, *What Went Wrong?*, draft for discussion, 19 November 2020, POL00175235

Of the 109 paragraphs of Fraser's Common Issues judgment that Grabiner had cited as biased, Coulson found that none were. Grabiner's arguments were "misconceived", "untenable", "without substance" and other versions of nonsense. But the verdict was delivered more in sorrow than anger. It was "a great pity", said the Law Lord, that the recusal appeal had delayed the Horizon issues trial. It "could have led to the collapse of [it] altogether" and he could "understand why the [sub-postmasters] originally submitted on 21 March that that was its purpose".[30] An appeal court judge appeared to suspect the Post Office's ulterior motive was to avoid justice. At least now it was failing to do so with increasing regularity. The Horizon Issues trial could resume.

Taint by numbers

The 2018/19 financial year, culminating in the March Common Issues defeat, was a shocker even by the Post Office's plummeting standards. So, when it came to rewarding those responsible, the handouts were almost as insulting to sub-postmasters as the litigation tactics used against them.

Executives led by Paula Vennells were docked just 20 percent of one element of their pay (a short-term incentive payment) because of the litigation's "impact on the business". For Vennells, that was a loss of £36,000. But her "long-term incentive" payment went up by £50,000 on the previous year to the maximum possible, despite her having wreaked such long-term damage on the institution. Overall, her pay stayed at £718,000 – the peak of an eight-year tenure at the top when the Post Office had obstructed justice and misled sub-postmasters, courts, parliament and public on a grand scale. (And, although nobody knew it at the time, the executive who might have merited a Worst Courtroom Witness of the Year award, Angela van den Bogerd, was also given a bonus.) Since becoming chief executive in 2012, over seven years in scandal and cover-up, Vennells bagged bonuses worth £2.95m and total pay of £4.95m.[31] Equating to several hundred pounds per victim, these were among corporate Britain's better rewards for failure.

Vennells's riches were largely determined by the financial returns of the Post Office, which helpfully counted the growing legal bills as "exceptional" and thus not a hit to day-to-day business performance. The accounts measuring the results were vouched for by auditor EY (until 2013, Ernst & Young), which didn't once express any doubts relating to the mounting threats from the Horizon scandal. This was despite the confidential 2011 "management letter" highlighting concerns over remote access, and despite Ernst & Young partner

---

30 Lord Justice Coulson, order made in *Bates v Post Office*, 10 May 2019
31 Post Office Ltd accounts 2012/13-2018/19, Companies House

Angus Grant having told Post Office chair Alice Perkins privately of "real risks" and about allegations of a "systems problem" from poor-quality IT – which it had known about since the turn of the century.

Since then, following Second Sight's investigations – and others – the risks and likely costs had loomed larger still. Because the Horizon system was not just a source of woe for the sub-postmasters but also the foundation of the Post Office's corporate accounting, the implications were serious. Money held in suspense accounts, for example – which might well have been payment for a false Horizon-generated branch shortfall and thus belong to a sub-postmaster – was appropriated to the Post Office's bottom line after three years.[32]

EY was required to consider risks of "material misstatement due to fraud or error". Yet in the lengthy annual reports of risks facing the business, it didn't mention anything related to Horizon, such as the liability this legalised theft might be creating, or the mounting chances of huge compensation bills. Only when EY's successor as auditor, PwC, signed the 2018/19 accounts in September 2019 – after Fraser's Common Issues judgment – did a cursory mention appear. If the beancounters had addressed the IT elephant in the accounting room earlier, pointing out the potential impact on the bottom line – which the Post Office really understood – its board and government shareholder would have been forced to pay attention. The cover-up of the scandal might well have been foreshortened.

IT hits the fan

By the time the Horizon Issues trial restarted in early June 2019, Alisdair Cameron had made changes to the legal team whose hyper-aggressive approach had proved disastrous. Out went the general counsel, Jane MacLeod, who had led it. Womble Bond Dickinson was also given the boot. It, too, had doubled down after the Common Issues trial, ignored its essential truths and blamed the judge. In the firm's place came financial-scandal veterans Herbert Smith Freehills.

None of the lawyers, old or new, evidently persuaded the Fujitsu staff who appeared as the Post Office's witnesses in the Horizon Issues trial to present an honest picture of the IT system. Mr Justice Fraser, unmoved, sat in court 26 of the Rolls Building over the spring and summer of 2019 and listened sceptically as Fujitsu's people took their turn to fudge and fib, sticking to the official Horizon story in the face of a wall of evidence disproving it. (The handful of witnesses from the Post Office now behaved themselves. Even Van den Bogerd, Fraser would later say, showed "a more realistic approach to the accuracy of her evidence".)[33]

---

32 For more details, see Ron Warmington, witness statement, 18 June 2024, WITN01050200
33 Fraser, *Bates v Post Office* Judgment No. 6, "Horizon Issues", 16 December 2019

The principal witness from Fujitsu was its "chief architect" on the Post Office account, Torstein Godeseth. It would have been Gareth Jenkins, had the Post Office not kept him away for fear of the trial becoming "an investigation of his role in [Seema Misra's] and other criminal cases".[34] Still, the shadow of the "distinguished engineer" hung unmistakably over the courtroom throughout the company men's evidence.

Godeseth got off to a poor pre-trial start, providing three written witness statements that Fraser would describe as "wholly misleading". He'd overlooked details of the Horizon system's many flaws from the outset, and on crucial questions concerning bugs in the system had completely misrepresented their significance. Particularly important was the Callendar Square bug that had been raised and dismissed in Lee Castleton's case in 2006/07 and had been said by Gareth Jenkins to be "irrelevant" in Seema Misra's in 2010. Godeseth had written that he agreed with this, but in court had to admit that the bug had been far more widespread, affecting scores of branches.

At least Godeseth did go on to give important testimony about Horizon's failings and accept that Fujitsu could remotely access branch accounts – even if he had initially said it couldn't, based on advice from Jenkins. This, Fraser would decide, was "extremely important evidence, both in resolving the Horizon issues, and indeed in the whole group litigation".[35]

Godeseth wasn't the only Fujitsu man voicing Gareth Jenkins's words, although he was the only one who disavowed them. Andy Dunks, the security analyst who had given evidence against Lee Castleton, proved a more faithful ventriloquist's dummy. In his witness statement, he repeated the embarrassingly outdated lines about Horizon's infallibility. Among them was that "at all material times the computer was operating properly or, if not, any respect in which it was not operating properly or was out of operation was not such as to effect [sic] the information held on it". These familiar words were exactly the ones, including the spelling mistake, used by Jenkins in Mrs Misra's and other cases. Yet Dunks denied there was a "party line", leading Mr Justice Fraser later to find he "expressly sought to mislead me". The Fujitsu man did, however, give the game away in one important respect, admitting that when he provided so-called ARQ audit data to Post Office investigators, he wasn't concerned with whether the data was fully accurate. When Bates's barrister Patrick Green QC put it to him that it therefore might not be the "gold standard to compare and investigate anomalies", Dunks agreed: "Possibly not."[36]

---

34 Ibid
35 Ibid
36 Ibid

"Gold standard" had been the description given to the data by the Post Office's external IT expert in the case, a theoretical physicist with a long career at Logica behind him. Even by the variable standards of expert witnesses appearing in Britain's courts in return for a suitable fee, Dr Robert Worden's performance was poor. He, too, relied extensively on what Gareth Jenkins had told him, and dismissed the sub-postmasters' experiences. Perhaps the low point of his evidence was some execrable statistical analysis suggesting that, given the rarity of bugs and the chances of them producing shortfalls, the probability of the affected sub-postmasters' problems being caused by them was "two in 10 million".[37] This was like finding a lottery winner and saying she must be a fraudster because the chances of her numbers coming up are so remote.

As Fraser prepared his judgment on this shambles towards the end of the year, appeal court judge Lord Justice Coulson reappeared with a timely reminder of how the Post Office weaponised the Horizon system. Alisdair Cameron's new legal team, advised by Herbert Smith Freehills, had sought to appeal the Common Issues judgment – albeit, wisely, dropping any claim of unfairness on Fraser's part. Coulson put the new bunch of lawyers back in their place. The application, he said in his judgment on 22 November, was "founded on the premise that the nation's most trusted brand was not obliged to treat their [sub-postmasters] with good faith". The Post Office thought it was "instead entitled to treat them in capricious or arbitrary ways which would not be unfamiliar to a mid-Victorian factory-owner".[38] It was a nice warm-up for the main Horizon verdict, about to come.

Robust decision

The following week, Fraser showed his Horizon Issues judgment to both sides. Its 1,030 withering paragraphs couldn't have been a stronger vindication of what Alan Bates and so many others had been saying for 20 years.

Crucially, found the judge, "it was possible for bugs, errors or defects" to have the potential "to cause apparent or alleged discrepancies or shortfalls", and "all the evidence in the Horizon Issues trial shows… it actually has happened, and on numerous occasions".[39] The Horizon system in place until 2010 "was not remotely robust". Its replacement, Horizon Online, was better but still "its robustness [a term defined over a mere 21 paragraphs] was questionable, and did not justify the confidence placed in it by the Post Office in terms of its accuracy". A handy "Bug Table" listed 29 separate bugs identified over

---

37 Dr Robert Worden, *Bates v Post Office* expert report, 7 December 2018
38 Coulson, *Bates v Post Office* judgment on PTA (permission to appeal), 22 November 2019
39 Fraser, *Bates v Post Office* Judgment No. 6

Horizon's lifetime, from one first seen in 1999 (the "data tree build failure discrepancies" bug) to one emerging in 2017 (the "bureau discrepancies" bug).

The judgment was a catalogue of denunciations of the Post Office, Fujitsu and their witnesses. The former's case amounted to "bare assertions and denials that ignore what has actually occurred". It was "the 21st century equivalent of maintaining that the earth is flat". Internal documents showed the Post Office to be verging on "institutional paranoia". The analysis of its expert, Dr Robert Worden, was "conceptually flawed". Fujitsu was in denial over its software's shortcomings "regardless of evidence to the contrary" and had provided multiple false statements. So secretive had Fujitsu been over the years that the "majority of problems and defects… simply would not have seen the light of day without this group litigation". [40]

When he delivered his judgment publicly a couple of weeks later, Fraser dropped another bombshell. The case had left him with "very grave concerns regarding the veracity of evidence given by Fujitsu employees to other courts in previous proceedings about the known existence of bugs, errors and defects in the Horizon system", both in civil and criminal cases. He was sending his papers to the Director of Public Prosecutions [41]

The Horizon contract may have been worth £100m a year or more to the company, and exposing it would certainly damage what was still one of the UK government's go-to IT suppliers. But it remained remarkable that so many of its staff would mislead the courts to protect their employer. The same defensive and dishonest culture found in the Post Office was mirrored at its IT supplier. Only one of them, however, was required to pay for its sins.

Settle down

Behind the scenes, Alan Bates, James Hartley and Patrick Green QC and their teams had been running the numbers for months. They'd managed to keep the case going past the point that the Post Office might have expected them to run out of cash, but they didn't have a bottomless pit of money. Further trials to translate the victories so far into damages would present a large legal bill too far. With the draft Horizon Issues judgment in hand, they decided now was the time to bank the wins. For the Post Office, haemorrhaging cash wasn't the main problem; it was the flow of reputation-trashing judgments that needed to be staunched. So, ahead of the publication of the latest mauling, the warring parties, with new chief executive Nick Read representing the Post Office, sat down to talk.

Days of haggling concluded with a settlement worth around £58m. Of

---
40 Ibid
41 Fraser, *Bates v Post Office* final hearing, 16 December 2019

this, however, the sub-postmasters would share only £12m. The remaining amount went to their lawyers (£15m), a support fund for immediate hardship (£750,000) and the rest to the litigation funders (£30m). The word was that the financial backers could have taken more under their terms of engagement. But that wouldn't have been a great advertisement for the business model. The Post Office's own costs ran to £43m, making the group litigation a nine-figure debacle for the taxpayer.[42]

At an average £20,000 per sub-postmaster, the payout obviously came nowhere near justice. (Nor, for that matter, would the gross amount before fees – around £100,000 each – have done.) Convicted sub-postmasters, who had their claims stayed pending criminal appeals, were omitted from the settlement, although compensated by the others *ex gratia*. A few considered it a kick in the teeth. Some complained about the absence of transparency. But it was close to the best that could have been achieved from the only process available. Bates secured a 25-point Post Office improvement plan, largely covering the way the Post Office trained and dealt with sub-postmasters, and also ensured that those who had not signed up to the action, many because they had not heard of it in time, would have a route to redress through a Horizon Shortfall Group that the Post Office committed to setting up.[43]

Even more importantly, *Bates & Others v Post Office Ltd* blew the scandal open, proving the culpability of a state-owned body and a major multinational company (one which reported a £700m worldwide profit that year) for an epic national scandal. Getting justice and compensation out of such deep pockets for *all* victims shouldn't, therefore, have required another battle.

"The figure has literally halved just now!"

---

42 committees.parliament.uk/publications/8841/documents/89132/default
43 onepostoffice.co.uk/media/47518/20191210-glo-confidential-settlement-deed-executed-version-redacted_-003.pdf

14

DRAMATIC DEVELOPMENTS

Campaigning sub-postmasters secure a public inquiry;
a TV drama forces government to act; but for too many
the ordeal goes on

THE Horizon Issues trial victory and settlement agreement just before Christmas 2019 provided some much-needed festive hope. "It would seem from the positive discussions with Post Office's new CEO, Nick Read," said Alan Bates, "that there is a genuine desire to move on from these legacy issues and learn lessons from the past."[1] The new boss promised "a reset in our relationship with postmasters".

Moving on would, however, require huge cultural change. The Post Office still employed many of the culprits, including former investigators referred to internally as "the untouchables" and dozens of staff given a "red rating" because of their prior involvement in the scandal.[2] The leadership itself hardly looked up to the task, either. Chairman Tim Parker didn't go in for critical self-reflection, judging that the exposure of the scandal he'd presided over for four years, covering the obstructive and dishonest conduct of the *Bates* litigation, was not a resigning matter. Welcoming Read to "execute the next crucial stage of the Post Office's turnaround into a more efficient, resilient and sustainable business",[3] Parker might as well have added: "Crisis? What crisis?"

Read would later agree that he'd been recruited "to focus on Post Office's commercial future", without any mention of the seismic litigation then still under way.[4] He had the kind of profile that appealed to the semi-detached chairman who recruited him. Both were privately educated sons of army fathers. Read had an MBA, Parker an MSc in business studies. Both had long corporate track records, Read's taking in Vodafone, Tesco and HBOS in the run-up to the 2008 financial crisis. He'd then run retail mutual Nisa for three

---
1 Joint press statement by parties in *Bates v Post Office*, 11 December 2019
2 See, for example, Henry Staunton, inquiry evidence, 1 October 2024
3 Post Office press release, 18 July 2019
4 Nick Read, witness statement, 13 September 2024, WITN00760300

years up to 2017, achieving a degree of commercial success but incurring the wrath of its members with the size of his bonuses.[5]

The new chief executive had arrived at the Post Office in September 2019, fresh from running an obscure and doomed electricity supplier, and set about trying to understand what he'd taken on. For a captain of industry of his vintage, this meant calling on the management consultants (in whose ranks he had served in the late 1990s). Read's preferred outfit was McKinsey, which started by testing the Post Office's "cultural maturity" – ironic, given its antiquated practices – against the consultants' "bespoke organisational health index". The firm set out a plan for "purpose, strategy and growth" that spawned further management initiatives of uncertain value.[6] When it came to the unhappy past, Read found his new colleagues playing down the significance of the devastating Common Issues judgment that had landed six months earlier. They felt, Read would later say, that the High Court finding of an "oppressive" organisation was "a matter for the Operations Team in Chesterfield [home of the Network Business Support Centre] who were conducting an internal review". This didn't look like an organisation ready to face up to the changes it desperately needed to make.

Wise head

The Post Office scandal ran for so long that it created a second generation of victims. While prosecutions based on Horizon evidence had all but ceased in 2013, a further 626 sub-postmasters were suspended over the following five years. (Around three quarters of them were subsequently sacked.)[7] About ten new victims a month, in other words.

One of them was Chris Head, who had become Britain's youngest sub-postmaster in 2006 at the age of 18. He'd been running the post office in West Boldon, near Sunderland, successfully – albeit with small discrepancies he'd funded himself – until shortfalls of tens of thousands began appearing from nowhere in 2014. The following year, he was suspended and pursued through the courts for five years. Chris became one of the 555 signed up to the group litigation and over the following years would, with Batesian persistence, become one of the most eloquent and effective advocates for a proper reckoning with the past and for fair redress.

His first target was a government whose response to the damning *Bates* judgments had been lukewarm at best. Once parliament returned after Boris

---

5 *The Grocer*, 7 October 2017
6 Read, WITN00760300
7 Fraser, *Bates v Post Office* Judgment No.3

Johnson's December 2019 re-election, four days before the Horizon Issues judgment, a new ministerial team dampened sub-postmasters' hopes for a meaningful examination of the scandal. There would be a "new national framework" for sub-postmasters, said jobbing junior minister Lord (Ian) Duncan in February 2020, but not the public inquiry that most wanted and that Mr Justice Fraser's findings demanded.[8]

Until, that was, Chris Head's MP, Kate Osborne, scored a direct hit at prime minister's questions a couple of weeks later. Would the PM, she asked, "assure Chris and others that he will commit to launching an independent inquiry?" Johnson replied, possibly unscripted and to general surprise, that he was "happy to commit to getting to the bottom of the matter in the way that she recommends".[9] While his statements from the despatch box weren't always scrupulous in their accuracy, he had at least put this on the record.

Head intensified his lobbying, delivering a petition to Number 10, calling for a full *public* inquiry. He wasn't heeded. When the latest postal services minister, Paul Scully, made a statement in the Commons in June 2020 to flesh out Boris Johnson's commitment from nearly four (Covid-interrupted) months earlier, the "inquiry" that the PM had endorsed became a "review". This would "understand and acknowledge what went wrong in relation to Horizon" and consider whether the Post Office was living up to its post-*Bates* promises.[10]

Chris Head and fellow campaigners weren't impressed. With an unambitious remit and no powers to compel witnesses or information, this was never going to get to the bottom of what caused the scandal or who was to blame. Bates's JFSA called the set-up a "whitewash" and said it wouldn't co-operate. James (now Lord) Arbuthnot described the review as "inadequate" and remarked that its "terms of reference have been designed to exclude all possibility of blame falling on the government".[11] The response from the government's Lord (Martin) Callanan, that the Post Office "has committed to co-operating fully", showed how pitifully little it had learned about the institution.

Short redress

The other pillar on which something resembling a fair resolution needed to be built, redress, wasn't hopeful either. In May, Scully launched the Historic Shortfall scheme – later renamed the Horizon Shortfall scheme, when sub-postmasters pointed out that this wasn't some annoying problem from the past but very much

---

8 *Hansard*, 4 February 2020
9 *Hansard*, 26 February 2020
10 *Hansard*, 10 June 2020
11 *Hansard*, 18 June 2020

a present struggle. It was drawn up with little input from sub-postmasters and was to be overseen by a "remediation unit" inside the Post Office. Not only was this a conflict of interest to kick off with – the body that had created the victims was now responsible for their redress – but 35 of those in the unit carried the "red rating" from their past roles. The scheme's design and operation, meanwhile, were entrusted to Herbert Smith Freehills, the law firm that the Post Office had switched to late in the group litigation process and which Nick Read admitted had "guided" him in the settlement negotiations with Bates.[12]

One document, which would emerge some years later, gave an indication of Herbert Smith Freehills' approach to compensation. In February 2020, the firm's partner Alan Watts had lobbied the Post Office's latest general counsel, Ben Foat, for the discretionary element of its fees on the litigation settlement two months earlier. He boasted of having achieved "a very positive result for Post Office", which "fell towards the lower end" of the possible settlement range. This was thanks to the firm's "quantum analysis which enabled us to negotiate credibly about the true value of the claims" and the use of specialist QCs to "manage the expectations of a volatile claimant group".[13] What they were good at, in other words, was belittling people and minimising payouts.

Those who knew of Herbert Smith Freehills' handiwork in other realms were alarmed by the appointment. The firm had made fortunes from acting for banks in the wake of the financial-crisis. A judge in one case involving RBS had called its £100m fees "staggering".[14] He added: "I'm not saying for a moment that Rolls-Royces aren't expensive to maintain. I'm saying that it would be an odd impetus for the court to give, that you can charge that to the other side." Another example was a review of a notorious loan fraud at the Reading branch of HBOS, for the purpose of compensating victims. This had been so poorly handled that it necessitated a review-of-the-review by a retired judge – whose findings, some time later, prompted Tory backbencher Kevin Hollinrake to tell the Commons that "legal advisers Herbert Smith Freehills are clear that they misled the Financial Conduct Authority" and advised "on some legal points incorrectly".[15] This was just three months before the announcement of the firm's role in the Horizon Shortfall scheme. Appointing it to run Post Office compensation was, said Hollinrake, "perverse and undermines any confidence that such [a] scheme can deliver a fair outcome to applicants".[16] They were to prove prescient words.

---

12 Read, WITN00760300
13 Email from Alan Watts to Ben Foat, 25 February 2020, POL00128937
14 Mr Justice Hildyard, *RBS Rights Issue Litigation*, 3 May 2017
15 *Hansard*, 14 February 2020
16 lawgazette.co.uk/news/herbert-smith-freehills-under-fire-for-post-office-advice/5105176.article

Appealing outcome

Things were looking brighter for those seeking to overturn convictions. In March, the Criminal Cases Review Commission had referred the 42 cases it had been sitting on, pending the outcome of *Bates v Post Office,* to the Court of Appeal. Given Mr Justice Fraser's comments, this hadn't been in doubt. But it was a welcome reminder of how high the stakes were for many.

In October, the Post Office announced that, of the 47 cases that had been referred to the appeal courts by then, it would not put up any contest in 44 of them. Half a dozen of these sub-postmasters had been convicted in magistrates' courts and were therefore to have their appeals heard in a Crown court.

Christopher Trousdale, Kamran Ashraf, Julie Cleife, Susan Rudkin, Vipinchandra Patel and Jasvinder Barang duly arrived at Southwark Crown Court on 11 December 2020. Within minutes of Her Honour Judge Taylor taking her seat, they heard the Post Office's counsel confirm that she'd be offering no evidence. The broad reason was that Mr Justice Fraser had found that "the Post Office did not routinely investigate or disclose the possibility that evidence of the Horizon system may be unreliable". [17]

Among the six were two of the scandal's earliest victims. Christopher Trousdale from Whitby, North Yorkshire, had been convicted of false accounting in March 2004 at the age of just 22. More than 16 years later, he stood outside court and said that he and his co-claimants "can take our first breath and look forward to being able to start to heal and rebuild". [18] Kamran Ashraf, convicted of theft from his post office in Hampstead in January 2004 and imprisoned, told reporter Nick Wallis: "It means everything. It's been 17 years… Way too long. Way too long."[19]

The other falsely convicted sub-postmasters, including Jo Hamilton, Noel Hughes and the late Julian Wilson, were to have their cases heard by the Court of Appeal the following March. *Hamilton & Others v Post Office Ltd* would take place in the grander setting of the Royal Courts of Justice and come with an added twist. Three of the convicted were arguing not just on the grounds of Horizon's concealed unreliability but also for a more profound reason.

Seema Misra, Tracy Felstead and Janet Skinner, all wrongly imprisoned, had been waiting a combined 44 years for justice and now claimed, in arguments developed *pro bono* by barristers Paul Marshall and Flora Page, that their prosecutions should never have taken place and had been so horrendously conducted that they were an abuse of process and "an affront

---

17 *R v Christopher Trousdale & Others*, 11 December 2020
18 itv.com/news/2020-12-11/post-office-apologises-as-first-postmasters-acquitted-after-horizon-it-scandal
19 Wallis, postofficetrial.com/2020/12/first-subpostmaster-convictions-quashed.html

to the public conscience".[20] Some thought the extra argument risked delaying the acquittals unnecessarily. The Post Office was resisting the point, through the senior barrister who'd played a part in keeping a lid on the scandal a few years before (and was now perhaps a bit conflicted), Brian Altman QC. But for the women, who had endured traumatic experiences even by the standards of the Post Office scandal, it was an important point to make.

They did exactly that when, the following month, Lord Justice Holroyd delivered the court's judgment. The Post Office's "failures of investigation and disclosure", he said, "were in our judgment so egregious as to make the prosecution of any of the 'Horizon cases' an affront to the conscience of the court."[21] They should never have been undertaken, not just against Seema, Tracy and Janet, but in all 39 of the cases in which convictions were overturned. (Another three, not relying entirely on Horizon evidence, were upheld.)

Arguing the case had an invaluable spin-off benefit, too. The disclosure process elicited the 2013 advice to the Post Office from barrister Simon Clarke, proving the fatal lack of credibility of the star prosecution witness from Fujitsu, Gareth Jenkins. (It spoke volumes about the Post Office's attitude to disclosure in the group litigation that this hadn't previously been handed over.) Dragging this episode into the light would prove pivotal to the public examination of the whole scandal to come.

On the April morning that 39 sub-postmasters emerged victorious into the London sunshine, the political ground shifted, too. A full 15 months after the last of the *Bates* judgments, the government could no longer resist calls for its review to become a full statutory inquiry. The "affront to the public conscience" of the state abusing the justice system to persecute its citizens demanded it.

One month later, postal affairs minister Paul Scully stood up in the Commons to make a statement. In light of "the gravity of the [Court of Appeal] judgment and the scale of the miscarriage of justice that it makes clear", Scully had agreed with the chair of the review, retired High Court judge Sir Wyn Williams, "that the context of the inquiry has changed". It would move on to a "statutory footing" with all the powers that entailed.[22] It was a resounding win for Seema Misra's, Tracy Felstead's and Janet Skinner's insistence on the Post Office facing the full extent of its culpability in court. (One other snippet of news came out the following week. ITV had commissioned a drama with the working title *People vs Post Office*.)

Despite the breakthrough in the Court of Appeal, the wheels of justice

---
20 Lord Justice Holroyd, judgment in *Hamilton & Others v Post Office*, 23 April 2021
21 Ibid
22 *Hansard*, 19 May 2021

continued to grind slowly. Six months after the *Hamilton & Others* judgment, only a further 27 convictions had been overturned.[23] At this rate it would take decades for all to receive justice. Some had already died without doing so. The courts had shown the government the depth of the scandal but the grim demographics seemed not to bother it, or at least not enough. However pedestrian the legal process, its exacting and time-consuming demands had to be respected at all costs. Sub-postmasters would just have to wait for justice – or die waiting. Progress on redress for victims who hadn't been prosecuted was no better and many were going to their graves without receiving anything. The most recent estimate is around 350 dying with no redress.[24]

Falling short

As Chris Head had put it in his petition, fair redress would mean "ensuring that all those affected are returned to the position they would have been in had they not encountered the Horizon scandal and compensated for the pain, trauma and suffering they have gone through including their families".[25] But with the assessment of claims in the hands of the adversarial Herbert Smith Freehills, applying principles used for more routine unfair-dismissal cases, this wasn't going to happen.

When the Commons business select committee, chaired by Darren Jones, looked at the Horizon Shortfall scheme at the end of 2021, there had already been 2,500 applications. Of these, fewer than a third had been made offers. The more complex and longer ago the case, the harder it was for claimants. One of their solicitors, Neil Hudgell, told MPs of the difficulty "establishing documentary support… because we are talking, in some instances, 20 years on".[26] Worse still, "the burden of proof is on the claimant to establish loss and, because of Post Office's actions, paperwork is very often not there and is unavailable". The MPs agreed that the idea of sub-postmasters having to prove their case and the Post Office sitting as "judge, jury and executioner" was too familiar. The system whereby it set compensation offers, with help from Herbert Smith Freehills, put the fox in charge of the henhouse.

Another striking unfairness was the exclusion from the shortfall scheme of the sub-postmasters who had signed up to the Alan Bates group litigation and received paltry payouts after legal costs. Paul Scully had insisted the settlement was "full and final", but Bates told the MPs they were "being

---

23 Letter from Scully to Darren Jones MP, 14 December 2021, committees.parliament.uk/publications/8292/documents/84425/default/
24 *Times*, 4 July 2025
25 change.org/p/biztradegovuk-post-office-scandal-full-compensation-and-accountability
26 Commons business, energy and industrial strategy committee, 14 December 2021

punished for bringing the case in the first instance". Why, he wanted to know, while thousands of others were now lining up higher payments, "should the 555, who dared to stand up to them and to expose the real truth in all of this, continue to be punished?"[27] The committee agreed. Scully accepted the point and belatedly set up a parallel scheme for the group.

Sub-postmasters with overturned convictions – including those in the group of 555 – were being invited to apply for more significant compensation under an "overturned convictions" scheme run by the Department for Business, Energy & Industrial Strategy (BEIS), and given an interim payment of £100,000 in the meantime. But getting them to come forward in the first place wasn't easy. This wasn't entirely surprising, given the breakdown in trust and the prospect of reliving their experiences in order to construct an appeal. Of the 736 people the Post Office had prosecuted and had now written to, just 160 had begun the process of overturning their convictions. There was a long way to go if justice on the scale demanded was to be delivered.

View from the chair

Righting such historic and now public wrongs might have been expected to be the government's number one priority for the Post Office – if only so that it could move on.

Yet, when BEIS's permanent secretary wrote to Post Office chairman Tim Parker in early 2022 setting out what, as its sole shareholder, she expected in the forthcoming financial year, her instructions were heavily qualified. Compensation, Sarah Munby told Parker, should be "fair for claimants and taxpayers". Delivery must be an "appropriate use of taxpayers' money" and the Post Office should "deliver redress in a timely manner and at a lower cost".[28] The message reflected the straitened post-Covid times – that spring, chancellor Rishi Sunak demanded "discipline on public spending" – but it was hardly conducive to handing sub-postmasters their dues without putting them through the wringer once again.

Administering justice and redress weren't exactly in prince of darkness Tim Parker's sweet spot, either. But he wouldn't preside over them for much longer. As the public inquiry began hearing its first witnesses in February 2022, he announced that he would be stepping down in six months' time. His replacement was to be Henry Staunton, a former PwC chartered accountant who had moved into the corporate world, culminating in nine years as chairman of WH Smith. The appointment came with a certain irony – the

---
27 Ibid
28 Letter from Sarah Munby to Parker, 1 May 2022, BEIS0000984

struggling retailer had subsumed scores of Crown post office branches on his watch, as part of the very Post Office cost-cutting drive that formed the backdrop to the scandal he was now stepping into.

When Staunton surveyed his new domain, he found what he would call a "mess" and a workforce that he sensed hadn't accepted Mr Justice Fraser's findings in the High Court. It was also, he thought, dragging its feet on redress payments and had "no appetite at all for exoneration [of sub-postmasters]". [29] All doubtless true, but not views that endeared the forthright new chairman to the Finsbury Dials faithful.

More bonus balls

While the public inquiry continued its long journey to the heart of the affair, Post Office HQ – where, incidentally, there were around 200 people on salaries above £100,000 – remained self-absorbed to the point of corporate narcissism.

One of Staunton's first steps as chairman had been to lobby business secretary Grant Shapps for a better pay deal for Nick Read. His salary was £415,000 and could be increased to a maximum of £788,000 with bonuses (he'd struggled by on £693,000 for the previous year). But this obviously wasn't enough. Read was "a prime target for other prospective roles not constrained by the public sector influence", said Staunton and, in handling the inquiry, had been "exemplary in his navigation through the sensitivities". [30] There was no evidence to support this; the Post Office was in fact being repeatedly criticised by the judge over egregious disclosure failings. Begging for more money when sub-postmasters whose lives had been ruined were having trouble getting their dues looked more like a two-fingered salute than sensitive navigation.

Staunton was in fact following his predecessor's lead and responding to Read's bellyaching. Tim Parker had repeatedly lobbied Shapps's predecessor Kwasi Kwarteng, who made one of the better financial calls of his career and refused Read a pay rise. The Post Office "chief people officer" from the time, Jane Davies, would soon write that "from the first day, I found a chief executive who was obsessed with his pay, to such an extent that it was a huge distraction from me establishing myself in my new position".[31]

Such was the fixation with remuneration more widely that even dealing with the inquiry became a bonus-generator for Read and 30-plus senior executives. The Post Office's accounts for 2021/22 reported "confirmation

---

29 Henry Staunton, inquiry evidence, 1 October 2024
30 Letter from Staunton to Grant Shapps, 11 November 2022, POL00448680
31 Letter from Jane Davies to Liam Byrne, 18 March 2024, committees.parliament.uk/publications/44373/documents/220654/default

from Sir Wyn Williams and team that Post Office's performance supported and enabled the inquiry to finish in line with expectations" as a contribution to one bonus scheme. The inquiry, of course, was nowhere near finished and Sir Wyn's team had said no such thing.[32] The chief executive hastily apologised and returned the relevant part of his bonus.

Hollinrake's progress

Staunton's arrival at the Post Office had coincided with that of a new postal services minister, Kevin Hollinrake, at the business department. This looked encouraging, since the MP for Thirsk and Malton had long campaigned against rapacious institutions and for sub-postmasters. His most important task would be accelerating the compensation schemes run by his legal *bête noire*, Herbert Smith Freehills.

Hollinrake did try to give the flagging programme some impetus, with mixed success from a frugal Treasury led by chancellor Jeremy Hunt. In September 2023, he was able to offer sub-postmasters who had their convictions overturned £600,000 on a take-it-or-leave it basis. Published figures suggested claims from this group that were considered in detail were producing an average £1m payout and, the previous year, Paul Scully had estimated total potential payments for overturned convictions of £780m, indicating something similar.[33] So this was hardly generous, but it may have encouraged some of the wrongly convicted to come forward.

But, even with an ally of the sub-postmasters in the ministerial hotseat, addressing the miscarriage scandal remained sclerotic. By the end of 2023, just 93 convictions had been overturned. At this pace, justice would stretch into the second half of the 21st century. Some £148m had been paid out in redress to all categories of victim.[34] Both totals were below 20 percent of what was forecast to be required.

Drama out of a crisis

Not many people would have guessed that the key to unlocking real progress, four years after Alan Bates's victory, would be a TV drama. But when the four-part telling of the story, made by the Little Gem production company, aired on ITV in the first week of 2024 it did just that.

Mr Bates vs The Post Office told the story through the sub-postmasters.

---

32 Sir Wyn Williams, chair's statement regarding Post Office 2021/22 annual report, 5 May 2023
33 Letter from Scully to Jones, 2 December 2022, committees.parliament.uk/publications/8841/documents/89132/default/
34 *Hansard*, 8 January 2024

Toby Jones portrayed Alan Bates's initial frustrations and then his long campaign; Monica Dolan showed the horrified panic of Jo Hamilton as shortfalls appeared on her screen; and Will Mellor captured the hounding and defiance of Lee Castleton. The intransigence of the Post Office in the face of their ordeals was personified by Lia Williams and Katherine Kelly re-enacting the cynical performances of Paula Vennells and Angela van den Bogerd in front of MPs nine years earlier.

The production achieved what serious (if generally belated) journalistic coverage over the previous few years had not. It showed to millions what it meant for a state institution to abuse its citizens on such a scale. Dramatisation appeared to make real what reporting, however personal, had not. Where there had been public indifference, there was now widespread sympathy for the sub-postmasters and anger with the Post Office, its leaders and government. The story moved to the top of the news agenda immediately, former sub-postmasters appearing on all the TV sofas and news programmes and movingly sharing their experiences.

In terms of the underlying injustice itself, nothing had really changed. The numbers of victims had been known for a long time, as had the way they had been treated. The inability of the courts to provide justice quickly enough had also been understood. As had the numbers awaiting redress. None of this had prompted the urgent action needed. But at the start of election year, with the public outraged, everything changed.

As early as 10 January prime minister Rishi Sunak announced a bill to overturn all Horizon-related convictions, remedying "one of the greatest miscarriages of justice in our nation's history". His government would "make sure that the truth comes to light, we right the wrongs of the past and the victims get the justice they deserve".[35]

The move wasn't universally welcomed among m'learned friends. It stepped across a constitutional line separating the executive and the judiciary, which guarded its authority over the law jealously. Without actually specifying the forthcoming legislation, Lady Chief Justice (Sue) Carr, head of the judiciary in England and Wales, told a press conference when asked about it: "The rule of law is clearly engaged, and it is for the courts to make judicial decisions."[36] She also went on the defensive when probed on judicial failings throughout the scandal. Legal journalist Catherine Baksi put it to her that judges – with the exception of Fraser – "have not behaved admirably", having "taken pleas from people where there is no evidence, sentenced innocent

---
35 *Hansard*, 10 January 2024
36 Lady Chief Justice of England and Wales, press conference 6 February 2024

people to lengthy times in prison, and also failed to spot a trend of hundreds of people being prosecuted by the Post Office". (She could have added to the list the overwhelming tendency to favour the prosecution on questions such as disclosure of evidence, such as in Seema Misra's landmark case, which seriously hampered the defence.) Would there be an investigation? Baroness Carr shot back: "I would resist any suggestion that there is any basis for implicating the judiciary in any of the very egregious failures that do appear to have gone on in terms of the prosecution of these sub-postmasters…".[37] It was almost Post Office-style knee-jerk denial.

The Post Office's own criminal lawyers also pushed back. Peters & Peters, which had been advising on appeals including the landmark *Hamilton & Others* case, wrote to CEO Nick Read just before Sunak's announcement, when the mass exoneration was being mooted. It was, the firm said, "highly likely that the vast majority of people who have not yet appealed were, in fact, guilty as charged and were safely convicted". The government risked "making incredibly important and expensive decisions on a completely false premise".[38] (The move would also, the firm didn't say, cost Peters & Peters plenty of appeal work.)

On the strength of this view, Read immediately wrote to justice minister Alex Chalk saying that there were at least 369 convictions in which "we would be bound to oppose an appeal". There was no explanation of this beyond "reliance on evidence unrelated to the Horizon computer system".[39] This "evidence" would generally have been confessions. Although Peters & Peters insisted it did not treat these as conclusive of guilt, they were hardly reliable, given the oppressive and coercive methods used to extract them and the imbalance of information.

Crisis out of a drama

With ultimate responsibility for the Post Office now in the hands of business secretary Kemi Badenoch, not always known for putting the greater good above her own political interests, the institution was plunged into its own psychodrama.

On 27 January 2024, the day before she was due to go on the BBC's Laura Kuenssberg show, the woman with the Tory leadership in her sights sacked Staunton. The timing didn't look coincidental; she could go on the programme and appear tough in the face of the public outcry. "It just wasn't

---

37 Ibid
38 Letter from Nick Vamos to Nick Read, 9 January 2024, POL00448701
39 Letter from Read to Alex Chalk MP, 9 January 2024, POL00448381

working," Badenoch said, so she'd acted decisively.[40] Staunton inevitably took his revenge. In an interview the following month with Oliver Shah in the *Sunday Times*, he made the incendiary claim that the government had asked the Post Office to stall compensation so it could "limp into the election" with limited costs.[41] He also said that the Post Office culture remained one of "toxic" mistrust of sub-postmasters, and that it was the tight-fisted shareholder body UKGI that had made Nick Read write his letter to the minister saying it would have opposed large numbers of appeals. Weeks of denials, claims and counter-claims followed, featuring racism, sexism and lashings of greed.

Post Office executives, meanwhile, were bailing out. In the summer, general counsel Ben Foat, who had faced criticism for the handling of the inquiry so far, took a paid "leave of absence". Finance director and former stand-in chief executive Alisdair Cameron had been off for months with stress. And in July, Read himself decided to step back, keeping his salary while he prepared for his appearance before the public inquiry in the autumn. He wouldn't return to the day job, eventually signing off entirely in March 2025.

Little less compensation

Corporate dysfunction wasn't delivering sub-postmasters the justice they deserved, when they deserved it. As promised, in May several hundreds of convictions were overturned in one fell swoop by the Post Office (Horizon System) Offences Act 2024. But, for hundreds of other victims, the compensation process was dragging on interminably, while Herbert Smith Freehills and the firm working on the scheme for the group litigation claimants, Addleshaw Goddard, quibbled with sub-postmasters.

A couple of months after the ITV drama, the Commons business select committee, now chaired by Labour's Liam Byrne, concluded that the Post Office was "not fit" to run the compensation schemes, having (still) paid out just one pound in every five that was budgeted for. The message fell on deaf government ears.

A new Labour government arrived in July 2024, professing its own commitment to the cause. With Byrne's select committee predecessor and sub-postmaster champion Darren Jones now holding the purse strings as chief secretary to the Treasury, hope sprung once again. Money wasn't going to be a problem. In her November 2024 budget, Jones's boss, chancellor Rachel Reeves, announced that £1.8bn would be set aside for redress. But no budget, however large, could help those banging their heads against the brick wall of

---

40 *Sunday with Laura Kuenssberg*, 28 January 2024, bbc.co.uk/news/live/uk-politics-68113424
41 *Sunday Times*, 18 February 2024

the legalistic compensation schemes. The Kafkaesque tales continued. One of the battles covered by the *Eye* illustrated the nightmare.

Back in 2006, Tony Downey had faced repeated false shortfalls at his branch in Hawkshead in the Lake District. After having paid around £35,000 from his own funds, a further phantom deficit of £7,000 forced him to resign and sell up. He and his wife Caroline became bankrupt and, with locals assuming he'd stolen the money, moved abroad and ended up living on benefits in Spain. The toll on the Downey family was extreme. Tony suffered years of depression and anxiety, leaving him unable to work. His daughter Katie, who had left her school and friends at the age of 11, also needed therapy for the trauma.

Tony's story typified that of a sub-postmaster and a family suffering life-altering consequences, without a criminal conviction, and demanding a fair assessment through the Horizon Shortfall scheme. When he received his first offer in 2022, however, it came in at £150,000 – after, the Post Office confirmed, consideration by "leading external law firm, Herbert Smith Freehills". Of this, £140,000 was to go to his bankruptcy trustee, leaving just £10,000. The gross figure was made up of what Tony had been forced to pay to cover shortfalls in the first place, miserly estimated lost earnings, £10,000 for "distress and inconvenience" and some interest. He rejected the insulting offer.

It took 18 months, and a television drama, for the Post Office and its lawyers to have a rethink. The revised offer was £293,000, almost double the original (but still minus the £140,000 for the bankruptcy trustee). The increase was accounted for by the absurdly belated admission that the Post Office had caused Tony's bankruptcy. Even then, it valued this at just £30,000. His tormentor also accepted – having previously refused to do so – that it had caused "personal injury", i.e. harm to mental health. This was rated at a mere £45,000. The Post Office continued to reject entirely claims for sums that would have gone a small way to putting the Downeys where they would have been had the Post Office not ruined their lives, such as the losses incurred by being forced to sell their home and the consequences of Mrs Downey's bankruptcy. Neither she nor their daughter counted in the brutal arithmetic.[42]

Behind the parsimony were legal methods unsuited to the injustice. Herbert Smith Freehills was using standard breach-of-contract principles applicable to more run-of-the-mill unfair dismissal cases.[43] The starting point for considering loss of earnings was the calculation used by the Post Office at the time for sub-postmasters whose branches were being closed under the "network transformation programme". This generally translated

---

42 Information provided to *Private Eye*
43 See, for example, Horizon Compensation Advisory Board meeting, 14 June 2023, RLIT0000250

into 26 months' salary. Lost appreciation of assets was largely ignored, as was the inability to work in a comparable role to the one they had lost. In short, the system was a million miles from placing victims in "the position they would have been in had they not encountered the Horizon scandal", as the campaigner Chris Head had put it. (He, too, was being offered derisory sums for having had his promising career cut short.)

The lawyers' methods were aggravating the hellish process. James Hartley of Freeths told Liam Byrne's committee MPs how the law firm running the scheme for the Bates group litigation claimants, Addleshaw Goddard, had queried medical evidence from one of his clients. When a consultant had "expressed the opinion that, on the balance of probabilities, the postmaster had suffered a condition of anxiety and depressive disorder", Addleshaw Goddard replied that this was "vague and lacking in detail" and sent "two pages of questions about this person's prognosis and their prior symptoms".[44] As Hartley observed, this was a long way from "giving the postmaster the benefit of the doubt" as the Post Office had promised. Although redress offers went through an independent advisory panel, the fact that they were often significantly increased if disputed showed the effectiveness of the lawyers' chiselling in the first place.

It was, of course, all stupendously profitable for the lawyers. By March 2024 they had been paid £136m for working on the redress schemes. Nearly £100m had gone to Herbert Smith Freehills on the Horizon Shortfall scheme, to add to something similar for other work including advising the Post Office on the group litigation and the public inquiry.[45] All told, by the summer of 2025, law firms had earned £350m from the government and the Post Office from fighting Alan Bates and co and handling the redress required by the scandal. While more than £1bn had been paid out to around 8,300 victims, it's fair to say the lawyers were doing better than them from the "legalistic approach".

Dying for justice

The concessions that had been forced on governments by the post-ITV drama furore, such as a fixed £75,000 up-front payment from March 2024 for anybody eligible for the Horizon Shortfall scheme, did boost the statistics. Total payouts trebled to £500m in 2024 and in June 2025 passed the £1bn mark, as thousands of former sub-postmasters – many of whom had suffered

---

44 Commons business and trade committee, 5 November 2024.
45 Commons business and trade committee report, 1 January 2025. Herbert Smith Freehills had earned £82m from the scheme by December 2024. By March 2024 Herbert Smith Freehills had earned total £163.5m for all its work for the Post Office (FoI), and £188m by March 2025.

POST MORTEM

hardship and stress but kept their jobs – came forward to collect the amount. The numbers of convicted sub-postmasters receiving a minimum £600,000 payout also moved past 500.[46]

But for those like Tony Downey, Chris Head and even Alan Bates – complex cases without convictions and deserving of far more than £75,000 – redress was still moving glacially. As late as September 2025, settlements were being reached in the 188 outstanding cases in the original cohort of Horizon Shortfall scheme claimants at the rate of four per month.[47] As Liam Byrne's select committee had reported on the first anniversary of the TV drama, payments were "so slow that people are dying before they get justice".[48] In July, it was the turn of another group of MPs to lament the ongoing travails of the sub-postmasters. Public accounts committee chairman Sir Geoffrey Clifton-Brown called it "deeply dissatisfactory to find these schemes are still moving far too slowly".[49] The oldest victim, 92-year-old Betty Brown, had to hold out until November 2025 for an offer she could accept. The same month, after years of back-and-forth over inadequate offers, Alan Bates also agreed a seven-figure settlement with the government's lawyers. But hundreds of others were still waiting for theirs.

More than six years after the Post Office had been judged "oppressive" towards sub-postmasters, the tortuous process of redress showed an organisation and successive governments unable to face the full consequences of the past. All while its dark truth was being pored over in a central London inquiry room.

"It's our most popular drama in years, I say we turn it into a franchise"

---

46 Post Office Horizon redress data for 2025: gov.uk/government/publications/post-office-horizon-financial-redress-and-legal-costs-data-for-2025
47 Ibid
48 Liam Byrne MP, comment on Commons business and trade select committee report, 1 January 2025
49 Sir Geoffrey Clifton-Brown MP, comment on Commons public accounts committee report, 25 June 2025

15

SEARCHING INQUIRY

A public reckoning and heroic attempts to evade it – 2,214,858 pages of evidence, 780 witness statements and 298 witness appearances. A few highlights, and plenty of lowlights…

THE Post Office Horizon IT Inquiry began its public hearings on 14 February 2022, in a modern office block near St Paul's Cathedral, with the most compelling testimony of its near three-year course.

The "human impact" phase of the inquiry heard from 68 former sub-postmasters, often in harrowing detail.[1] Along with nearly 100 others who submitted detailed witness statements, they gave first-hand evidence of the Post Office's conduct and opened the search for how and why the scandal had happened. While each story was uniquely appalling, it was the patterns – for example of having been told they were the "only one" experiencing difficulties with Horizon – that hammered home the systemic abuses of the Post Office and its accomplices.

The very first witness, who had been sacked after shortfalls appeared in his Brentford branch soon after Horizon was launched, personified the public-spiritedness and stoicism of the many who followed him. "We never had any problems," Baljit Sethi told the inquiry's lead counsel, Jason Beer QC, and its avuncular but sharp chairman, Sir Wyn Williams. "Of course, we had seven armed robberies but my wife was very brave and they didn't take a single penny from the Post Office."[2] The Sethis had been "commended many times" and encouraged by the Post Office to take on more branches. By the time they were forced out, one branch was showing a surplus of £40,000. They refused to take anything out. "It was not right," said Mr Sethi, "and we, being honest, we said, 'No, there's no way this money belongs to us and we're not going to withdraw this money.'"

Mr Sethi described the unbearable fallout from the Horizon shortfalls.

---

1 Transcripts and videos of sub-postmasters' evidence can be found on the Post Office Horizon Inquiry website, postofficehorizoninquiry.org.uk, and transcripts on postofficeinquiry.dracos.co.uk. The Human Impact hearings ran from 14 February to 19 May 2022
2 Baljit Sethi, inquiry evidence, 14 February 2022

"Our reputation was in shreds. People who used to hold us in high esteem thought we were thieves, we were robbing from the Post Office. People who used to stop us in the street to say hello turned their face the other way… and we had no way [to] tell anybody that this is wrong". As so many did, he "contemplated suicide".

The impact of such experiences was written in the faces of those who appeared, and borne out by their words.[3] These included:

> "I can't get motivated with anything, it's just always there in your mind, it doesn't go away."
> "I find it very difficult to be in a room with people now."
> "I wake up in the morning and I'm actually disappointed that I've woken up."
> "I still think about it every day. I mean there's not a day goes past that you don't go past a postie, you don't go past a Royal Mail van, you don't pass a red pillar box."
> "I had a really good relationship with my mum and yeah, for her to think that I'd robbed from the Post Office, you know that's… she took that to the grave."
> "I've let [my children] down, I've been unable to do what I should have as a parent, and it's just been very difficult."
> "I don't want to talk to anyone, don't want to see anyone."
> "When it gets to cashing up at the charity shop [where I now work], if it's out, I get… there was one time it was £20 out and I couldn't stop crying."
> "It affected my eldest child quite a lot because there was rumours going around. She used to come home and say 'Daddy, are you going to jail?'"
> "I lost my dignity, personality and my soul in the end."
> "You know, we're all exhausted, we've had almost 20 years of fighting and people aren't with us that should be."

Missing documents

The final words were spoken by Jo Hamilton[4] and should, like all the others, have told the Post Office management that now, finally, it was time to face the music openly and honestly. There had been any number of commitments to

---

3 For a collation of excerpts of sub-postmaster evidence, see postofficehorizoninquiry.org.uk/news/stories-human-impact-post-office-horizon-it-inquiry
4 Josephine Hamilton, inquiry evidence, 14 February 2022

change since then but, when it came to the difficult past, the inquiry showed that the Post Office's adversarial and defensive culture lingered.

On the question of disclosing essential evidence, proven failings in criminal cases and in the *Bates* litigation ought to have made the Post Office commit to a thorough, professional approach this time round. This wasn't some dry legal process. As Jason Beer put it, documents were the "lifeblood of the inquiry".[5] Yet, from the outset, the Post Office and its adviser Herbert Smith Freehills failed in basic disclosure tasks, such as mapping where in the organisation information was to be found, and took an excessively narrow approach to searches.

By 2023, a couple of years after the inquiry had officially kicked off, the failings were causing mayhem. In July, one of the key witnesses, Fujitsu's Gareth Jenkins, had to be stood down as thousands of potentially relevant documents were found 12 hours before he was due in the witness chair. After surveying the performance that summer, chairman Sir Wyn Williams rebuked the Post Office and its lawyers, plus consultants from KPMG dealing with the IT, for "grossly unsatisfactory" performance.[6]

Yet, a few months later, the same problems delayed the appearance of Jenkins again and of five Post Office investigators, including **Steve Bradshaw**. Even the usually unflappable Beer showed his exasperation. "This is, of course, the latest in a series of disclosure failings by the Post Office... etched in the memory of those who sit on this side of the room," he told Sir Wyn, reeling off a litany of incompetence and dereliction of duty.[7]

Clueless Clouseaus

Unluckily for Bradshaw, his appearance was rescheduled for 11 January 2024.[8] He would be the first witness since the final episode of ITV's *Mr Bates vs The Post Office* had aired seven days previously. The scriptwriters couldn't have choreographed it any worse for him. When he arrived at the inquiry's new venue of Aldwych House, round the corner from the Royal Courts of Justice, the country's eyes were trained on the real-life embodiment of the persecution

---

5 Christopher Jackson, inquiry evidence, 12 January 2022
6 Williams, consideration of Post Office disclosure failings, 10 July 2023
7 Bradshaw, inquiry evidence, 7 November 2023
8 As with all witnesses appearing at the inquiry, transcripts and videos are available on the official site, and transcripts on postofficeinquiry.dracos.co.uk. The inquiry was split into phases, into which the evidence is assembled. Witnesses concerned primarily with the Horizon system itself appeared in Phases 2 and 3, those with the investigation of sub-postmasters in Phase 4, and those with the response to the scandal, including appeals, in a merged Phase 5 & 6. Phase 7 concerned present and future governance of the Post Office. Not all hearings slotted neatly into their phase, for example because witnesses were delayed through disclosure failings.

they had seen on their TV screens the week before. It was still pantomime season – and here was the villain.

Bradshaw and the other Post Office investigators who would appear at the inquiry faced a major disadvantage in defending themselves: their job title. They should have *investigated* the possible causes of any given shortfall. When there was no sign of theft, that would have included considering whether the IT system that was showing the shortfall could have been at fault. Having never done this, they now had nowhere to turn. Most resorted to insolence and occasional belligerence.

For Bradshaw, it started with his witness statement. He had been asked to supply evidence about nine cases he'd investigated, including those of Janet Skinner, Noel Thomas and Khayyam Ishaq, all falsely imprisoned. In response to each, Bradshaw had written: "There were no concerns, the investigation was conducted in a professional manner at all times," followed by "I have no other reflections about this matter."[9]

Inquiry counsel Julian Blake asked Bradshaw if he had "given enough thought, over the past 20 years, as to whether you may have been involved in what has been described as one of the largest miscarriages of justice in British history?" He hadn't. The problem was simply "not being given any knowledge from the top downwards, that if any bugs, errors or defects was [sic] there, it's not been cascaded down from Fujitsu, the Post Office board, down to our level".[10] Bradshaw claimed that he was "not technically minded" and couldn't have been expected to question the system himself. This was despite agreeing with one of the lead counsel for the sub-postmasters, Ed Henry KC, that investigators had been "drenched in information that Horizon wasn't working from the very beginning".

Bradshaw denied allegations of more brutish behaviour, such as having called a female sub-postmaster a "bitch" and forcing another who used a wheelchair to enter a small parcel lift to get to her interview in a Royal Mail sorting office. His demeanour, however, left most observers preferring his accusers' versions. And the non-technically minded investigator couldn't escape another serious allegation: that he had signed a statement for a prosecution avowing "absolute confidence" in Horizon based on a generic script. He should, "in hindsight", he admitted, have added "these are not my words". In a strong field, it was one of the more ambitious uses of the H-word – "hindsight" – during the inquiry.

Scottish investigator **Raymond Grant** had to be summoned under threat

---

9 Bradshaw, witness statement, 11 January 2024, WITN04450100
10 Bradshaw, inquiry evidence, 11 January 2024

of criminal sanction and provided a witness statement that was a well-spaced two pages long. He had given priority, he said, to activities with the Salvation Army and, during the December month that he should have been reading the papers, had been busy with "carol services, Christmas dinners, various other bits and pieces". Then "I was going home, walking my dog…"[11] He'd been unable even to answer the inquiry's first written question of when he started working at the Post Office. (Answer: 1982, as a postman.) After Grant had finished with his excuses, made to disbelieving laughter in the room, Jason Beer drily remarked: "Well, let's see if we can improve on it today, now that carol services and dog-walking are out of the way." Alas, things didn't improve. On the one issue Grant *had* covered in his witness statement, his role in the prosecution of a sub-postmaster in the Outer Hebrides, he remained unrepentant. In fact, he knew better than the High Court of Judiciary in Scotland that overturned the conviction. "Do you remain of the view that he's guilty of the crime?" asked Beer. "Yes, I do," replied Grant.

At the time of that case, Grant had been one of just two evidently productive investigators who operated in Scotland. The other was **Robert Daily**, who faced questions about the prosecution of Peter Holmes from across the border in Jesmond in Newcastle. The policeman turned sub-postmaster, who died before he was posthumously exonerated, had been convicted despite Daily's investigation finding no sign of the supposedly missing funds. Sir Wyn asked: "In the absence of any success in discovering the whereabouts of the money, what did you do to investigate whether, in fact, there had been a loss?" Daily remained mute for a full 11 seconds before the chairman said: "I think silence…" At this point Daily offered: "I'm not really quite sure how to answer that, sir." [12]

Public evisceration was still not enough to shift the mindset of a Post Office investigator that had calcified over decades. When Christopher Jacobs, counsel for Mr Holmes's widow Marion, asked: "Do you accept any personal responsibility for what happened to Mr Holmes?" Daily answered: "No, I was only doing my job." [13]

With another investigator, blaming everyone else turned into nauseating self-pity. The inquiry heard how **Gary Thomas**, who had led the case against another man who didn't live to see justice, Julian Wilson from Worcestershire, had appeared to want compensation for *himself*. The same man who in 2015 had emailed a colleague saying "there is FFFFiiinnn no 'Case for the Justice

---

[11] Raymond Grant, inquiry evidence, 24 January 2024
[12] Robert Daily, inquiry evidence, 23 January 2024
[13] Ibid

of Thieving Sub-Postmasters'",[14] wrote to chief executive Nick Read six years later. The scandal "now sits somewhat on my conscious [sic] because of my employer," said Thomas. "Whilst compensation is being correctly awarded now to these sub-postmasters, I feel the employees instructed to conduct these prosecutions, arrests and searches have been completely overlooked."[15]

Such sentiments, along with repeated refusals to face up to their complicity in the scandal, betrayed the investigators' limitations. Many weren't very bright, all were poorly trained and few seemed to have it in them to contemplate whether their actions were just or fair. Incentivised to produce results, and thus implicitly told that prosecutions and financial recoveries were the be all and end all, they were unwilling and perhaps incapable of asking the questions that might have challenged their working methods. This, of course, suited those further up the Post Office hierarchy just fine.

System failures

The prosecutions that the investigators generated relied on an equally blinkered outlook from their opposite numbers at Fujitsu.

When he finally made the witness seat, **Gareth Jenkins** was, like Steve Bradshaw before him, advised of the "privilege against self-incrimination". He didn't have to answer anything that risked helping a criminal case against him. There was, however, no warning against desperate attempts at self-exculpation. These largely involved the IT engineer claiming that his flaky evidence against sub-postmasters had been addressing narrower or different questions from the ones put to him. When Beer asked if knew that as a witness in prosecutions he was required to tell the "whole truth", Jenkins replied that he had "told the whole truth, as far as the Horizon system was operating in the specific branches at the specific times that I'd looked at data".[16]

In Seema Misra's prosecution, Jenkins had been asked if there were "any known problems with the Horizon system that Fujitsu are aware of". He now claimed that, at the time, he thought that this related solely to Mrs Misra's branch. Beer pointed out that it "plainly doesn't say that though, does it?" Jenkins acknowledged, "I realise that now."[17] At the time, it must have been a misunderstanding.

This wouldn't wash with Seema Misra, sitting with her barrister just a few metres away. Her counsel, Flora Page, read out Jenkins's self-appraisal for the

---
14 POL0017652
15 Email from Gary Thomas to Nick Read, 9 May 2021, POL00113304
16 Jenkins, inquiry evidence, 25 June 2024
17 Jenkins, inquiry evidence, 27 June 2024

year of her client's conviction, in which he'd recorded as personal a success: "The defendant was found guilty of theft and Horizon was given a clean bill of health." Page remarked: "You knew that the *Misra* trial was a test case for Horizon, didn't you?" Jenkins replied that he "realised that afterwards". [18] Enlightenment, as ever, came well after the event.

The IT engineer reflected on having consistently misunderstood what was required of him. At one point he claimed he "got trapped into doing things that I shouldn't have done but that was not intentional". He was "better with systems and things than people". When Sam Stein KC asked what Fujitsu should have done better, Jenkins ventured: "Probably not put me in the situation that I was put in."[19] The former sub-postmasters packed into the room almost certainly agreed.

If it was possible, Jenkins's lesser-known IT security colleague **Andy Dunks** was even more hapless. He had to admit to routinely signing witness statements that were based on what other more expert but court-shy people had told him and conceded Beer's suggestion that he "couldn't know whether what they were telling you was right or wrong".[20]

These were just a couple in the parade of Fujitsu staffers whose direct role in false convictions, and indirect one in the wider oppression of the sub-postmasters, emerged in forensic detail. Their exposure to the inquiry's glare exposed the depth of the company's complicity in the scandal and therefore, when their time came to appear, the paucity of Fujitsu's leaders' response.

Lawyers unto themselves

One group had even less justification for being ethically rudderless than the bone-headed investigators and myopic technicians. These were the lawyers whose profession existed to serve justice but who had somehow subverted it into the miscarriage of justice.

The man most deeply implicated in arguably the worst case, the Seema Misra show trial, was senior Post Office criminal solicitor **Jarnail Singh**. The investigators might have set a low bar with their evidence, but Singh appeared determined to get under it. First came a correction to his witness statement. "As far as I recall, I had very limited involvement with Mr Jenkins," he'd initially written.[21] After mountains of evidence contradicting this emerged, it now read: "As far as I recall, I had more or greater involvement with Mr Jenkins."[22]

---

18 Jenkins, inquiry evidence, 28 June 2024
19 Ibid
20 Dunks, inquiry evidence, 16 July 2024
21 Singh, witness statement, 6 October 2023, WITN04750100
22 Singh, inquiry evidence, 30 November 2023

On his multiple contributions to the scandal, Singh could offer few excuses and even less self-reflection. Asked why he had drafted a misleading email in June 2014 repeating his 2010 view that sub-postmasters were "jumping on the Horizon bashing bandwagon"[23] and that Seema Misra's conviction was sound even though he knew that Jenkins was fatally undermined, all he could say was: "Well, look, sir, the position then and now is completely different" – the difference being that he'd now been found out. "So I can only apologise to everybody, maybe it's hurt their feelings or even hurt them deeply, but I can't explain, sorry." The "maybe" said a lot. As a final mark of his credibility, when Beer accused Singh of a "big fat lie" – after a risible account of not seeing a document he'd printed off and saved – nobody in the inquiry room was taken aback.[24]

There were moments of self-awareness from the lawyers. The barrister with whom Singh had worked in Mrs Misra's prosecution, **Warwick Tatford**, showed what appeared genuine contrition and acceptance of where he'd gone wrong. He admitted "there are many failings [in disclosure of information] that I had ignored on my part".[25] He accepted his share of responsibility for Jenkins's not understanding of his role as a witness and said, amid countless superficial expressions of regret at the inquiry, what few managed: "I apologise unreservedly for what happened."

Simon Clarke, the lawyer who had informed the Post Office that Jenkins was "fatally undermined" (and whose work the Court of Appeal in the *Hamilton & Others* case had commended), also admitted one significant failing. Not disclosing his findings to Seema Misra and other convicted sub-postmasters was, he agreed, an "error".[26] But the grander the lawyer, the harder it became to find much humility.

Lord (Anthony) Grabiner, who had advised the Post Office on the application to get rid of the judge in the *Bates* litigation, which the Court of Appeal called "misconceived", appeared irked at being in the witness chair answering questions for a change. Confronted by Beer over his animosity towards Mr Justice Fraser, Grabiner added obtuseness to the pomposity. "Was this becoming personalised?" asked Beer. Grabiner: "What do you mean by that?" Beer: "No more and no less than the question." Grabiner: "Well, what do you mean by – personalised as between whom and whom?" Beer: "You and the judge." Grabiner: "Me and which judge?" (There was only one it could have been.) Beer: "The judge that you were applying to recuse himself?" Grabiner:

---

23 Email from Singh to Sophie Bialaszewski, 11 June 2014, POL00113015
24 Singh, inquiry evidence, 3 May 2024
25 Warwick Tatford, inquiry evidence, 15 November 2023
26 Clarke, inquiry evidence, 9 May 2024

"Absolutely not. My view was that he had made a mess of that case and that was my position…"[27] He didn't resile from the view, even though the entire legal establishment (apart from members of it that were paid by the Post Office) had recognised Fraser's judgments in the *Bates* cases as exceptional pieces of work.

The Post Office's own senior lawyers were the most uncomfortable under spotlight. **Rodric Williams** twitched and ummed and ahhed through his evidence. He was forced to admit his central role in the denial of justice to sub-postmasters. Sir Wyn summarised his involvement in the 2014 exchanges with Jarnail Singh. "When, on any sensible reading of [Simon] Clarke's advice of July 2013, there was a problem about Mr Jenkins's evidence, the Post Office and you personally appeared still to be asserting to the world that the conviction was safe… and those two things don't sit very easily together, do they?" Williams agreed. "No, they don't, sir."[28] His half-baked apology – "I'm truly sorry, you know, that I've been associated with this… I'm truly sorry" – was swiftly rejected by Ed Henry KC, the sub-postmasters' lead counsel. "You weren't associated with it, Mr Williams," he growled. "You were in the middle of the web and you were part of it."

Williams's boss **Susan Crichton**, who had been accused by Paula Vennells of having "put her integrity as a lawyer above the interests of the business", but had done so far from perfectly, cut a sad figure. While trying to do the right thing she had acquiesced in the will of Vennells and others, especially in limiting the work of Second Sight and was, she admitted, "too shortsighted".[29]

At least these lawyers showed up. **Jane MacLeod**, the general counsel from 2015 to 2019, refused to travel from her home in Australia to answer about her deep involvement in matters such as the suppression of the Swift review and the cynically fought Bates case. Given the consequences for thousands in justice delayed and denied, this was the ultimate contempt from a lawyer who deserves particular ignominy recorded next to her name.

Wonky chairs

The two Post Office chairs during the concerted cover-up felt much more betrayed by the professionals around them than by their own negligence.

Alice Perkins, chair from 2011 to 2015, was quick to blame general counsels Susan Crichton and Chris Aujard for not giving her board the information it needed about matters such as the Clarke advice. But she was far less assured when taken through her own actions, such as excluding

---

27 Lord (Anthony) Grabiner KC, inquiry evidence, 11 June 2024
28 Rodric Williams, inquiry evidence, 19 April 2024
29 Crichton, inquiry evidence, 23 April 2024

Crichton from the 2013 board meeting at which Second Sight's findings were discussed and Simon Clarke's findings should have been. Questioned about her complaint that the lawyer had not "marked" the awkward investigators closely enough, Perkins insisted she meant merely "liaison". Other evidence – never mind the dictionary – suggested otherwise.

As for why the lawyers and other officials had told her board so little, Perkins claimed to be "a believer… in the cock-up rather than the conspiracy theory of life". She tended "not to think that people in large, complex organisations are conspirators".[30] Those watching wondered whether, for the chair of a body fairly obviously conspiring to suppress the truth and certainly being accused of doing so, a little more openness to the idea might have helped.

Beer reminded Perkins of how, as soon as she'd arrived in 2011, auditor Ernst & Young had confided in Perkins about the ropey IT system. "You're told that the auditor has concerns over whether it captures data accurately and then you're told that suspects are suggesting that it's a systems problem," Beer summarised. "Aren't those things linked together?" Perkins sought to mitigate her failure to make the connection by explaining that she was new to the job and "I didn't read *Private Eye* and I didn't read *Computer Weekly.*" Not only was this quite possibly the gravest admission in the inquiry, it was also an obvious deflection. As Beer pointed out, given what she'd been told, she shouldn't have needed to.

The ex-mandarin had subsequently asked some questions, largely thanks to James Arbuthnot MP bending her ear, which she felt entitled her to claim she had "lifted the rock".[31] But Catriona Watt, the barrister representing the National Federation of Sub-postmasters (no longer in denial, post-George Thomson), added the bit that Perkins had left out: "What then happened is you put the rock back down and just became part of the corporate reputation protection."

Former NFSP general secretary **George Thomson** put in his own stupefying appearance at the inquiry. The essence of it came when he was confronted with evidence of him "tipping off" the Post Office's communications chief Mark Davies about media interest back in the day. "I have made the point, time after time today, that Horizon is a robust system," he pointed out, almost comically contradicting perhaps the most thorough judicial examination of an IT system on record.[32]

The only contribution of any note by Perkins's insouciant successor **Tim Parker** in his seven long but barely-there years as chairman had been to

---

30 Perkins, inquiry evidence, 5 June 2024
31 Perkins, inquiry evidence, 6 June 2024
32 George Thomson, inquiry evidence, 21 June 2024

commission the damning report from Jonathan Swift QC. He'd then buried it on the strength of legal advice from Jane MacLeod. Asked by Beer about shunting work from the Swift review into the "legally privileged" workstream of the *Bates* litigation and thus away from prying eyes, Parker drawled: "So it's a very difficult question because, you know, when you look at these things in hindsight, you say, well, you could have spent some more time discussing it, or you could have had your own view, or you could have done this." He wasn't finished. "The problem with experts or specialists is, how do you judge the view of the specialist? Do you get another specialist to advise you on the specialist or do you draw the conclusion that your judgement of the specialist was wrong and the specialist you got is no good…"[33]

For a veteran businessman, Parker seemed remarkably unaware that it might have been his, rather than his lawyer's, role to set the direction on such matters and that the top job involved challenging such advice. Yet the captain of industry enjoyed nothing more than delivering long business tutorials from his reclined position. "Can I also… just explain to you a little bit about the perspective of being a chair and time, and what makes an effective chair, based on the experience that I've had," he began when asked about his minimal time commitment. "So being a chair is about a number of different things… [*cont p.494*]"

Chief culprit

By the time **Paula Vennells** appeared in May 2024, the former chief executive had been pilloried in front of millions, handed back her CBE, lost her non-executive directorships and was no longer preaching in the church. The only time a police escort was required for a witness arriving at Aldwych House, it ushered into the building a broken woman. But one for whom potential criminal proceedings loomed and who therefore had more to worry about than a tattered reputation.

Beer opened his questioning by running through 18 separate critical events or facts – such as Simon Clarke's watershed advice – that she had claimed in her witness statement not to know about. "Ms Vennells," the KC wanted to know, "in the light of the information that you tell us in your witness statement you weren't given… of the documents that you tell us in your witness statement that you didn't see and… the assurances that you tell us about in your witness statement that you were given by Post Office staff, do you think you're the unluckiest CEO in the United Kingdom?" Vennells could

---

33 Parker, inquiry evidence, 3 July 2024

respond only that "I was too trusting."[34] She later named those she over-relied on. "I trusted the people who gave me the information, so on the IT side, Lesley Sewell, and Mike Young… and, on the legal side, the general counsels, Susan Crichton and Chris Aujard and, later, Jane MacLeod."[35] Oddly, one man she didn't throw under the bus was her PR man Mark Davies, whom she'd once thanked for "guiding us through stormy waters of all kinds" and who was possibly more influential in her big decisions than all those others.

On the key events of her tenure, Beer pointed out, Vennells tended to "lack recollection in relation to facts that might be damaging to the Post Office" – she used the expression "I don't recall" 44 times over the three days of her evidence – but "when you refer to a recollection of a conversation that's unminuted, undocumented, not referred to in any email, there are always things that exculpate you, that reduce your blameworthiness". Vennells claimed this "isn't the approach I've taken".[36]

One such undocumented and exculpatory exchange had taken place (or not taken place, depending on who was believed) with IT boss Lesley Sewell in May 2013, as Second Sight prepared to reveal a couple of bugs and the taint of Gareth Jenkins was becoming known at senior Post Office levels. Vennells maintained that Sewell had told her that Jenkins was being stood down because he'd failed to disclose "one or two bugs" but these were "not relevant to the case he had been giving evidence on".[37] This became the convenient justification for her sustained subsequent refusal over the following years to admit that Horizon was the source of the sub-postmasters' woes. Ed Henry KC wasn't having it and bluntly put it to Vennells that the conversation was a "creation of yours". She didn't agree.[38]

For Sam Stein KC, also representing sub-postmasters, the commercial transformation of the Post Office explained Vennells's record. "You papered over the cracks and dragged… the Post Office into financial profitability over the debris that your firm had made of the lives of the sub-postmasters," he told her. Vennells admitted that her objective had been "commercial sustainability" but insisted she "was noted within the organisation for caring about sub-postmasters". One of her "huge regrets" was that "I did not do that for the sub-postmasters affected in this way, and that will be with me."[39]

Paula Vennells seemed to have learned far too late that no warm words,

---

34 Vennells, inquiry evidence, 22 May 2024
35 Vennells, inquiry evidence, 24 May 2024
36 Vennells, inquiry evidence, 22 May 2024
37 Ibid
38 Vennells, inquiry evidence, 24 May 2024
39 Ibid

cultivated reputation or encomia about her virtue could counter years of suppressing the most difficult issues. As her finance director from 2015, Alisdair Cameron, put it in his statement to the inquiry, "Paula did not believe there had been a miscarriage and could have not got there emotionally."[40] Evidence was no match for blind faith.

Mismanaging directors

For their different reasons, both the Post Office and Fujitsu consistently needed to hear that all was well with Horizon. One way to get this comfort was to tell each other. Vennells wrote in her witness statement that "both Simon Blagden [Fujitsu UK chairman] and Duncan Tait [Fujitsu UK and then European chief executive from 2011 to 2019] assured me that the Horizon system was safe and secure and not at fault".[41] At the same time, **Duncan Tait** told the inquiry, "Post Office executives including Ms Vennells… never escalated to me any issues regarding Horizon integrity. Indeed, I heard repeatedly that the sub-postmasters' claims regarding Horizon integrity were unfounded and that the system was working well."[42] It became clear that there was a self-reinforcing cycle of delusion and denial at the top of both organisations.

Complacency served Tait well for a decade, as he watched the revenue flow from his company's cornerstone contract, but was comprehensively exposed by the inquiry. He admitted that, when the "Horizon Issues" judgment in the *Bates* case landed in December 2019 (around the time he was pocketing a £2.6m payoff), he was "shocked to read in the media that… Horizon could and did cause discrepancies in branch accounts".

Given the extent of knowledge of Horizon's flaws in his company, this was extraordinary. But after what was revealed of his approach, not surprising. In February 2011, the Post Office's chief technology office Mike Young had sent Tait (then Fujitsu managing director and about to be promoted) a link to Nick Wallis's first film for BBC *Inside Out South*, telling him and the Fujitsu manager on the Post Office account: "I need you to take a look at this if you haven't seen the programme already." Tait didn't watch it, relying, he said, on a line from Young that "nothing has surfaced that suggests there is any evidence that the system is flawed in anyway [*sic*]"[43] – even though plenty had emerged, of course.

Inquiry counsel Julian Blake took Tait through a series of other reports

---

40 Alisdair Cameron, inquiry evidence, 17 May 2024
41 Vennells, witness statement, 8 March 2024, WITN01020100
42 Duncan Tait, witness statement, 21 May 2024, WITN03570100
43 Email from Mike Young to Tait, 8 February 2011, FUJ00174417

and broadcasts, none of which had moved the Fujitsu boss to act beyond ensuring that defensive PR lines were in place. "It's an old allegation which I believe is totally false, however, it is on the news," he told his head of marketing in June 2012, for example.[44] "It's like *Groundhog Day*," said Blake. "It's year, after year, after year, exactly the same thing comes up. There's a national report about Horizon integrity, and all there is is an email with a line that says everything is OK. Why wouldn't you, as managing director and then CEO, not actually put a significant investigation in place?" Tait reeled off a list of committees that constituted "good governance" but admitted "with hindsight, we absolutely should have done something about it because the media were absolutely spot on."[45] Once again, for "with hindsight", read "if we'd done remotely the right thing rather than act in our immediate corporate interest".

Tait's refusal to take responsibility for the damage caused by his product fitted in a dishonourable Fujitsu tradition, judging by the attitude of the chief executive when the company had sold a flawed system to the Post Office a quarter of a century earlier. When Flora Page put it to **Richard Christou**, by then 79, that his company had "failed to deliver… an accounting system that was fit for purpose", he replied that "fitness for purpose was never part of the codified agreement. It was specifically excluded."[46] Asked if he felt any responsibility for the ensuing scandal, he answered "No." Christou was "aggrieved that what I felt to be a good system has been put into such disrepute. But I'm not responsible for it."

The latest occupant of the Fujitsu top seat, appearing a couple of weeks after the ITV drama, couldn't get away with such insensitivity. **Paul Patterson** acknowledged deep corporate knowledge of Horizon's flaws and, having told a committee of MPs the week before that his company accepted a "moral obligation" to contribute to redress, now conceded what was obvious but previously denied, that "right from the very start of deployment of this system, there were bugs, errors and defects which were well known, to all parties, actually".[47] Hiding them from courts was, he agreed, "shameful".

The question hanging over Fujitsu, given its admitted culpability, was what it was going to do by way of recompense. A group called Lost Chances had been set up by former sub-postmaster Tony Downey's daughter Katie and two daughters of convicted sub-postmasters, Rebekah Foot and Katie Burrows, to campaign for sub-postmasters' children (now adults). Despite

---

44 Email from Tait to Simon Carter and others, 21 June 2012, FUJ00168523
45 Tait, inquiry evidence, 19 June 2024
46 Richard Christou, inquiry evidence, 19 June 2024
47 Paul Patterson, inquiry evidence, 19 January 2024

dealing with huge personal consequences, they weren't eligible for publicly funded redress. Would Fujitsu, Sam Stein KC wanted to know, help them out? "We will do everything we can do to address those wrongs in whatever way we can," intoned an earnest Patterson.

Between this promise in early 2024 and Patterson's second appearance at the inquiry nearly a year later, Fujitsu made around £1bn profit worldwide and earned tens of millions of pounds from the UK taxpayer despite a moratorium on new contracts (but not extensions of existing ones). On its commitment to Lost Chances, however, it had delivered precisely nothing. Fujitsu was, droned Patterson, "struggling to find out how we can be more creative, frankly, because that's not something that we've got any experience in".[48] A quarter of a century after selling the defective IT, a full six years after this had been found "not remotely robust" and with thousands of victims in its wake, Fujitsu had still to cough up a penny to anybody. The acceptance of a "moral obligation" – not a legal one, note – was shown up as a boilerplate PR strategy to avoid real consequences.

Government whipped

For world-class, systemic responsibility-dodging, nowhere rivalled Whitehall. The Post Office's "arm's-length" status distanced successive governments from accountability, even if, as inquiry counsel Jason Beer noted wryly at one point, "sometimes the arms get longer when it suits government and then get shorter when it doesn't".[49]

The telescopic mechanism was operated by the Shareholder Executive, which became UK Government Investments from 2016. It acted as steward for the government's interests in around 20 companies and had its own bureaucratic thicket in which to hide bad news. Potential trouble at any of its companies was entered on risk registers and "heat maps". One risk, recorded while Second Sight was doing its stuff, was that "if the [Horizon] system were to show up as defective then potentially the criminal convictions could be overturned and compensation from [the Post Office] sought."[50] Incredibly, the Shareholder Executive board did not consider this ticking timebomb, as it wasn't deemed a "significant risk". As the chief executive from the time, **Mark Russell**, admitted to the inquiry, "And weren't we wrong?"[51] Corporate processes that were supposedly there to address serious threats instead

---

48 Patterson, inquiry evidence, 11 November 2024
49 Richard Callard, inquiry evidence, 12 July 2024
50 Notes from the Shareholder Executive's eleventh risk and assurance committee, 19 February 2014, UKGI00042124
51 Mark Russell, inquiry evidence, 9 July 2024

consigned them to spreadsheets – and absolved those nominally in charge of doing anything about them.

The "risk" had been downplayed by the Shareholder Executive/UKGI official holding the Post Office brief and sitting on its board from 2014 to 2018, former Deloitte accountant **Richard Callard**. He was unrepentant about ensuring that his political masters didn't receive bad news, telling the inquiry "my job as a civil servant, with my civil servant hat on, is to try and deal with and protect ministers from undue – or even due, sometimes – criticism."[52] This was a cynical and incorrect view of his role, as if he'd prepared for government service by watching *Yes Minister* as an instructional video. The effect, in any case, was not to protect ministers but to keep them in the dark and lay them open to greater embarrassment later on. Callard didn't, for example, share Second Sight's final report with Jo Swinson, the postal affairs minister for most of 2013 to 2015, because, he told the inquiry, "She's then got to take a view." Which might have been different from the ultra-defensive view taken by the Post Office. In 2013, Callard had told Swinson that Second Sight had "'gone native' and are unduly taking the side of [Bates's group] the JFSA" and played down their findings.[53] Swinson wasn't best pleased, telling the inquiry that Callard was "using his departmental position, access and contacts to work on behalf of [the Post Office] to seek to persuade me to do what [it] wanted". It was the Shareholder Executive, she thought, that had "gone native".[54]

Jo Swinson had been a relatively long-serving exception to a rapidly revolving door of ministers with plenty of other priorities. The Shareholder Executive/UKGI had little difficulty pulling the wool over all their eyes. Some ministers, including Swinson and Baroness Neville-Rolfe, did ask searching questions but were, perhaps too easily, fobbed off. Swinson admitted some specific regrets, more thoughtfully than the generic ones of many others. "I should have met with… Alan Bates", she told the inquiry. "I wished I'd asked to meet with Second Sight directly. I wish, on a couple of occasions, I had pushed more and probed more."[55]

Others were more forgetful. Neville-Rolfe's successor **Margot James** was in post for two years as the Post Office fought the Alan Bates case. She made no mention to the inquiry that she'd been made aware of what she'd described in a parliamentary committee hearing in 2012 as "a lot of problems with [Horizon]" and that "it does not allow [sub-postmasters] to find where

---
52 Richard Callard, inquiry evidence, 12 July 2024
53 Patterson, briefing for Jo Swinson MP, 10 September 2014, UKGI00002472
54 Swinson, witness statement, 19 July 2024, WITN10190100
55 Swinson, inquiry evidence, 19 July 2024

an error has occurred and to rectify the error before having to repay losses".[56] This was just four years before becoming the minister responsible. Her inquisitors hadn't picked up on this, accepting her written evidence that "when I was appointed as minister with responsibility for postal affairs, I had no knowledge of any of the issues I have been asked to comment on."[57] She went on to tell the inquiry that it wasn't until six months after taking the job that she became "uncomfortable" with the defensive lines she was continuing to trot out about Horizon being "fit for purpose".[58]

The Post Office scandal was a political failing but, rather than one that was to any great extent down to particular ministers, it was one that went back a couple of decades to the notion that government could shed responsibility for state-owned companies and institutions. The business secretary when the *Bates* litigation was at its most febrile in early 2019, **Greg Clark**, was especially critical of the "arm's-length" arrangement and scathing of the body interposed between the elected government's ministers and a public service business. In the decision to seek Mr Justice Fraser's removal as judge, he told the inquiry, UKGI had "contrived to keep the unambiguous view of ministers from the Post Office". This was "outrageous".[59]

The shareholder body, said Clark, was "a private equity-type organisation [and] I think the people in it, structurally, are kind of keen to do deals and to do the things that you do in corporate finance". It "talks about its 'assets' the whole time," he added. Sub-postmasters with computer problems were clearly on the wrong side of the balance sheet: liabilities to be eliminated.

Good fellas

The smattering of good guys appearing at Aldwych House gave their own, sometimes world-weary insights. **Ian Henderson** of Second Sight told the inquiry how he believed his firm's work with the Post Office had started as "a shared commitment to seek the truth".[60] This had morphed into obstruction and, when he'd started to find uncomfortable truths, the "thinly veiled threat" from Chris Aujard to bankrupt him. "What had happened to the shared desire to seek the truth…?" asked Beer. "I think we'd moved on from that!" replied Henderson.

His colleague **Ron Warmington** was blunter. His written evidence revealed that when Susan Crichton had refused to use a new firm of lawyers to look at the prosecutorial misconduct Second Sight was finding, because the board

---
56 Commons business, innovation and skills committee hearing, 15 May 2012
57 Margot James, witness statement, 26 June 2024, WITN10910100
58 James, inquiry evidence, 24 July 2024
59 Gregory Clark, inquiry evidence, 25 July 2024
60 Henderson, inquiry evidence, 18 June 2024

wouldn't bear the expense, he'd told her "you're all fucking mad".[61] He was more restrained in the witness chair but, asked whether he stood by comments from 2014 that the Post Office's conduct was "the worst corporate behaviour I've ever come across",[62] confirmed that "it's exactly what I felt then and still feel now."[63]

The parliamentarian who had confronted this behaviour a decade before, **Lord (James) Arbuthnot**, provided a useful picture of it when asked 16 successive questions about whether key pieces of information, concerning internally known bugs and other proof of Horizon's faults, had been given to him during his extensive dealings with Vennells and Perkins early in the campaign. He answered "no" to all of them.[64] Arbuthnot was also one of two witnesses whose appearances had to be accompanied by a warning from Sir Wyn Williams to the public gallery not to applaud. The other was the leading man in this drama.

Two months away from becoming *Sir* **Alan Bates**, the chief protagonist told his story engagingly. He hadn't "set out to spend 20 years doing this," he explained. But "once I'd started my individual little campaign in there, we found others along the way and, eventually, we all joined up [and]… as you got to meet people and realised it wasn't just yourself, and you saw the harm and injustice that had been descended upon them, it was something that you felt you had to deal with."[65] His appearance also provided one of the lighter moments, when Jason Beer KC read the words of a Post Office executive claiming that he had been sacked because he "became unmanageable" and "struggled with the accounting".

The saving grace of the Post Office Horizon IT scandal was that Alan Bates never gave up the struggle to hold the Post Office to account.

"I was only obeying postal orders"

---

61 Ron Warmington, witness statement, 20 May 2024, WITN1050100
62 Transcript of conversation between Warmington and Alun Jones, 22 August 2014, SSL0000109
63 Warmington, inquiry evidence, 18 June 2024
64 Arbuthnot, inquiry evidence, 10 April 2024
65 Bates, inquiry evidence, 9 April 2024

16

CONCLUSION

Ending the litany of scandal…

SO PERVASIVE and systemic were the failings in the Post Office Horizon scandal that the word "scandal" hardly seems adequate to describe them. It wasn't just a few executives who bought into the Horizon lies; it was pretty much all of them. It wasn't just a handful of lawyers who executed the improper litigation strategy, driven by the financial imperatives of their client at the price of overriding justice; it was the vast majority of them. Much the same can be said of the civil servants and the technicians who hid the Horizon system's flaws, as well as the accountants. Almost everybody with any involvement in Horizon, or the Post Office's actions based on its output, played along in some way.

Sub-postmaster Tim Brentnall was undoubtedly right in saying "it was people", rather than an IT system, at fault.[1] But it is also impossible to argue that the scores of seriously culpable individuals were all exceptionally amoral or worse. They were in general relatively ordinary people who somehow inflicted extraordinary damage on others. It is also hard to believe that either of the principal organisations to blame, the Post Office and Fujitsu, were uniquely predisposed to such appalling conduct, even if their corporate cultures were certainly conducive to it.

What the Post Office Horizon scandal showed is that, in certain circumstances, behaviour by and within institutions can deteriorate catastrophically. It provides a case study in how this happens and should be examined as such in the years to come.

~

Action against the potentially criminal perpetrators of the injustice, largely within the Post Office and Fujitsu, will not be swift. Although the Metropolitan Police has 100 officers on its Operation Olympus investigation into the scandal and has

---
[1] Timothy Brentnall, inquiry evidence, 1 March 2022

said it is looking at 45 individuals, by the summer of 2025 it had interviewed just four of them and any cases are unlikely to reach court before 2028.

The putrefaction of cultures within the Post Office and Fujitsu, to the point that people in positions of responsibility hid evidence and lied to sub-postmasters, politicians, their own board and even to judges and juries, demands a more immediate response.

At a minimum, executive and non-executive directors of the Post Office and Fujitsu, whose job it was to prevent the spiral of denial, groupthink and eventually blind faith that rendered the truth impossible to confront, need to face the consequences of their dereliction. They surely failed in their fiduciary duties, which under the 2006 Companies Act include considering long-term consequences, the interests of employees, the impact on the community and environment, and maintaining a good reputation.[2] This should lead to meaningful sanctions from company regulators, such as long bans and the reputational harm that comes with them. At the very least, the conduct of Post Office managing directors Alan Cook (2006-2010), Dave Smith (2010) and Paula Vennells (2011-2018), plus Fujitsu chief executive Duncan Tait (2011-2019), needs to be assessed against these standards. Similarly, the records of Post Office chairs Alice Perkins (2011-2015) and Tim Parker (2015-2022) ought to be measured against the requirements of the position to challenge – if not quite to be a "guarantor of good behaviour", as Parker grandly put it, then certainly to promote high standards and question groupthink. If these figures are not held accountable, the notion of enforceable corporate standards means nothing.

The consequences under individuals' contracts should be followed through, too. Paula Vennells and other executives had "clawback" clauses in their contracts allowing for bonuses to be repaid "in the event of misstatement of the accounts, error or gross misconduct".[3] These need to be enforced if the framing of directors' contracts and extravagant remuneration packages isn't to be just a game that the top dogs always win.

∽

Further down these organisations, there were any number of managerial structures that were supposed to head off or highlight faults. Fujitsu's Duncan Tait told the public inquiry: "We had delivery assurance in place. We had assurance teams… We had audit and risk committees in place and each one of these could have brought to the attention of the [chief executive] that we

2 legislation.gov.uk/ukpga/2006/46/pdfs/ukpga_20060046_en.pdf
3 Post Office annual report and financial statements, 2012-13

needed to do something about [Horizon]."[4] Paula Vennells explained that she had instigated a "bad news is good news" initiative and a "pre-mortem" system to ensure "lessons learned" and to "read into actions going forwards where things might go wrong".[5] No number of committees and no amount of management-speak, however, can compete with subtler messages coming from the top that the real "bad news" must not be mentioned.

The only antidote to secretive and censorious environments of the sort found in the Post Office, in which unethical or even unlawful instructions cannot be countermanded, is the possibility of speaking out. The Post Office scandal proves the need for laws both to require and protect the disclosure of wrongdoing. The Labour government's forthcoming Hillsborough Law must translate into a real requirement for transparency, candour and frankness for public officials – not just during inquiries into scandals but at all times, so as to prevent them happening in the first place. This should be accompanied with greater protections for whistleblowers – and even rewards for them – so that those tempted to act in the way many Post Office and Fujitsu employees did would fear the prospect of being exposed. Speaking up needs to be a better option than covering up to avert a crisis or defer it until it is somebody else's problem – a pattern that leads to generational scandals such as this and the even longer-running one over infected blood transfusions.

It isn't just insiders who should feel bound to voice concerns; so should those brought in from outside when they find serious failings that are being ignored or denied. Deloitte's consultants produced thorough reports under the codenames Zebra and Bramble, but remained conspicuously silent when the Post Office and Fujitsu gave testimony in the High Court shortly afterwards that they would almost certainly have been aware of, and which they knew to be false. Auditor EY was also aware of the failings in Horizon that were being denied in court. A duty of candour on professional advisers in such circumstances should accompany that for employees.

~

The legal profession, meanwhile, will need to ask what caused so many of its members to relegate their professional obligations below commercial incentives. Although disciplinary action awaits some involved in the scandal, this is unlikely to produce the transformation required. The Post Office story perhaps demonstrates a need for a wholesale review of how to ensure solicitors

---
4 Tait, inquiry evidence, 19 June 2024
5 Vennells, inquiry evidence, 22 May 2024

and barristers serve the interests of justice in an adversarial legal system. It also throws up a host of other legal questions – such as whether private prosecutions without independent oversight by large organisations should be consigned to history, or at least seriously curtailed. And, whether the Lady Chief Justice likes it or not, the fact that criminal and civil trials heard highly partial (in both senses) cases against sub-postmasters demands a look at the role of the judiciary when the evidential cards are stacked against one side – especially when it comes to control of computer evidence.

The importance of a functioning and objective legal system was powerfully demonstrated by Alan Bates. It was the only mechanism that could ever have got to the truth and eventually performed its task very well. But it did so only in the exceptional circumstances of Sir Alan having lined up hundreds of victims, without whom the case would never have got off the ground. Access to justice needs to be radically improved for those in similar situations in future.

∽

The scandal has also exposed a yawning gulf in political accountability for the Post Office. It proved impossible even for MPs to get adequate answers, never mind action, from government about a major public body with a social purpose. The distancing of Post Office Ltd from its shareholder in Whitehall, with the Shareholder Executive/UK Government Investments sitting in between, blocked democratic oversight. The intermediary body was incapable of stewarding a company with more than just a commercial purpose. Given the depth of its shortcomings, and the range of companies with sensitive or nuanced objectives that UKGI oversees – including Britain's main nuclear companies, Channel 4, a nationalised steel company, the UK's defence equipment supplier and more than a dozen others – it could well be time to end the 22-year "arm's length" experiment and for UKGI to join the list of quangos being scrapped by the government. At the same time, publicly owned companies should invariably become "public interest companies" rather than more narrowly commercial ones.

The Post Office itself faces an uncertain future. While it was sacrificing sub-postmasters for its commercial objectives, other operators were eating further and further into its business. Mail and parcel deliveries, click and collect, and ubiquitous online government and financial services leave some asking what the point of the Post Office is any more. The one thing that it had was the Post Office brand. The greatest irony is that, in seeking to protect this, it has come close to trashing it.

The Post Office name isn't completely destroyed, however. It is steeped in history and there could still be a demand for hubs in communities providing basic services under the Post Office umbrella. But it needs to be radically different from the command-and-control organisation it has become. A green paper published by the government in July 2025 again raised the prospect of mutualisation. This time it needs to be tried seriously, putting those who understand the needs of their communities at the heart of the business.

The other chief corporate culprit, Fujitsu, has failed woefully to account, never mind pay, for its role. It is perhaps all too aware that a tarnished brand comes with few consequences when its clients are corporations and public-sector bodies. While the government has imposed a moratorium on bidding for new contracts, so embedded is the company that permitted renewals and extensions of existing ones are enough to tide it over. Ministers should be far more reluctant to agree such deals as long as the company, still making billion-pound profits globally, refuses to put its hand in its pocket for its role in the scandal. Governments should never again become so dependent on a major IT company. And, as public bodies excitedly hand out deals for the latest wave of transformational IT (from artificial intelligence to data platforms), they should look back 30 years to what happened in the last wave of techno-enthusiasm and treat the latest hyperbolic promises with some scepticism.

It is worth reflecting on some things that *did* work, however imperfectly. The law eventually proved its worth, notably through the Alan Bates litigation that exposed the truth. This in turn enabled the extent of the Post Office's misfeasance – the "affront to the public conscience" – to be recognised in the Court of Appeal. This then brought about the statutory inquiry that has unearthed so much of how the scandal happened. No episode could better demonstrate the need for the wheels of justice to keep turning – and for impediments to this to be removed.

Representative democracy, despite efforts to shield the Post Office from it, was also essential in this process. Through debates, questions and direct engagement with the Post Office, the sub-postmasters' parliamentary champions secured the first independent scrutiny of the Horizon system in the shape of Second Sight's work. This and the publicity given to the sub-postmasters' cause provided crucial grounds for the legal action to go ahead. It wasn't quick, and it was far from perfect, but the chain of events at least demonstrates to members of parliament what they can achieve by campaigning on the real issues hitting their constituents hardest.

Journalism also, to some degree, did its job. The story wasn't the easiest to pick up, with the Post Office gleefully pointing to court verdicts against the sub-postmasters to deter reporting. But *Computer Weekly*, the BBC through Nick Wallis's *One Show* reports, *Taro Naw* in Wales and later *Panorama*, and *Private Eye* showed it was perfectly feasible to raise and examine complaints. While fawning interviews not mentioning the affair were conducted with Paula Vennells, there was little other significant coverage until judgments in the Alan Bates case opened the floodgates. This is an indictment of the media and its apparent lack of interest in the lives of the ordinary people who constituted the scandal's thousands of victims. It is hard to imagine a similar indifference if they had been a more eye-catching group. But the press got there eventually, and for the last few years has spotlighted the cause well.

Throughout the scandal, governments have listened less well and paid less attention to the details than they needed to. They too readily accepted the dismissal of media reports by the Post Office and its ciphers in the Shareholder Executive/UKGI, rather than consider the stories critically. Investigative journalism needs to be taken seriously and judged on its merits rather than dismissed as axe-grinding by the "usual suspects". (Disclosure: this is a usual suspect grinding an axe.)

Nothing made this point more forcefully than the Sunak government's response to ITV's *Mr Bates vs The Post Office*. Between the end of 2023 and the drama's conclusion a few days later, no new facts about the scandal emerged. But, when ministers realised the nation now understood the story, they acted with something closer to the required urgency.

Justice arrived only because of the campaigning of the sub-postmasters portrayed on the country's TV screens. The good that emerged from the Post Office Horizon scandal was the sub-postmasters' triumph.

Acknowledgements

THE story of the Post Office Horizon IT scandal from within the Post Office, Whitehall and Fujitsu can be told only because of the wealth of information unearthed by the statutory inquiry. I owe the sub-postmasters, campaigners and politicians who made this happen the greatest debt of thanks for thus providing most of the raw material for this book. I have tried to bring out the role of some, but far from all of them, in its pages.

Through their stewardship of this inquiry and expert forensic examination of the mountain of evidence, Sir Wyn Williams's inquiry team brought out the shocking facts of the story, on which much of this account is based. Legal teams acting for sub-postmasters drew out many of the most telling revelations and themes. Most of the underlying evidence has been made available through the inquiry's website, postofficehorizoninquiry.org.uk, and has been made searchable through the extremely helpful site set up by IT specialist Matthew Somerville, postofficeinquiry.dracos.co.uk.

Other crucial information has been brought out by unheralded campaigners, notably Eleanor Shaikh. She was inspired by the fate of her local sub-postmaster in Surrey, Chirag Sidhpura, who was sacked as late as 2018 over a false shortfall. Eleanor's freedom of information enquiries revealed a huge amount about the political and technical origins of the scandal and some of the most damning, but buried, evidence of Horizon's failings.

I am also grateful for illuminating discussions with many of those who have put their shoulder to the wheel of turning this scandal into justice and ensuring its grimmer aspects were not lost, in particular campaigning barrister Paul Marshall and campaigner "Monsieur Cholet".

Along with the support and encouragement of *Private Eye*'s editor Ian Hislop and managing director Geoff Elwell, I have been very lucky to have an ace *Eye* team producing this book. Glenn Orton has applied his design genius; Stephen Patience has proved a case study in nominative determinism and helped greatly with his editing, along with his collegue Simon Edmond; Peter McNamara's indexing is invaluable; and our lawyer Lizzie Greene has expertly helped ensure we get this terrible tale out.

One important episode recounted in this book involves Royal Mail chairman Donald Brydon raising *Private Eye*'s first report on the scandal with the Post Office board, after which forensic accountants Second Sight were brought in and started on the long road to the truth. I want to thank all my colleagues – from production staff to joke writers, editors and assistants, cartoonists, business managers and everybody else – for ensuring those with any sense read the *Eye* and enabling me to tell this story of the Post Office Horizon IT scandal.

Appendix 1

Key officials

Post Office leaders

Managing directors/chief executives

John Roberts chief executive 1995–2002

David Mills chief executive Apr 2002–Dec 2005

Alan Cook managing director Mar 2006–Mar 2010

David Smith managing director Apr–Sept 2010

Paula Vennells managing director Oct 2010–Mar 2012; chief executive Apr 2012–Mar 2019

Alisdair Cameron acting chief executive Apr–Sept 2019

Nick Read chief executive Sept 2019–Mar 2025

Neil Brocklehurst chief executive Apr 2025– (acting chief executive from Jun 2024 while Read dealt with public inquiry)

Chairs

Neville Bain chair Post Office Group Mar 1998–Dec 2001

Allan Leighton chair Consignia plc (formerly Post Office Group, then from Nov 2002 Royal Mail), Jan 2001–Mar 2009

Donald Brydon chair Royal Mail Mar 2009–Aug 2015 (and chair Post Office Ltd May 2009–Sept 2011)

Alice Perkins chair Post Office Ltd Sept 2011–Jul 2015

Tim Parker chair Post Office Ltd Oct 2015–Sept 2022

Henry Staunton chair Post Office Ltd Dec 2022–Jan 2024

Nigel Railton chair Post Office Ltd May 2024–

Other Post Office officials

Chris Aujard general counsel Oct 2013–Mar 2015

Keith Baines contracts manager 1990s–2000s

Susan Crichton head of legal and general counsel Jan 2010–Sept 2013

Belinda Crowe Project Sparrow programme director Oct 2013–Mar 2015

Mark Davies communications director Jul 2012–2019

Ben Foat general counsel May 2019–Apr 2024 (and from 2016, legal director)

Rod Ismay head of branch accounting Jun 2006–Mar 2016

Alwen Lyons company secretary Jul 2011–Aug 2017

Tony Marsh head of security Sept 1999–Dec 2006

Jane MacLeod general counsel Mar 2015–May 2019

David Miller Horizon programme director Jan 1998–early 2000, then managing director Post Office Network to Feb 2021

Jarnail Singh head of criminal law Apr 2012–Mar 2015

John Scott head of security Jan 2007–Sept 2016

Lesley Sewell head of IT and chief information officer Apr 2010–Nov 2015

David Smith head of IT (later change and information systems) Feb 2005–Mar 2010

Mandy Talbot civil litigation team leader 2004–2011

Angela van den Bogerd senior network positions 1996–2012; head of partnerships 2012–2013; programme director, branch support programme 2013–2015; then other roles including business improvement director 2018–2020

Rodric Williams litigation lawyer Aug 2010–2017; head of legal (dispute resolution and brand) 2017–Aug 2020; head of legal remediation unit 2020–

Rob Wilson head of criminal law May 2002–Apr 2012

Mike Young operations director Aug 2008–Oct 2010; chief operating officer Oct 2010–Apr 2012

Fujitsu leaders

Richard Christou chief executive Fujitsu Services Ltd Jul 2000–Apr 2004 (having been commercial and legal director mid-late 1990s)

David Courtley chief executive 2004–2008

Roger Gilbert chief executive 2009–2011

Duncan Tait chief executive Apr 2011–Jul 2019 (until Mar 2014 UK, then Europe & Middle East)

Simon Blagden self-styled Fujitsu UK chairman and chair Fujitsu Telecoms UK, and political consultant for Fujitsu Services Ltd 2005–2019

Paul Patterson chief executive Fujitsu Europe Jul 2019–

Other Fujitsu staff

Andy Dunks customer service Post Office account security team 2002–

Jan Holmes audit manager Horizon programme 1997–2008

Gareth Jenkins software engineer 1973–2015 (from mid-1990s "distinguished engineer")

Colin Lenton-Smith commercial and finance director Horizon Mar 2001–Oct 2007

External legal advisers

Brian Altman KC advised on the post-Clarke advice review of disclosures and acted for Post Office in Court of Appeal in *Hamilton & Others*

Simon Clarke barrister with Cartwright King advising Post Office from Apr 2013

Lord (Anthony) Grabiner KC barrister representing Post Office on application to remove judge in *Bates*

Gavin Matthews senior litigation partner Womble Bond Dickinson May 2013–Apr 2021

Andy Parsons senior associate Womble Bond Dickinson 2012–May 2016; partner May 2016–

Jonathan Swift KC author of Swift report confirming remote access 2015–16

Shareholder Executive/UKGI officials on Post Office board

Susannah Storey Apr 2012–Mar 2014

Richard Callard Mar 2014–Mar 2018

Tom Cooper Mar 2018–May 2023

Postal services ministers

Ed Davey May 2010–Feb 2012

Norman Lamb Feb–Sept 2012

Jo Swinson Sept 2012–May 2015

Baroness (Lucy) Neville-Rolfe May 2015–Jul 2016

Margot James Jul 2016–Jan 2018

Andrew Griffiths Jan–Jul 2018

Kelly Tolhurst Jul 2018–Feb 2020

Paul Scully Feb 2020–Jul 2022

Jane Hunt Jul–Sept 2022

Dean Russell Sept–Oct 2022

Kevin Hollinrake Oct 2022–Jul 2024

Gareth Thomas Jul 2024–Sept 2025

Blair McDougall Sept 2025–

Appendix 11
Timeline of events

May 1996 ICL, then 80 percent owned by Fujitsu, awarded £1bn PFI contract to run benefit payment card system for Post Office and Benefits Agency

May 1999 Benefits payment card dropped; Horizon now to be just a Post Office branch accounting system; Post Office collectively writes off nearly £900m; Alan Bates becomes sub-postmaster in Craig-y-Don, north Wales

Oct 1999 Horizon roll-out begins

Oct 2000 Horizon installed in Alan Bates's post office; discrepancies first arise a couple of months later

Mar 2001 Post Office group becomes public limited company and "arm's-length" body, outside ministerial control

Sept 2003 Shareholder Executive (later UK Government Investments) created to manage government shareholdings in public companies such as Post Office

Nov 2003 Alan Bates's contract terminated; he soon sets up Postofficevictims website

Jan 2004 Independent IT expert Jason Coyne tells Post Office that, having looked at Horizon in the Cleveleys branch in Lancashire, the system "was clearly defective in elements of its hardware, software or interfaces"

Mar 2006 Lee Castleton suspended over a £26,000 shortfall; nine months later he is bankrupted

Sept 2006 Noel Thomas pleads guilty to false accounting and is jailed for nine months

Feb 2008 Jo Hamilton pleads guilty and is spared jail

May 2009 *Computer Weekly* publishes its first article: "Bankruptcy, prosecutions and disrupted livelihoods – postmasters tell their story"

Nov 2009 Alan Bates convenes the first meeting of Justice for Subpostmasters Alliance at Fenny Compton village hall in Warwickshire

Aug 2010 Post Office head of branch accounting Rod Ismay produces his "whitewash" report

Oct 2010 Paula Vennells becomes Post Office managing director; Seema Misra convicted of theft, then sentenced to 15 months in prison while pregnant

Feb 2011 BBC *Inside Out South* and reporter Nick Wallis air first TV report

Sept 2011 James Arbuthnot MP and Ernst & Young audit partner alert new Post Office chair Alice Perkins to Horizon flaws; *Private Eye* publishes its first story: "Computer says no"

Apr 2012 Post Office becomes independent of Royal Mail; Paula Vennells now chief executive

Jul 2012 Second Sight appointed to examine operation of Horizon system in specific cases and advise on mediation through special working group

Jul 2013 Second Sight submits interim report, finding two bugs, multiple problems with training and support; barrister Simon Clarke advises Post Office that Fujitsu engineer Gareth Jenkins's "credibility as an expert witness is fatally undermined"

Oct 2013 Privatisation of Royal Mail, not mentioning Horizon troubles; report for Post Office from Detica consultants finds "Post Office systems are not fit for purpose in a modern retail and financial environment"

Jun 2014 Project Zebra report from Deloitte identifies the possibility of remote access to branch accounts

Aug 2014 Second Sight's draft final report concludes that Horizon is not fit for purpose

Dec 2014 Arbuthnot uses parliamentary debate to dismiss "sham" mediation process

Feb 2015 Paula Vennells makes her only appearance before a parliamentary committee, insisting there was no evidence of miscarriages of justice

Mar 2015 Second Sight sacked by Post Office and mediation working group shut down

Aug 2015 BBC *Panorama* airs *Trouble at the Post Office*, in which former Fujitsu engineer Richard Roll reveals that the company altered branch accounts remotely

Oct 2015 Tim Parker succeeds Alice Perkins as Post Office chair and follows postal services minister Baroness Neville-Rolfe's order to commission a review of Horizon

Feb 2016 Review from Jonathan Swift QC finds remote access "poses real issues" for Post Office and demands further investigations

Apr 2016 Having secured funding and insurance, Alan Bates files papers in the High Court and begins *Alan Bates & Others v Post Office Ltd*

Jan 2017 At first hearing in *Bates*, Post Office admits remote access possibility to correct branch errors

Oct 2017 Further report from Deloitte, Project Bramble, providing proof of remote access without sub-postmasters' knowledge; the paper is not disclosed

Nov 2018 Mr Justice Fraser finds Post Office "attempting to restrict evidence for public relations reasons"

Dec 2018 Paula Vennells awarded CBE in 2019 New Year honours list

Jan 2019 Paula Vennells ceases to act as chief executive

Mar 2019 In his "Common Issues" judgment, Fraser finds the Post Office guilty of "oppressive behaviour" towards sub-postmasters and destroys basis of false accounting charges; as "Horizon Issues" trial starts, Post Office alleges Fraser is biased and seeks to de-bench him

May 2019 Appeal court judge Lord Coulson dismisses the application as "untenable"

Sept 2019 Nick Read becomes Post Office chief executive

Nov 2019 Coulson also rejects Post Office bid to appeal Common Issues judgment, likening the organisation to a "mid-Victorian factory owner"

Dec 2019 In his "Horizon Issues" judgment, Fraser finds Horizon until 2010 was "not remotely robust" and Horizon Online, from 2010, was more robust but also contained bugs. Post Office and the group led by Alan Bates agree a settlement, leaving the sub-postmasters with an average £20,000 after legal costs; compensation for other sub-postmasters also to be set up

May 2020 Prime minister Boris Johnson agrees to inquiry into the scandal, which is soon clarified as a non-statutory review under retired judge Sir Wyn Williams

Dec 2020 First (six) convictions based on Horizon evidence overturned at Southwark Crown Court

Apr 2021 Thirty-nine convictions overturned at Court of Appeal, all adjudged an "affront to the public conscience"

May 2021 Government announces inquiry will be statutory

Feb 2022 Inquiry begins hearing evidence, starting with sub-postmasters; Tim Parker announces resignation as Post Office chair

Jan 2024 ITV airs *Mr Bates vs The Post Office*; prime minister Rishi Sunak announces legislation to overturn all Horizon-related convictions; Fujitsu European chief executive Paul Patterson admits "moral obligation" to compensate victims – still unfulfilled

May 2024 Paula Vennells makes tearful appearance at inquiry and says she was "too trusting"; Post Office (Horizon System) Offences Act 2024 is passed, acquitting hundreds of sub-postmasters

Sept 2024 Nick Read announces he is stepping down as Post Office chief executive

Jan 2025 Parliamentary committee reports that for many redress process remains "so slow that people are dying before they get justice"

Jul 2025 Sir Wyn Williams publishes first volume of his report, outlining devastating personal consequences of the scandal, including link to 13 suicides, and demanding drastic improvements in redress scheme

Index

A

Addleshaw Goddard, 170, 172
Allen, Lisa, 50
Altman, Brian, 106, 114-117, 129, 163
anomalies: see bugs
Arbuthnot, James, 9, 67, 69, 89, 90, 92, 100, 109-110, 118, 125-126, 128-130, 183, 191; leafy constituency, 134; Jo Hamilton's MP, 67-68, 86, 122; meetings with Vennells and Perkins, 91, 119, 122; and Second Sight, 98-100, 102-103, 112, 119; faith in mediation scheme, 117; loses faith in mediation scheme, 122-123; stands down as MP, 128-129; elevated to peerage, 160; calls for full inquiry, 160
Argos, 83
Ashraf, Kamran, 162
audit record queries (ARQs), 27, 55, 77, 154
Aujard, Chris, 116-120, 122, 124, 128, 136, 182, 185, 190; threat of legal action against Second Sight, 119, 190

B

Badenoch, Kemi, 169-170
BAE Systems, 111
Bailey, Adrian, 125-126
Bain, Neville, 15-16, 42, 45
Baines, Keith, 19, 30, 32
Bajaj, Amar, 66
Baker, Simon, 100
Baksi, Catherine, 168
Barang, Jasvinder, 162
Bardo, Matt, 131, 132

Bates, Alan, 2, 4, 9, 48, 65-66, 68-69, 86-87, 91-92, 103, 112-113, 117-119, 122, 127, 129-131, 134-135, 137, 141-144, 155-158, 164-165, 173, 191; termination of sub-postmaster contract, 33-34; founds JFSA, 6, 133, 160; persistence, 33, 131, 159; writes to Allan Leighton, 46; writes to Ed Davey, 82-83; select committee appearance, 126; files High Court claim, 139; *Alan Bates & Others v Post Office Ltd*, 2-3, 74, 135, 141-146, 148-149; Court of Appeal victory, 58; knighted, 191
BBC, 42, 86, 100, 121-122, 131, 133, 169, 197
Beefeater, 83
Beer, Jason, 174, 176, 178-179, 180-181, 183-185, 188, 190-191
benefit payment card, 11, 13-15
Benn, Tony, 8, 11, 41
BHS 46, 150
Binley, Brian, 127
Birkenshaw, West Yorkshire, 96
Birmingham Six, 104
Blagden, Simon, 113, 117, 121, 186
Blair, Tony, 13-14, 42-43, 47, 68
Blake, Julian, 177, 186-187
Bond Dickinson (now Womble Bond Dickinson), 35, 101, 105-106, 109, 114-115, 118, 139, 141-142, 149, 153
Bond Pearce: see Bond Dickinson

Bourke, Patrick, 132
Bowyer, Harry, 93-94, 96, 115
Bracknell, Berkshire, 27-28, 46, 92, 128, 133
Bradshaw, Steve, 55, 57, 58, 60-61, 74-75, 96; Noel Thomas case, 55; Janet Skinner case, 57; Jacqueline McDonald case, 74-74; not technically minded, 177
Bramble, Project: see Deloitte
Brander, Graham, 52-53, 60-61
Breedon, John, 38, 145
Brentnall, Tim, 74, 192
Bridgen, Andrew, 91-92, 122, 133-134
Bridlington, East Yorkshire, 34
Bristow, David, 68, 87, 90
British government, xi, xii, 4, 16, 18, 43, 67-68, 87, 108, 110, 113, 135, 137, 148-149, 156, 159-160, 164-165, 168, 172; under Harold Wilson, 11, 41; under Margaret Thatcher, 41; under John Major, 11, 42; under Tony Blair, 12-15, 42, 46; under David Cameron, 81, 91; under Boris Johnson, 159-160; under Rishi Sunak, 197; under Keir Starmer, 170, 194; stake in Post Office, xii, 6, 9, 18, 43-44, 47, 71, 83, 188; stalling compensation, 170
Brown, Alan, 66
Brown, Betty, 173
Brown, Gordon, 13
Brown, Tom, 123
Brydon, Donald, 81, 88, 90, 111, 206
BSkyB, 46

207

bugs: 6, 19-21, 28, 39, 55, 62, 72-73, 76, 79, 95-96, 100, 102, 104-105, 108, 112, 117, 131-132, 155-156, 177, 185, 187, 191; bureau discrepancies, 156; Callendar Square bug, 28, 37, 66, 77-78, 154; Dalmellington bug, 136-137; data tree build failure discrepancies, 28, 156; Girobank discrepancies, 28; phantom transactions, 28; receipts/payments mismatch issue, 72-73, 79, 82, 100, 132; table of, 155-156; Paula Vennells dislikes term, 4, 100
business select committee (House of Commons), 125-128, 164, 170, 173
Butoy, Harjinder, 62
Byers, Stephen, 13, 18, 43-44, 68
Byrne, Liam, 170, 172-173

C

Cable, Vince, 81-82, 96, 110, 125
Callanan, Lord (Martin), 160
Callard, Richard, 118, 135, 137, 147, 189
Callendar Square, Falkirk: see bugs
Camberwell Green, London, 30
Cameron, Alisdair, 150-151, 153, 155, 170, 186
Cameron, David, 91
Campbell-Smith, Duncan, 16
Canada Post, 81
Capture IT system, 5
Carr, Lady Chief Justice (Sue), 168-169,
Carroll, Lewis, 146
Cartwright King, 93-96, 104-108, 114-116, 129
Castleton, Lee, 9, 77, 141, 154, 168; trial, 34-37, 56; contacts *Computer Weekly*, 65-66; case cited in defence of Post Office, 69, 72
Cavender, David, 143, 147, 150-151
Chalk, Alex, 169
Chambers, Anne, 37-38, 56
Channel 4, 44, 195
Charles II, 7
Chisholm, Alex, 147-148

Christou, Richard, 20, 187
Clark, Greg, 149, 151
Clarke, Ken, 12, 42
Clarke, Simon, 104-108, 113-115, 117, 127, 163, 181-182, 184
Clegg, Nick, 81
Cleife, Julie, 162
Cleveleys, Lancashire, 28-29, 31
Clifton-Brown, Sir Geoffrey, 173
Collins, Tony, 65
Computer Weekly (magazine), 65, 67-68, 74, 76-77, 86, 121, 137, 183, 197
Cook, Alan, 63-64, 66-67, 70, 193; earnings, 64
Cooper, Tom, 147-149, 151
Costa Coffee, 83, 109
Cottingley, West Yorkshire, 146
Coulson, Lord Justice (Peter), 151, 152, 155
Court of Appeal, 3, 73, 105, 141, 162, 181; *Hamilton & Others v Post Office*, 162, 163; convictions overturned, 58
Courts and Tribunals Service, 151
Coyne, Jason, 29-30; eponymous report, 29-32, 35, 39
Craig-y-Don, Wales, 2, 33-34
Crichton, Susan, 90-92, 104-107, 115-116, 182, 185, 190; and Second Sight review, 93, 95, 98, 101; left sitting in corridor outside meeting, 108, 183; integrity as lawyer, 109, 116, 182
Criminal Cases Review Commission (CCRC), 103-106, 114, 117, 129, 141, 162
Crocker, Michael, 125
Crowe, Belinda, 118, 123
Crown Prosecution Service, 21, 23
Crozier, Adam, 45-46, 81
Cwmdu, Swansea, 24

D

Daily, Robert, 62, 178
Dalmellington, Ayrshire: see bugs
Darling, Alistair, 13-14
Davey, Ed, 82-83, 90

Davies, Jane, 166
Davies, Mark, 100-102, 110, 122-124, 126, 134-135, 137, 147-148, 183, 185; guides Vennells through stormy waters, 101, 147, 185; goes nuclear, 131
Dearing, Ron, 41, 45
Deloitte, 90, 92, 120, 132, 135, 138-139, 189, 194; Project Bramble, 140, 194; Project Zebra, 120, 132, 138, 194
Department for Work and Pensions, 59
Department of Social Security (DSS), 12-15
defects: see bugs
Detica, 111-112
Dilley, Stephen, 35-37
Dixons, 83
Dolan, Monica, 168
Downey, Tony, 171, 173, 187
Duncan, Lord (Ian), 160
Dunks, Andy, 35-36, 56, 80, 154-155, 180

E

Edwards, Martin, 100, 102
electronic point of sales system (EPOSS), 19-20, 30
Elizabeth II: privatisation of her head, 41; said to be miffed, 44; Vennells a potential embarrassment to, 148
Ernst & Young, 17, 64, 70-71, 88-90, 152-153
errors: see bugs
exceptions: see bugs
EY: see Ernst & Young

F

Fagan, Mary, 66
faults: see bugs
Felstead, Tracy, 9, 24, 30, 162, 163; wrongly imprisoned as 19-year-old, 9; asked to demonstrate how she did not steal money, 24
Fenny Compton, Warwickshire, 68
Financial Conduct Authority, 161
Flemington, Hugh, 95, 101, 104, 106, 114
Flinders, Karl, 137

Foat, Ben, 161, 170
Ford, Julie, 66
Foster, Richard, 129
Fraser, Mr Justice (Peter), 142-154, 181-182; endorsement of Alan Bates, 145; Post Office applies for his recusal, 151-152, 181-182; Horizon Issues judgment, 155-156
Freeman, George, 133-134
Freeths, 130, 134-135, 141, 143, 172
French, Jane, 86
Fujitsu, 4, 6, 11, 15, 27-32, 35-38, 47, 52, 55-57, 62, 69, 72, 76-80, 87-88, 89, 94, 104, 105, 113, 116-117, 121, 131-132, 143, 153-154, 163, 176-177, 179-180, 186-188, 192-194, 196; HQ, 27-28, 46, 92, 128, 133; support centre, 39, 58, 80; knowledge of bugs, 6, 28, 37, 72, 77, 79, 143; remote access to Horizon, 13-1, 92, 103, 120, 131-132, 142, 154; "moral obligation" to compensate victims, 187-188

G

Gaerwen, Anglesey, 54-55
Gibson, Will, 110
Gilliland, Kevin, 113
Girobank, 28, 41
glitches: see bugs
Glover, Amanda, 87
Godeseth, Torstein, 154
Grabiner, Lord (Anthony), 150-152; apparent obtuseness at inquiry, 181
Grant, Angus, 88-89, 153
Grant, Raymond: unrepentant of role in prosecution, 178; busy with carol services and dog-walking, 177-178
Granville, Mike, 83
Green, Patrick, 135, 142, 154, 156
Greene, Moya, 81, 88, 90
Griffiths, Gina, 125
Griffiths, Martin, 124-125
Griffiths, Oliver, 71
Grocer (trade magazine), 66
Groundhog Day, 187

H

Hall, Alison, 122
Hall, Tony, 132
Hamilton, Jo, 6, 55-58, 66, 92, 132, 168, 175; HGV licence, 51; trial, 51-54; appears on BBC television, 86, 123-124; constituent of James Arbuthnot, 67-68, 86, 122; *Jo Hamilton & Others v Post Office Ltd*, 162-164, 169, 181
Hampstead, 162
Harding, Susan, 48
Hartley, James, 130, 134-135, 156, 172
Havery, Richard, 36-37
Hawkshead, Cumbria, 171
HBOS, 158, 161
Head, Chris, 159-160, 164, 172-173
helpdesk, 28-29, 56, 75
Henderson, Ian, 92, 99, 103, 108, 112-113, 118-120, 129, 131-132, 135, 190; receives threat, 119, 131, 190; deadpan select committee appearance, 127-128; see also Second Sight
Henry, Ed, 8, 177, 182, 185
Herbert Smith Freehills, 153, 155, 161, 164, 167, 170-172, 176; staggering fees, 161
Heseltine, Michael, 42
Heywood, Jeremy, 14
High Court, 163, 178; *Alan Bates and Others v Post Office Ltd*, 135, 139, 141, 144, 159, 166; Lee Castleton, 35-36, 38
HM Revenue & Customs, 21, 59; formerly Inland Revenue, 21, 92
Hollinrake, Kevin, 161, 167
Holloway, HM Prison, 9
Holmes, Jan, 19-20, 29-30, 31, 62
Holmes, Marion, 62
Holmes, Peter, 61-62, 178
Holroyd, Lord Justice, 163
Hooper, Sir Anthony, 118
Hooper, Richard, 81
Horizon IT system, 14-17, 19, 26, 35, 37, 39, 43, 47, 48, 52-53, 55-56, 61, 65, 88-89, 106-107, 153; unveiled, 11-12; Tony Blair briefed on risks, 13; roll-out by Post Office, 43-44; early problems, 17-18; detects non-existent crimes, 49; remote access to, 28, 73, 79, 82-83, 92, 103, 120, 126, 132-133, 135, 137-139, 142, 153-154; robustness, xi, 3-5, 13-14, 18, 49, 68, 70-72, 76, 90, 94-95, 105, 156, 183, 188; not fit for purpose, 99, 112, 120; Post Office aware of problems, 2, 15, 17, 19-21, 27, 31, 48, 66, 100
Horizon Shortfall scheme, 157, 160-161, 164
HSBC, 45
Hudgell, Neil, 164
Hull, East Yorkshire, 57

I

IBM, 11
ICL: see International Computers Ltd
Independent Police Complaints Commission, 24
Inland Revenue: see HM Revenue & Customs
Inside Out South (BBC series), 86-87, 186
International Computers Ltd (ICL), 11-21, 27, 29, 38, 43, 76; ICL Pathway, 12, 17, 22
Ishaq, Khayyam, 96, 177; wrongly imprisoned, 96
Ismay, Rod, 37, 70, 74, 80, 89, 91, 125; eponymous report, 71-73, 82
IT faults: see bugs
ITV, 3, 6, 81, 167, 170, 172, 176, 187, 197; commissions Post Office drama, 163

J

James, Margot, 189-190
Jenkins, Gareth, 37-38, 72-73, 76-79, 94-95, 154-155, 163, 176, 179-182, 185; distinguished engineer, 76, 79, 94, 154; expert witness, 37, 55-56, 63, 77, 79-80, 94, 105-106, 115-116; knowledge of Horizon remote access, 103; credibility as witness "fatally undermined", 104-106, 108, 116, 127, 154, 163, 181-182, 185

Jesmond, Newcastle-upon-Tyne, 178
Johnson, Alan, 44
Johnson, Boris, 136, 159-160
Jones, Darren, 164, 170
Jones, David, 68-69
Jones, Kevan, 123-124, 134
Jones, Toby, 168
Justice for Subpostmasters Alliance (JFSA), 2, 6, 69, 86, 91-92, 102-103, 109, 118, 126, 129, 133, 135-136, 160, 189

K

Kafka, Franz, 7, 24, 33, 53, 171
Kelleher, Ronan, 95-96
Kelly, Katherine, 168
Kipling, Rudyard, 123
Kirkham, HM Prison, 54
KPMG, 15, 176
Kuenssberg, Laura, 169
Kwarteng, Kwasi: makes good financial call, 166

L

Lamb, Norman, 83, 96
Lastminute.com, 46
Law Commission, 21
Law Society, 29
Leeds, HM Prison, 96
Leeds United FC, 46
Leighton, Allan, 45-46, 81
Lenton-Smith, Colin, 30, 31
Letwin, Oliver, 91, 122
Lilley, Peter, 11
Linklaters, 119
Linnell, Kay, 92, 118, 126-127, 134
Little Gem (production company), 167
Lock, Geoffrey, 24-25
Lock, Pamela, 24-25
Logica, 155
Longman, Jon, 80
Lord, Jonathan, 82-83
Lowther, Sue, 70
Lyons, Alwen, 90, 98-99

M

MacLeod, Jane, 136, 138, 142, 149-150, 153, 184-185; refuses to attend inquiry, 182, 185
mafia: Post Office likened to, 26; investigators likened to, 60, 74

Major, John, 11, 42
Mandelson, Peter, 14, 18, 68, 81
Marsh, Tony, 39, 63
Marshall, Paul, 162, 205
Matthews, Diane, 55, 57
Matthews, Gavin, 106, 114, 115
McCartney, Ian, 13, 18
McCausland, Neil, 99, 101
McCormack, Tim, 136, 137; part-time Nostradamus, 148
McDonald, Jacqueline, 60, 74, 75
McDonnell, David, 19
McFadden, Pat, 68
McFarlane, Juliet, 57
McInnes, Tim, 110
McKelvey, Maureen, 26-27, 58
McKinsey, 159
McLachlan, Charles, 77-78, 80
McLean, Andy, 66
mediation scheme, 112-113, 115, 117-120, 122-123, 126-127, 129, 132, 134, 141; pitiful output, 129; killed by Post Office, 134, 141
Mellor, Will, 168
Merritt, Tracy, 93
Metropolitan Police, 192-193
Michael, Alun, 82
Mill, John Stuart, 96
Miller, David, 16, 18-19, 31, 39-40
Mills, David, 40, 45-46, 63
Ministry of Defence, 89
Misra, Davinder, 86
Misra, Seema, 9, 79, 94-95, 98, 115-117, 132, 163, 169, 179-181; trial, 75-80, 82-83, 181; wrongly imprisoned while pregnant, 9, 91; and *Private Eye*, 87; and Horizon Issues trial, 154; *Hamilton & Others v Post Office*, 162
Moloney, Tim, 6
Montague, Adrian, 13; eponymous report, 14
Moores, Mike, 71
Moran, Tom, 142
Morgan, Richard, 35-36
Mr Bates vs The Post Office (ITV drama), 6, 167-168, 176, 197
Mulgan, Geoff, 13-14, 16
Mull of Kintyre Chinook disaster, 65
Munby, Sarah, 165

N

Naruto, Michio, 14
National Audit Office, 15
National Federation of Sub-postmasters (NFSP), 52, 61, 65-66, 90, 92, 126, 133, 183; officials aware of Horizon problems, 18
National Health Service (NHS), 12, 47
National Lottery, 13, 47, 49; scratchcards, 125
Network Business Support Centre helpline, 24, 34, 49, 52, 57, 75, 125
Neuberger, Lord (David), 150-151
Neville-Rolfe, Baroness (Lucy), 133-138, 140, 148, 189

O

Odiham, Hampshire, 68, 87
Official Secrets Act, 146
Olympus, Operation, 192-193
One Show (BBC series), 123, 197
Orwell, George, 54; reference to works of, 4, 100, 145
Osborne, George, 82, 99
Osborne, Kate, 160
Owen, Les, 90, 110

P

PA Consulting, 19
Page, Flora, 162, 179-180, 187
Palmer, Suzanne, 49-50, 57, 58
Panorama (BBC series), 131, 135-136, 197; *Trouble at the Post Office*, 132-133
Pardoe, David, 59; *There Must Be Some Mistake* (thesis), 5, 59
Parker, Steve, 29, 30
Parker, Tim, 147, 150-151, 158, 165-166, 182-184, 193; "prince of darkness", 136, 165; warned of Horizon problem, 136; reaction to Swift review, 137-139; semi-detached chairman, 151, 158, 183; luscious bouffant, 135
Parliamentary Office of Science and Technology, 47
Parsons, Andy, 105-106, 109, 114-115, 118, 139, 141-143
Patel, Priti, 82

Patel, Vipinchandra, 162
Patterson, Paul, 187-189
Peach, Mik, 56
Perkins, Alice, 88-90, 108-110, 117-118, 120, 122, 127, 135, 153, 182-183, 191, 193; meeting with Arbuthnot, 90-91; recommends hire of Mark Davies, 101; Royal Mail privatisation, 96, 111; and Second Sight, 98-101, 108, 119; member of BBC executive board, 115, 131; watches *One Show*, 123; does not read *Private Eye*, 183
Peters & Peters, 169
PFI (private finance initiative), 12-15, 44, 47; Libra IT system, 46
Phillips, Steve, 123, 124
Pinder, Brian, 56
Police Service of Northern Ireland, 26
Postal Services Act 2000, 43, 81
Postcomm (Postal Services Commission), 43
Post Office: "arm's-length" business, 9, 43, 71, 118, 149, 188; auditors, 2, 17, 19, 34, 50, 52; chairs, 182-184; containment, 100, 103, 114, 118, 129, 131, 141, 147; convictions, 25, 40, 58, 74, 82, 88, 104; culture, 6, 8, 17, 39, 148, 159, 170, 176, 192; dispensing pensions and benefits, 11; doublethink, 98; internal audit, 90; investigators, 23-27, 38-39, 52, 55, 59, 60-63, 75, 120-121, 176-179; lawyers, 180-182; not fit to run compensation schemes, 170-172; overturning convictions, 4, 162, 165; prosecutions, 2-3, 5, 22-23, 32, 57-59, 75, 93, 95, 119; protection of brand, 29-31, 35, 38, 53, 74, 84, 94, 101-102, 114, 124-125, 128, 131-132; renamed Consignia, 44; restricting information, 127-128, 138, 143; security division, 24, 26; social value, 6; stalling compensation, 170;
suppression of evidence, 52-53; treatment of sub-postmasters, 1, 3, 5, 23, 38, 40, 62, 91, 135, 155
Postofficevictims website, 34, 65
private finance initiative: see PFI
Premier Inn, 83
Private Eye, xi, xii, 1, 6, 9, 28, 87-90, 102, 110, 113, 120, 171, 183, 197
Proceeds of Crime Act, 59
public accounts committee (House of Commons), 46, 173
PwC, 44, 153, 165

R

racism, 39, 170
Read, Nick, 161, 169-170, 179; becomes chief executive, 156, 158-159; pay rise, 166
Reeves, Rachel, 170
reversals: see bugs
Richardson, Simon, 101
Ridge, Elaine, 52
Riposte messaging system, 13
Roberts, John, 16, 40, 42
Robinson, Anthony de Garr, 139
Robinson, Tim, 132
robust: see bugs
Roll, Richard, 27-28, 131-132, 135, 142
Roosevelt, Theodore, 123
Rose, Helen, 34, 36
Royal Bank of Scotland, 161
Royal Commission, 23
Royal Mail, 41-42, 44-46, 63, 66, 68, 80, 88, 90, 105, 108-109, 175, 177; history of King's Mail, 7-8, 23; *Modernise or Decline*, 81; split from Post Office, 93, 96, 102; privatisation, 83, 85, 99, 109-111; Horizon dropped from prospectus, 111, 126
Royal Mint, 44
Royal Society for the Prevention of Cruelty to Animals (RSPCA), 23
Rudkin, Michael, 92, 133
Rudkin, Susan, 162
Russell, Mark, 188-189

S

Sabir, Mohammad, 146
Saddiq, Shazia, 60
Scott, John, 63, 70, 111; and typed minutes, 106-107
Scully, Paul, 160, 163-165, 167
Second Sight, 92-93, 96, 98-102, 106, 110, 112-113, 115-121, 127, 132-133, 135-136, 153, 182, 185, 188-191, 196; brought in by Post Office, 92-93, 95; interim report, 100-103, 105, 108-109, 111, 116-117; Post Office campaigns against, 113, 118-119, 128-129; *Initial Complaint Review*, 120-121; warned off, 131; prevented from attending meeting with MPs, 134
Sercombe, Suzanne, 33
Sethi, Baljit, 174
Sewell, Lesley, 71, 91, 100, 104, 112, 126, 185
Sewell, Peter, 35-36
sexism, 170
Shah, Oliver, 84, 170
Shapps, Grant, 166
Shareholder Executive, 44, 71, 82-83, 96, 103, 110, 118, 133, 134-135, 148-149, 188-190, 195, 197; renamed UK Government Investments (UKGI), 149, 170, 188, 195
Shoosmiths, 87, 89, 92
Singh, Jarnail, 50, 93-95, 104, 106, 115, 180-182; and Seema Misra, 76-77, 79-80; distinctive prose style, 93, 95, 107
Skinner, Janet, 57-58, 162-163, 177; wrongly imprisoned, 57
Smith, David (head of IT), 16, 48, 69, 91
Smith, David (managing director), 71, 73, 80
Smith, Martin, 94, 104, 106-107, 115,
South Wales Evening Post, 25
South Warnborough, Hampshire, 51, 68, 87, 92
Sparrow, Project, 118, 120, 125, 133
Staunton, Henry, 165-167, 169-170
Stein, Sam, 6, 180, 185, 188

Straw, Jack, 101
sub-postmasters, xi, xv, 1-3, 7, 25, 33, 47-48, 50, 52, 58, 128, 153; historical precursors, 7; imbalance of power in contract, 8, 33, 38, 48-50, 66, 84, 112, 121, 127, 130-131, 134, 142, 144-146, 155-156, 174-175, 193; told "you're the only one", 26, 52, 55, 60, 65, 69, 74, 174; theft/false accounting two-card trick, 49-51, 57-58, 74-75; *Hamilton & Others v Post Office Ltd*, 162; overturning convictions, 162-164, 167, 170-171; compensation schemes, 165, 171; second-generation victims, 159
Sunak, Rishi, 165, 168-169, 197
suspense account, 25, 33, 47-48, 50, 52, 58, 128, 153
Sweeney, John, 131
Sweetman, Stuart, 18
Swift, Jonathan, 137-139, 182, 184; eponymous review, 137-139
Swinson, Jo, 103, 109, 112, 123, 129, 189

T

Tagg, Elaine, 29
Tait, Duncan, 87, 186-187, 193; earnings, 87
Talbot, Mandy, 31, 35, 37, 69, 70
Taro Naw (S4C series), 66, 197
Tatford, Warwick, 76, 78-80, 181
Thomas, Gary, 61, 63, 178-179
Thomas, Noel, 58, 63, 66, 95, 123, 177; trial, 54-57; wrongly imprisoned, 54
Thomas, Penny, 56, 77
Thompson, Laura, 133
Thomson, George, 126-127, 183
Thomson, Rebecca, 65-66
Threlfall, Rita, 60
Today programme (BBC Radio 4), 122, 130
Todd, Keith, 19-20
Tolhurst, Kelly, 148-149, 151
Treasury, 13, 15, 42, 167, 170
Trouble at the Post Office: see *Panorama*
Trousdale, Christopher, 162

U

UK Government Investments (UKGI): see Shareholder Executive

V

Van den Bogerd, Angela, 54, 89, 91, 112-113, 118, 122, 125, 127-129, 132, 137-138, 144, 146, 148-149, 152-153, 168; and Noel Thomas, 54; leads branch support programme, 112; sullen drone at select committee, 128; "disregard for factual accuracy", 144-145; pay bonus, 152
Vaz, Valerie, 82
Vennells, Paula, 4, 6-7, 64, 83-85, 88, 90-91, 96, 98-102, 104, 108-113, 117-129, 132-134, 136-139, 146-148, 150, 152, 168, 182, 184-185, 191, 193-194, 197; becomes managing director, 80, 83; becomes chief executive, 84-85; select committee appearance, 84-85, 125-128; shelves "lessons learned" review, 109; weighs in on Royal Mail privatisation prospectus, 110-111; as TV critic, 123; importance of faith, 83, 88, 117, 121; blind faith in Post Office, 186; earnings, 84, 152; awarded CBE, 101, 147; hands back CBE, 184
Voltaire, 8-9

W

Wallis, Nick, 19, 86-88, 122-123, 131, 135, 162, 186, 196
Ward, Graham, 55-56, 59-60, 63
Warmington, Ron, 92, 98, 100, 103, 108, 113, 118-120, 129, 190; exasperation at Post Office, 103; see also Second Sight
Watts, Alan, 161
West Boldon, Tyne and Wear, 159
West Byfleet, Surrey, 76-78
Whitbread, 64, 83
Whitby, North Yorkshire, 162
Whitehall, xi, xii, 4, 13, 44, 67, 70, 108, 109, 188, 195
Whitehead, Michael, 83
Willetts, David, 12
Williams, Betty, 46
Williams, Lia, 168
Williams, Rodric, 115, 125, 137, 142-143, 182
Williams, Sir Wyn, 163, 167, 174, 176, 191
Wilson, Harold, 11, 41
Wilson, Julian, 61, 63, 123, 162, 178
Wilson, Karen, 61
Wilson, Rob, 70, 73, 89,
Winter, Suzanne, 26-27, 38
Wolstenholme, Julie, 28-33, 35, 39
Womble Bond Dickinson: see Bond Dickinson
Wood, Mike, 91, 122
Worden, Dr Robert, 155-156

Y

Yes Minister (BBC series), 189
Yetminster, Dorset, 93
Young, Mike, 63, 71, 87, 185-186

Z

Zahawi, Nadhim, 128
Zebra, Project: see Deloitte